ENGRAVED BY T.B. WELCH. DAGUERREOTYPED BY RICHARDS.

REV. ANDREW MANSHIP.

Yours affectionately
Andrew Manship

THIRTEEN YEARS' EXPERIENCE

IN THE

ITINERANCY.

BY

REV. ANDREW MANSHIP,

MEMBER OF THE PHILADELPHIA ANNUAL CONFERENCE.

"Preach the word; be instant in season, out of season; reprove, rebuke, exhort, with all long-suffering and doctrine."—2 TIMOTHY iv. 2.

"I am made all things to all men, that I might by all means save some."—1 CORINTHIANS ix. 22.

PHILADELPHIA:

HIGGINS & PERKINPINE,

No. 40 NORTH FOURTH STREET.

1856.

STEREOTYPED BY E. B. MEARS. PRINTED BY SMITH & PETERS.

TO

MY FATHERS AND BRETHREN

OF

THE PHILADELPHIA ANNUAL CONFERENCE,

TO

THE MEMBERS OF THE METHODIST EPISCOPAL CHURCH

IN MY SEVERAL FIELDS OF LABOUR,

AND TO ALL

"AMONG WHOM I HAVE GONE PREACHING THE KINGDOM OF GOD"

DURING THE THIRTEEN YEARS OF MY

ITINERANT MINISTRY,

THE FOLLOWING WORK IS RESPECTFULLY AND AFFECTIONATELY

DEDICATED,

BY THE AUTHOR.

PREFACE.

THE following work originated and assumed its present form under peculiar circumstances. Hedding Church, Philadelphia, had been completed and dedicated to Almighty God. On the day of dedication, an amount had been subscribed sufficient, or nearly so, to meet all the remaining pecuniary liabilities of the trustees on the house, and everything looked cheering. But a sad and unlooked for change had taken place. Many of these subscriptions, and some of an earlier date, amounting in all to some four thousand five hundred dollars, had become unavailable; for though made in good faith, the subscribers, being persons in humble circumstances, and depending on the results of their business and daily toils to meet their obligations, had been, through the unhappy embarrassments which had arisen in the financial and business affairs of the city, rendered unable to pay them. What was now to be done? How was so large an amount of money to be raised? While Brother Manship was anxiously deliberating on this question, and devising measures to meet the emergency, the thought suddenly arose in his fertile mind to draw up and publish an account of the Plank Church, which had excited so much attention in Philadelphia and elsewhere, and had been the means, under God, of doing so much good, and to apply the avails, or a large portion of them, to the object now engrossing his attention. He had already adopted various unusual expedients to accomplish this desirable object, and the church had realized from them a considerable sum. Now the thought was presented to him to turn author, and try to make something for the church in this way. What should he do? He felt embarrassed. He had given but little attention to literary labour, and had not written much besides letters to friends and outlines for the pulpit. He did not, however, long hesitate—for "to do and to dare" is characteristic of this brother, when good is to be accomplished. Accordingly he proceeded to collect materials and to prepare for his work. As he progressed, however, the original conception gradually enlarged itself, taking a wider and yet wider range, until at length "The History of the Plank Church" rose to the more dignified dimensions of "Thirteen Years' Experience in the Itinerancy:" and in this form it has been stereotyped, and made into a book.

This book I have read in manuscript, every word of it. It is characteristic of its author: sprightly, earnest, energetic; full of allusions, incidents, anecdotes, and biographical sketches; all tending to lead the sinner to Christ and to Heaven. It is, indeed, a fair transcript of the author's mind, of his modes of thinking, and of expression. In short, *it is Rev. Andrew Manship under the name and form of a book.* To his friends, it will be, I have no doubt, a great treasure; while to others, it will not fail to afford the means of filling up leisure moments both agreeably and profitably.

I hope this book may have a large sale; it is worthy

of it, not only in itself, but also on account of the benevolent end which the proceeds, in great part, are intended to subserve. Indeed, I cannot but hope that, beyond his being reimbursed in the thousand dollars which, in anticipation, he has already nobly secured to the Hedding Church, the author may realize a respectable sum to add to the comforts of his family, and his means of usefulness in other directions. L. SCOTT.

WILMINGTON, *Nov. 14th*, 1855.

CONTENTS.

CHAPTER I.

CHAPTER II.

CHAPTER III.

CHAPTER IV.

CHAPTER V.

CHAPTER VI.

CHAPTER VII.

CHAPTER VIII.

CHAPTER IX.

CHAPTER X.

CHAPTER XI.

CHAPTER XII.

CHAPTER XIII.

CHAPTER XIV.

THIRTEEN YEARS' EXPERIENCE

IN THE

ITINERANCY.

CHAPTER I.

Conversion—Rev. William Spry—Susceptibility of Youth—Hear a living Man's Funeral preached—The Stars seemed to be falling—Thought the Day of Judgment had come—Appointed Class Leader for the People of Colour—First Exhortation to white People—Sent by Presiding Elder to Frederica Circuit—Barratt's Chapel—Sacrament administered by Dr. Coke—Joyful Meeting between him and Mr. Asbury—Rev. Dr. Bond—Rev. William Connelly—Camp Meetings—Pastoral Visiting—Fighting with a Beast—Churches enlarged—Visit a Quaker Lady's House—Deeply pious coloured Couple—Sea Captain converted—Recommended to Annual Conference—In favor of the Itinerancy.

THE title of my book is "Thirteen Years' Experience in the Itinerancy;" yet my readers will not, I trust, deem it improper for me to give an account of my conversion. This glorious event, and one that never will be forgotten by me, took place in August, 1835, when I was a very small boy, at a camp meeting held in what was called the Three Bridges Woods, some three miles from Denton, Caroline county, Md. I heard a sermon preached on that occasion by Rev. Charles Pitman, that reached my heart, and proved to be the power of God unto my salvation. I was so small and so young, that some had but little faith, if any, in my sincerity, and rather repulsed than encouraged me; but, in making this effort, I found a true friend in Rev. William Spry, who practically manifested that he did not "despise the day of small things." He has gone from earth to heaven doubtless, yet he lives in my memory, and I hope in eternity to rise up and call him blessed, for the instruction he gave me, and the interest he took in a poor orphan boy's spiritual prosperity. Not only did I find that the Saviour was precious, but many of my young associates also experienced the smiles of Jesus. We were, on our return home in the town of Denton, formed into a class, which class was almost exclusively composed of very young persons, and Rev. William Spry did not think it beneath his dignity, though the preacher of the Circuit, to become our leader. And truthfully it may be said, he "led us beside the still waters," and we did "lie down in green pastures."

The Church sustained a great loss in the premature death of this deeply pious minister. Judging from his venerable and sedate appearance, and from his almost snow-white hair, some concluded that he was quite an aged man. It was not an uncommon circumstance for him to be addressed "Father Spry" by persons much his senior, and, in some cases, old enough to be his father. In all my intercourse with men (and I had much with him), I never knew a man that spent so much time upon his knees. The closet to him had many attractions. In his family, there was not only morning and evening devotion, but also at noon, he, with his family, worshipped God under his own vine and fig-tree. I was, in the year 1840, for some months in Lewes, Delaware, a resident in this Christian family, and I can truly say it was like the house of Obededom, where the "ark of the Lord rested." He was a model pastor—"into whatsoever house he entered," he said, "Peace be to this house." He won the hearts of all both small and great, and had a suitable word to address to all the inmates of the family; and, when he came amongst the families of his charge, an angel could not have been more welcome. His influence was felt, not only in the pulpit, but everywhere, and in every charge, where he was called upon to labour, he was compassed about with a cloud of devoted friends. And the most impious were attached to this dignified, devoted Christian minister, and delighted to attend his ministry. He had seals to his ministry, as my readers would naturally conclude. It was only to know him, to love him. He could sing almost like an angel, and his lady was also greatly gifted in this respect; and conjointly their performances, in this interesting part of worship, was sufficient to allay the evil spirit in any man, and make one feel that he was "quite on the verge of Heaven." His last field of labour was on the Eastern Shore of Virginia, shortly after the unhappy division of our Church in 1844. His circuit was on the border. It required a very prudent man to occupy successfully that field. In the hands of Rev. William Spry the appointing power felt that everything will be done decently and in order. All felt that he had the spirit of his Master, that all will be harmony, and the most glorious results will follow. He more than met the expectations of his friends on that then difficult field of labour. But his career here was short. To the grief of many a loving heart, he there "fell in the work, he died at his post." The loss of his family and of the Church was his infinite gain.

My impression is, we ought to encourage the young. Well do I recollect the powerful convictions I had for several years before my soul was converted. I saw an old man hung when I was about ten years of age. I heard a minister of Christ preach his funeral sermon. How awful it was to hear his own funeral discourse! The text was, "The wages of sin is death, but the gift of God is eternal life through Jesus Christ our Lord."

Rev. Mr. Stockton was the speaker. Under his sermon, I shed many tears; but, at that time, no one specially "cared for my soul." About this period I learned the hymn, beginning,

"And am I born to die?
To lay this body down?
And must my trembling spirit fly
Into a world unknown?"

I committed the whole of it to memory, and I used to sing it mournfully to myself, and in my heart did wish I had never been born. I suppose scarcely any one thought of such a thing relative to myself; but many a sleepless night did I spend from my tenth year until the time I was converted to God. I was afraid to close my eyes in sleep frequently, thinking I might awake up in hell. There are few children now, in this day, but have better opportunities for being instructed in the good way than I had. And as I felt I was in the downward road to ruin, had I been encouraged by the pious, and pointed to the sinner's Friend, I might have been converted several years earlier. Therefore I argue that our children are, in early life, susceptible of divine impressions, and we ought to labour for, and with them, more than we do, and revival after revival ought to take place in our Sunday schools.

In the autumn of 1833, the very remarkable meteoric

phenomena occurred. Early in the morning, before the day broke in the country where I lived, the family arose affrighted and dismayed. We saw the stars flying, shooting, and apparently falling in every direction. There were none in the family versed in astronomy, and we could not assign a cause for it. But there were a number of poor sinners in the family, greatly terrified; for we supposed "the great day of wrath had come, and we were not able to stand." No one, out of the bottomless pit, I thought, could be more miserable. And all with whom I was associated, were terrified awfully; because we knew we were not prepared for "the day of vengeance of our God." I then felt, though a very insignificant boy, between eleven and twelve years of age, if I could I would have given all the world for religion, a preparation to meet my God. After finding that our conclusions were incorrect, I again vowed to the Lord to be his servant. Some two years passed before I paid this vow; as I have already stated to my reders, I gave my heart to God in the month of August, 1835, at the camp meeting, by simple faith in the Redeemer. "This poor" boy "cried, and the Lord heard him, and saved him out of all his troubles."

I desire to present to my readers another incident in my history, which occurred while travelling my first field of labour. I was spending the night at the house of a worthy brother, who was the postmaster in the town where it occurred. It was the time of the Millerite excitement. The night was dismal, the thunders roared terrifically, the lightnings flashed vividly; and, just at the height of the storm, the four-horse stage, carrying the United States Mail, came dashing at almost full speed to the house where I was lodging, and being refreshed by "nature's sweet restorer." The bell, that was to arouse the postmaster, was suspended just over my head, and the stage driver brought all his muscular power to bear upon it. This, in connexion with the other circumstances, aroused me suddenly. I sprang from the bed hastily; and, for the time being, I felt "this is the end of the world." But I had gone to rest that night in a happy frame of mind; and, though for the moment I realized, in my feelings at least, that I should soon see the Judge descending upon his great white throne; yet I was enabled to say, feeling I was through riches of grace in Christ Jesus ready,

"Hallelujah, God appears on earth to reign."

Though I had no father or mother to help me on my religious course (my good old Quaker mother, who was very much attached to her children, dying when I was very young, and my father soon following after), yet the Lord and the Methodist Church have taken me up. The leaders of prayer meetings and ministers, early in my career, began occasionally to call on me to pray in public.

It was somewhat novel to see a small boy thus officiating. And, when I was very young, the preacher in charge appointed me to lead class for the people of colour in the town of Denton. In this sphere, I learned much, and found it was good for me to be there. One of the first efforts I made in the way of exhortation, among the white people, was in the church at Denton, on a certain Sabbath evening, when, from some cause, the minister failed to be at his post. I was much embarrassed; and, having been in the habit of labouring among the coloured people exclusively, I forgot my position, and, over and over, I addressed the audience as "coloured friends." I did not know that I had made such a mistake, until a kind old friend told me of it after the meeting was over. But the people threw the mantle of charity around me, and winked at this matter, owing to the circumstances.

In the year 1841, there were several vacancies on the Caroline Circuit. That year, three ministers on that field of labour died; viz. Rev. Wm. Torbert, Rev. Wm. W. Williams, and Rev. Wesley Henderson; and it may justly be said they were all faithful and true men, and the loss which their families and the Church sustained was their gain, for they were "ready to be offered." The Presiding Elder of the district, to my surprise, desired me to fill a vacancy there, and sent me an official paper to that effect. Circumstances would not admit of a compliance with this request. My business arrangements were against it; but, mainly, I did not feel that I was qualified for the great work, and sensibly felt I had not tarried sufficiently long at Jerusalem.

Having been licensed as a local preacher at the Quarterly Conference, for Denton Circuit, in January, 1842, I consented, the following May, to accompany Rev. Daniel Lamdin, the Presiding Elder, to Frederica Circuit, Kent county, Delaware, and, by him was appointed junior preacher for that circuit, as there was a vacancy.

The object the Elder had in view in going in person to Frederica Circuit, was to hold the first Quarterly Meeting for that Conference year. We found the attendance very large, even on Saturday. I was introduced to the brethren and the preacher in charge, and received kindly and treated affectionately.

The evening appointment for Saturday was to be filled by myself. I did the best I could from "Is there no balm in Gilead?" &c. The effort, however, was greatly mortifying to myself, and, I have no doubt, also to others. I had but little sleep that night; but, on Sunday morning, the clouds dispersed, and, in the love feast, my soul did "swell unutterably full of glory and of God." At the close of the love feast, so great was the crowd that it was deemed proper to request the coloured people to vacate the gallery for the whites; and an arrangement was made for them, and those whites who could not get a seat in the church, to hear the word of the Lord under the trees with which the church was surrounded. And the lot fell upon me to perform this service. I had for my pulpit a wagon, and I endeavoured to lift up my voice like a trumpet from "Go ye into all the world, and preach my Gospel to every creature." This was the largest congregation to which I ever had tried to preach. We found the presence and power of God was not confined to the edifice, but, under the foliage of those stately trees, he manifested himself to us most gloriously. I verily believe good seed was sown that day, and that it found a lodgment in good ground.

The point at which this Quarterly Meeting was held was "*Barratt's Chapel*," one mile from the town of Frederica. This place is the most celebrated, decidedly, for large Quarterly Meetings of any on the peninsula. A person attending a meeting of this kind at this point would see all the interest of a quarterly visitation that characterized such occasions generally forty and fifty years ago, especially in reference to attendance. And, God be praised! Quarterly Meetings here are still interesting in a religious aspect. At this period, we deemed it proper, from "the signs of the times," to continue our meeting for several days, which resulted in the conversion of a number of precious souls; among whom was a Quaker lady, who had recently located with her husband in this neighbourhood. This was the first soul over whose conversion I was permitted to shout in my itinerant life; but, thank God! I have rejoiced over many since.

Barratt's Chapel is an interesting spot on many accounts. It was built at an early period, viz. 1780, mainly through the labours and means of Philip Barratt, who had been a Presbyterian, as one of his descendants informed me; and, hearing the early Methodist preachers, fell in love with them and their doctrine, and resolved to bid them God speed, and open for them an effectual door, by building a house of respectable size and quality, in which the word of the Lord could be faithfully preached, and the sacraments duly administered. It was at this very place where Rev. Dr. Thomas Coke first met the faithful Asbury, who had taken a most active part in bringing about the erection of this place of worship, this church in the wilderness. They met joyfully, saluting each other, before the vast congregation, with a holy kiss. Here the holy sacrament was first administered *regularly* to the Methodists in this country. This was done by Dr. Coke, on the 14th of November, 1784, to between five and six hundred persons. Mr. Wesley had recently set him apart for this work and labour of love, and the complete organization of our societies into a regular Church. It was at this place the calling of the preachers together in a General Conference capacity was resolved upon; which event took place in the city of Baltimore, December 24, 1784. This was styled the

"Christmas Conference." Rev. Thomas Coke and Rev. Francis Asbury were, according to Mr. Wesley's wish and appointment, chosen Superintendents.

Mr. Asbury had been several years previously labouring day and night on this continent in his Master's cause, and, even when the war broke out between the mother country and the colonies, he did not desert the sheep and leave them without a shepherd. He found it necessary for his personal safety not to appear in public for a while, and found in this time of trial, an asylum at the house of Judge White, who was a resident of the state of Delaware, some twenty miles from Barratt's Chapel. Methodism, from its first introduction into this part of the country, has always had, and now has, men of wealth and great influence, who have felt, and now feel it to be their highest honour to sustain this child of Providence, or as Dr. Chalmers calls it, "Christianity in earnest."

As Barratt's Chapel was being built, the size was objected to, and it was asked by an enemy, "what is the use of building the house so large? for in a little while a corn crib will hold all the Methodists." But we see from the last census (unfaithful as we have been), this body of Christians is the largest in our country, and the corn crib would have to be of mammoth dimensions to hold us all. This was not the first, and, by no means, the

DRAWN BY A.T. SCOTT. T.B. WELCH.

BARRATT'S CHAPEL, KENT COUNTY, DELAWARE.

last false prophecy put forth relative to the people called Methodists.

As that spot is memorable in the history of Methodism, and as it stands now "as it ever hath stood," so far as its exterior is concerned, I have thought it would be very acceptable to my readers to give them a steel engraved view of the original Barratt's Chapel. This spot is interesting to me on many accounts, and amongst others, it was, as my readers have seen, the place where I commenced my itinerant life. This edifice has been revised inside and improved; the same seat, however, is retained in the pulpit on which Asbury, Coke, Whatcoat, Garretson, and others (of whom the world was not worthy), sat. In the spring of 1845, when the Philadelphia Conference was held in Milford, not far from Barratt's Chapel, Rev. Dr. Thomas E. Bond, "the hero of a hundred battles" in behalf of the Methodist Episcopal Church, had the privilege of standing in this temple, which was to him a great gratification. He doubtless thought of the men of precious memory, who had, in the very dawning of Methodism, stood here upon the walls of Zion; their characters, aspersed by the enemies of truth and righteousness, and their glorious cause, he had vindicated. The Church will remember and respect him as long as he lives. This has frequently been shown in the past; and, when he fights his last battle, and shouts in death "don't give up the ship,"—thousands and tens of thousands will say, "well done, good and faithful servant." Dr. Bond's sermon on this occasion proved him to be an able minister of the New Testament. The circumstances apparently inspired him, and the younger ministers who were present were awed into reverence, and felt like praying that the mantles of our ascended Elijahs might fall upon them.

My colleague, Rev. William Connelly, was much of a gentleman. His kindness I can never forget. He was greatly beloved on the Circuit. The people considered it a great privilege to hear him preach, and his congregations were always large. He was powerful also in exhortation; and he could stir a congregation, and affect to tears beyond his brethren generally. He was a man of one book, in this respect like Wesley; and, as it was said of Apollos, so it might be said of him, "he was an eloquent man, and mighty in the Scriptures." In the year 1844, August 8th, in the town of Denton, Md., he finished his course. He "rests from his labours." His last words were "glory to God."

As my colleague was favourable to camp meetings, and as the people were in this respect like their minister, and none more so than myself, therefore we had two on the Circuit, one at Pratt's Branch, and one at Combe's Woods. And I do not exaggerate, I think, when I say there were at least three hundred souls converted at the camp meetings. The people were well paid for their labour and expense. I remember an interesting case at one of the meetings referred to. The aged father of one of our valuable ministers earnestly cried for mercy. How imposing was the scene! one in which angels themselves took an interest. The son, an able minister of the New Testament, with tear-bathed cheeks, plead with God in behalf of his aged father, at the mourner's bench.

I have many reasons which I could assign in favour of this means of grace, this soul-saving arrangement. One of the prominent reasons why I would advocate their perpetuity amongst us is, that we have hundreds and thousands, through this agency, brought under our preaching that otherwise we should not be able to reach. And when they come, although it may not be in their thoughts to be benefited, arrows, shot from Jehovah's quiver, penetrate their hearts, and they are won to the Saviour. To establish this position, I will mention a few cases which have come under my own observation. I knew at one of our camps a tavern-keeper, a man at least fifty years of age, who had "destroyed much good," and who went to the meeting not to be spiritually benefited, but his heart was affected by camp meeting influences, and, when he struggled for mercy, it was "strangely warmed."

At a camp meeting, I recollect a certain distiller, who was no friend to the Methodists, or Methodist institutions, and who was, at mid-day, by the powerful preaching of the Gospel, Saul-like, brought to the ground, and who was not only killed, but also made alive. Both the persons referred to have, to to this day, proved faithful, and are prominent members of the Methodist Episcopal Church. The business in which they were engaged was abandoned *instanter*, they promptly "ceasing to do evil, and learning to do well." It is incompatible with the spirit of a child of Jesus either to sell or drink ardent spirits. The Christian feels the force of the passage, "Woe unto him that giveth his neighbour drink, that puttest thy bottle to him, and makest him drunken also." Dear readers, let us resolve that we will neither give, sell, nor drink this article, believing, with Dr. Adam Clark, "if we drink it down, the devil will drink us down."

The grove, when the weather is mild and calm, is the best place for preaching in the world. I have known, from some cause, preachers, by one effort at a camp meeting, to do more apparently in the way of getting souls converted, than they would accomplish for the entire year in the ordinary way, in the regular station. I believe the preaching at camp meetings is better, and more effectual than anywhere else. "The forest and the open heavens are friendly to the spirit of devotion, while the sound of prayer, of praise and instruction from the pulpit, spreads in open space, without the obstruction of walls, like the circular wave on smooth water."

I once knew a Christian sister, so ardently attached to this means of grace, that she craved the privilege of dying at a camp meeting, and going directly from the tented grove, the Church in the wilderness, to the Church triumphant in Heaven. She had years previously obtained, at a camp meeting, the pardon of her sins, and at the period of which I now speak, her health was feeble, so much so that her physician and her friends remonstrated with her, and told her plainly, if she went to the meeting, it would cost her her life. "None of these things moved her." She went "in the strength of the Lord," and felt anxious from that spot to ascend to the heights of Mount Zion. Her wish was gratified. In a tent, near the altar, while the meeting was in progress, she was enabled triumphantly to depart and be with Christ. She arose from that spot, dear to her, with Jesus, amidst a shining convoy of angels, and the shouts of the sacramental host around her, who did "with the spirit and understanding also" sing—

> "Sink down, ye separating hills,
> Let sin and death remove,
> 'Tis love that drives my chariot wheels,
> And death must yield to love."

This remarkable occurrence gave new life to the meeting; and, doubtless, was the most effectual preaching that took place on that camp ground. If all were as much attached to camp meetings, as was the sister referred to, they could not fail to be powerful in their results for good.

Dear readers, much good has been accomplished to saints and sinners, to our own and other churches by camp meetings; and what has been done, can be done again. Therefore let us, preachers and people, wake up to this subject. "As a Church we need to be drawn into closer and stronger fellowship. We are getting too cold and ceremonious. We must have the fires of Christian fellowship replenished. Let us fly away to our annual feast of tabernacles, and look into each other's faces and press each other's hands. Let the rich and worldly come, the proud and those whose Christian affections have declined. And if there be any upon whom jealousy, or envy, or evil surmising, has begun to prey, let them come. It is time they looked upon other scenes, and came under better influences. Let them come from the tops of the mountains, and the hill-sides; from the fertile valley, and the sterile plain; from the farm and shop, the factory and the counter; from the lonely cot, and the city mansion; the poor and the rich; let them come up to the tented grove, let them 'bow down and worship together.'"

I sensibly felt my insufficiency for the work of the

ministry. I felt that my efforts in the pulpit were exceedingly feeble; and did try, as much as possible, to atone for this lack of service, so far as quality was concerned in the preaching, by holding prayer meetings, leading class, and pastoral visiting. I will venture to suggest to my young brethren in the ministry, that it is not the better way to depend exclusively upon our preaching for success. While the preaching of the gospel is the great instrumentality for converting the sinner from the error of his ways, it is not the only means to be employed. I would venture to take the ground that "warning people from house to house with tears," is a means that can be successfully employed in accomplishing the great end of our ministry, viz. the conversion of souls. There are difficulties in the way of pastoral work, and we find it hard to surmount them; and nothing but the grace of God will enable us to enter promiscuously into the houses of our people, and "warn every man, and teach every man"—not neglecting the children—the way of salvation. But sowing seed thus, an abundant harvest is reaped, thirty, sixty, a hundred fold. By pursuing this course in the proper spirit, the people are impressed with the feeling, "our ministers care for our souls." The preaching may be but ordinary, yet it is efficient, because the audience believes "our report, and the arm of the Lord is revealed." And I hesitate not to say, that a faithful pastor, even with ordinary preaching powers, will always have large congregations, and be a successful minister of the New Testament.

I feel inclined here to notice a day spent on this Circuit in this service. It was in a portion of our Circuit where the people had been unaccustomed to this order of things; but, in nearly every case, I was treated well by both saint and sinner. I did indeed meet with one family who declined to accept my prayers. I exhorted the family to seek the Lord, and invited them all to come to church. At another place where I visited that day, and the last I visited pastorally, I was somewhat alarmed by a large mastiff, who made a strong effort to bite me when I first went up to the house. A temporary quietus was put to him, however, by the interposition of one of the family. While I was seated in the family, and trying to urge them to become religious, he rallied, and made the second attempt to bite me, and was not far from accomplishing his purpose. He was again repulsed, and from the effort made I thought he was driven off the plantation. After awhile we went to prayer, and, losing sight of the dog and earthly things, I did ardently try to lead the minds of the members of the family to the cross, but, in such a moment as I thought not, again this ferocious animal rushed upon me with the fury of a lion or tiger, and his open red mouth came in close proximity with my throat. This was a trying moment. I had to defend myself as well as I could. I fought him on my knees; and the lady of the house rose from her devotions, and heroically fought him with the poker, exclaiming, "in the name of God, who ever saw the like before!" I passed away, after recovering my equilibrium and finishing my prayer, thanking God that I had escaped unhurt. My reflections were, if I have not "fought with beasts at Ephesus" like Paul, I had fought with one powerful beast. I also reflected that, on a certain occasion, the devil was permitted to enter into the swine, and I concluded that he had been permitted to enter into this dog, as he did not wish the family to desert his service; and as the poet speaks of him as

"Ruling this lower world,"

my readers will not blame me for thinking this wily foe, who is capable of the most consummate meanness, used this dog as an instrument to rebut the feeble efforts that I was making to snatch this family as a brand out of the fire? And in holy indignation I said to him, "The Lord rebuke thee, O Satan, even the Lord that hath chosen Jerusalem rebuke thee."

Our churches on the Circuit, with a very few exceptions, were small, and by no means sufficiently capacious to contain the people who from every quarter flocked to hear the word. At Banning's, where we had an extensive revival, and where "much people were added unto the Lord," it was necessary to enlarge the house. This was done also at Purnell's Chapel, mainly through the energy and industry of my much-respected and enterprising colleague, who was not only an excellent minister, but a first-rate mechanic, and laboured with his own hands to enlarge the places of worship. At Banning's, particularly, God's work was revived. At this point there was, among others, a young Quaker converted. His friends at first felt opposed to this matter, but they saw plainly that he was under the influence of the Holy Spirit. They saw in him the grace of God. He persevered in well-doing. The heart of his aged mother was touched, and she became so favourably impressed towards the Methodists that the young man felt free to invite me to his mother's house. I accepted the invitation, and was treated most affectionately by this female Friend. After sharing in the hospitalities of the family, and before taking my departure, we knelt in prayer, the precious old lady doing so likewise. We had a memorable season, and I was most agreeably disappointed in hearing the Quaker lady give vent to her feelings in ascriptions of praise to "the Lamb of God that taketh away the sin of the world." I left her and her son happy in the Lord. I feel inclined to mention a little circumstance in this connexion. When I was leaving the Circuit, I accidentally met her in the streets of Camden, and, from the fulness of a pious heart, she accosted me with the holy salutation of primitive Christianity. I cannot but feel a warm attachment for the Friends, many of whom have been, and now are, bright examples of Christian perfection.

I found in preaching and leading class for the coloured people, which I did whenever I had an opportunity, that on our Circuit we had many of this class that were deeply devoted to God; and I could say with Peter, "of a truth I perceive that God is no respecter of persons: but in every nation he that feareth him, and worketh righteousness, is accepted with him." In one of our societies, we had a very venerable couple that had for more than half a century been consistent members of the church, and for deep piety none surpassed them. They were esteemed by all. I used to visit them with much comfort. One circumstance will show how highly they were thought of. A gentleman of the highest respectability in the community was convicted, and earnestly sought for pardon. Although he had the greatest regard for the ministry, he did not go to them for counsel and prayer. He did not seek to satisfy his disquieted mind by observing the stated forms of religion. He, in the solemn hour of night, with a heart "burdened, sick, and faint," visited the humble abode of this patriarchal pair, in whom he had great confidence. The old folks had retired. The gentleman stood at the door and knocked; and the pious old mother in Israel said, "I know who you are; I have been praying for you. Come in." He sprang in, fell upon his knees, and cried, "God be merciful to me a sinner." He was, by these humble but faithful servants of the Most High God, prayed for and instructed, for they had been with Jesus and learned from him. And it was not very long before he could sing,

> "Salvation in abundance flows,
> Like floods of milk and wine."

It was in this place that he felt that he was newly born; and, from that day till the present time, he has "gone on his way rejoicing." And, through time and in eternity, while he gives the glory of his salvation to him "that cometh from Edom, with dyed garments from Bozrah," he will hail that simple-hearted, pious coloured woman as the instrument which was employed in bringing it about. Dear reader, let us think upon the foregoing circumstance, and "humble ourselves in the sight of the Lord, and he shall lift us up." When a penitent reaches the point at which he feels willing to have religion in any way, or anywhere, he is not far from the kingdom. This gentleman was at the time, or had been, the high-sheriff of the county where this occurred, and it did not lower him in the estimation of anybody.

There was much interest on the subject of religion at every appointment. Some sought, but to this day they have not found. The reason is, those precious souls have not been mindful of the direction, "consecrate yourselves to-day to the Lord." For, when this is fully done, we shall, in every case, be accepted of the Lord. Many, however, did so, during the year on Frederica—my first Circuit; and perhaps no man, that I had the pleasure of seeing converted to God, did then enjoy himself more than a noble-hearted sea captain, who was enabled to step on board the "old ship Zion." Talk with him about the voyage, his prospects, &c. He will tell you there is land ahead; and he hopes safely, after awhile, to get over the bar, though the breakers may run mountain high, and he may receive a stroke which will shiver all his timbers, start every bolt, and open every seam. I would say, cheer up, ship-mate, for the next sea will float you high over all.

"The rougher the blast,
The sooner 'tis past;
The tempests that rise
Shall gloriously hurry us home to the skies."

At length the time came for me to take my departure. The Quarterly Conference recommended me to the Annual Conference, so far as I know, unanimously. I found it one of the greatest trials of my life, up to that time, to sever my connexion from the kind friends of Frederica Circuit, with whom I had spent so pleasantly

4

the first year in my new relation. But then I did not murmur, nor since have I ever complained, at our itinerant sytem, which, I believe, is Christ-like and apostolic; and every one can see its adaptation to the world at large, but particularly to our own country. "We go forth weeping, bearing precious seed;" but we "shall doubtless come again with rejoicing, bringing our sheaves with us."

CHAPTER II.

Received by the Philadelphia Conference—Rev. Joseph Lybrand—Funeral Sermon of Bishop Roberts—Sent to Centreville Circuit—Rev. James Allen—Liberality of Ebenezer Methodist Episcopal Church, Philadelphia—Should decently bury our Dead—Bishop Whatcoat's happy Death—His Remains—Anecdote of James Hopkins—Rev. Solomon Sharp casts out the Devil—Anecdote of him on leaving an Appointment—He cures a penurious Class Leader—Rev. Dr. Roberts' prophecies—A revolutionary Soldier converted—An interesting Youth called as Samuel—End of a young Sabbath Breaker—Bad Company leads to Ruin—Kindness to coloured People—Major Massey—Funeral Sermons—Ministers need Encouragement—Novel Means for converting a Soul—New Church dedicated—Institution for the Poor well managed.

IN 1843, at the Conference held in Trinity Methodist Episcopal Church, Philadelphia, I was received, with several other young preachers, on trial. To this class of brethren I became ardently attached. The examinations for four years continuously brought us together, and caused us to be intimately acquainted. Several of the class had a short, but, I trust, useful career; at least three of them have crossed over Jordan, into Canaan, brothers Campbell, Titus, and Ray. The residue of us are scattered broad-cast over the land. One is now in South America, as a missionary—Rev. G. D. Carrow. May his health and life, and the health and lives of his family, be spared! And after we shall have done battle in the service of the King of kings, may we all be victors, and our class of the spring of 1843 hear it said, in each case, "Well done, good and faithful servant!"

With no circumstance, which took place at this Conference, was my heart more affected than with the speech made by the lamented Joseph Lybrand, upon retiring from the effective ranks. He had, from his boyhood, been connected with this body, starting when he was about eighteen years of age. Perhaps no man had fewer faults or fewer enemies; his character was untarnished, and now that he sleeps in death, it may be said, with the utmost propriety, he has left to his children the legacy of "a good name, which is better than precious ointment." He filled many of the most important appointments in the Conference, and always with the greatest acceptability and profit to the Church. In the office of Presiding Elder he was pre-eminently useful. He was comparatively a young man, too, when placed in this position first, but all felt that he was mindful of the direction of the apostle, "Let no man despise thy youth," for he certainly was "an example of the believers in word, in conversation, in charity, in spirit, in faith, in purity." His quarterly visitations on the district were anxiously looked for, and the whole community felt it a high privilege to listen to his burning words, which were eloquently spoken, and proved to be "like apples of gold in pictures of silver." Such a man, retiring from the regular work, made an impression. He took his relation of supernumerary amidst the sobs and gushing tears of his brethren in the ministry, after delivering an interesting address to the Conference; closing his remarks by saying, "If I could have my choice, I could desire—

'My body with my charge to lay down,
And cease at once to work and live.'"

He did not long live after this relation was taken, but long enough to see one of his sons join his own beloved Conference. This son, like his revered parent, is greatly esteemed for his many excellent traits of character, and he promises much usefulness to the Church. Thus were the words of Charles Wesley fulfilled, "The workmen die, but the work goes on." The last sermon he ever preached was in Harrisburg, Pa., April 2, 1843. His text was, "And the very God of peace sanctify you wholly," &c. The last words he uttered were addressed to his companion, as follows: "Last night I had sweet and precious communion with God, and now I close my eyes to sleep, hoping that, sleeping or waking, my thoughts will be of Him, and with Him." He calmly sunk to sleep in Jesus, April 24, 1845.

"O may I triumph so,
When all my warfare's past,
And, dying, find my latest foe
Beneath my feet at last."

The Conference was a pleasant one. Several of the Bishops were present, viz., Bishops Hedding, Waugh, and Morris. The funeral sermon of Bishop Roberts, who had recently died, was preached, by request of the Conference, in St. George's Church, by the venerable Bishop Hedding. It was a weeping, memorable time. Thank God! all of our Bishops that have died a natural death, have been victorious, through the blood of the Lamb. Bishop Emory was thrown from his carriage, and never spoke afterwards, but his life entitles us to the belief that he, too, rests in Abraham's bosom. Is not this a high commendation? Our Church has always been blessed with excellent men in the episcopacy. Dr. Emory had preaching talent of a high order. He was, before elected to the episcopacy, sent, as a delegate from our General Conference, to the British Conference, and before that august body preached a sermon replete with Jesus Christ and him crucified. After the sermon was concluded, the great Adam Clark addressed Mr. Emory as follows: "Is that the doctrine you preach in America?" The American minister replied, "Yes, sir, that's the doctrine." "Then," said Dr. Clark, "that's the doctrine that will take the world."

My appointment was read out for Centreville Circuit. I was much cast down at this. I knew the people were very intelligent, none more so, perhaps, in our work. I knew there were other denominations, and there must be considerable competition in that place, and I feared and trembled, and did not feel sufficient for these things. I was much relieved in my mind by the kindness of Rev. James Allen, the preacher in charge, who, the night the Conference closed, showed me much respect and affection; and the spirit that characterized him then, continued through all our period of sojourn together, as fellow-labourers in the vineyard of the Lord. He was a colleague much to be desired by any young preacher—willing and able to instruct. At his house his colleague always had a pleasant home, always received a cordial welcome, both on his part and on the part of his family. Rev. James Allen was a man of more than ordinary preaching abilities; he was a strong Methodist, and competent to defend the doctrines and polity of the Church of his choice. A man of studious habits, and, considering that his early advantages were limited, the amount of information which he possessed was remarkable. His aim was to be useful; he was abundant in labours. He never missed an appointment, however humble it was. He was ready to go to a week-day appointment; he was ready, whenever an opportunity offered, to preach the Gospel to the people of colour. And he would not allow his colleague to outstrip him in pastoral visiting, or in any other respect. But God, in his providence, saw fit to call this useful minister, in the prime of his days, from the walls of Zion, while pastor of the Ebenezer station, in the city of Philadelphia, in the summer of 1850. Rev. James Allen, like most of his brethren in the ministry, had not much of this world's goods. He left a widow and several children. And be it spoken to the credit of this weeping Church, sister Allen was requested to occupy the Parsonage till the ensuing Conference, a period of about seven months, and receive the salary which had been estimated for him. A single man was chosen, Rev. H. F. Hurn, to fill the vacancy, till the Conference should convene the following spring. A thousand dollars was also raised by this noble church, and appropriated to her and her children. The church further manifested their attachment to my dear friend, by burying him in front of their church edifice, and erecting over his remains a beautiful marble monument. How commendable! The patriarchs attached much importance to the burial of their dead properly, and did not spare expense. It is a matter of grief to me that so little attention is paid to this subject by many at the present day. No stone, nor hardly a hillock of grass, to mark the spot where the dust of some flaming herald of salvation rests! And there are those who abound in wealth, and allow the family grave-yard to be neglected, not even an enclosure to protect the graves of their sires from being trampled upon by horses, cattle, hogs, &c. In regard, however, to those who have slept in Jesus, they are not forgotten by Him

"Who watches all their dust,
Till he shall bid it rise."

On this subject allow me to call especial attention to the course pursued in this matter by Abraham, and I refer my readers to the twenty-third chapter of the book of Genesis.

I was greatly gratified with the course recently pursued by our lay brethren in Dover, Delaware, and the members of the Philadelphia Annual Conference, in reference to the remains of Rev. Richard Whatcoat, the third Bishop of the Methodist Episcopal Church, who finished his course in that town, at the house of Richard Basset, Esq., a prominent citizen, and afterwards the Governor of Delaware. The end of Bishop Whatcoat, which took place the 6th of June, 1806, was peaceful, and his last night was spent in prayer and praise. He frequently prayed to the Lord in this time of need, and was often heard during the night to exclaim, "Bless the Lord! Bless the Lord!" A murmur never escaped his lips. A dear servant of God, and a friend of mine, Thomas Stevenson, Esq., who still lives, has informed me that he was with him the last night he lived, and though it was a most solemn time (for there was a corpse in the house), "it was," says he, "the happiest night I ever experienced." His remains were deposited immediately under the altar of the Methodist Episcopal Church of that place. His funeral sermon was preached by Rev. Dr. Chandler. Great respect was shown to this valuable minister, though a stranger in a strange land. A slab of marble, with an appropriate inscription, was inserted in the wall of the church, to mark the spot where he rested.

The brethren and friends of our Church, in the city of Baltimore, have with them the remains of Bishop Asbury, Bishop Emory, and Bishop George, and by Baltimorians, of course, who are ready for every good word and work (where Methodism is strong and second to none on earth in quality), due respect has been shown to these apostolic men. To visit their resting-places, and see the attention that has been paid, one would be ready to conclude, these friends have paid attention to the teaching of the word, which directs that we should "not love in word, neither in tongue; but in deed and in truth." Their arrangements being made for the remains of the deceased Bishops, they nobly—a few years since—asked the brethren in Dover, and also the Philadelphia Conference, the privilege of removing the remains of Bishop Whatcoat to that spot. We appreciated their kindness, but felt compelled to answer in the negative; both laymen and ministers desiring that the rest of this servant of God should not be disturbed, "till waked by the trumpet's sound." We covet the privilege of rising with him in the resurrection morn. As he had laboured in that region and died there, and as he was on his way to attend the Philadelphia Conference, we conjointly feel it a great privilege to retain his remains; and since the old church in Dover has been demolished, and a new one built in the central part of the town, a monument has been erected over this conquering soldier of the cross, that is not surpassed in neatness and durability by any monument erected over the remains of any officer of our Army or Navy, who may have distinguished himself for military prowess. We will not neglect, readers, those, in death, who have, in life, heroically led us on to victory.

I now have on my mind a faithful leader in our Israel, who fell near Salisbury, Maryland, a few years since. His remains were disinterred, and conveyed to the "Bethel Methodist Episcopal Churchyard," in Cecil county, Maryland, near the Delaware line, where he sleeps quietly with Rev. Lawrence Laurenson, and others of precious memory. This servant of God was respected in life, and in his death and burial not neglected. Too much credit, however, cannot be ascribed to his two affectionate children, who regarded it, to my certain knowledge, as no little pleasure, and honour also, to thus respect their deceased father. *Children, love your parents.* This faithful man was not only beloved by his children, but by all who knew him—his praise was in all the churches. He had seals to his ministry in every field of labour he occupied. I refer to Rev. John S. Taylor, of the Philadelphia Conference. His labours and usefulness in Bethel Methodist Episcopal Church, Philadelphia, will never be forgotten. He was the means of the building of that church. He there laid the foundation of his disease and death, by his *abundant labours.* He was admirably adapted to the sons of the ocean—his influence over them was almost unbounded. He could, however, not only give satisfaction to this *important* class of society, but his practical, earnest, and experimental manner of preaching, made him acceptable in any sphere. I will give one instance. While he was pastor of Mariner's Bethel, Rev. Levi Scott (now Bishop) was Presiding Elder of the South Philadelphia District. It so happened that the Elder could not, for some good causes, attend one of his Quarterly Meetings in a remote part of his district. Brother Taylor was earnestly requested by the Elder, to go in his place and hold the Quarterly Meeting. He did so, greatly to the satisfaction and admiration of the people. It was in the time of the war with Mexico. In that war the names of *Scott* and *Taylor* were conspicuous. The delighted people sent word to the Elder to this effect, "When *General Scott* can't come, *General Taylor* will do just as well!" Mr. Taylor died in great peace, August 21, 1849, in the 44th year of his age.

Kent Island was to me a deeply interesting part of our Circuit. We had two regular preaching places on the island. We preached on Saturdays at Father James Hopkins's. This was an old appointment, and Father and Mother Hopkins were amongst the oldest of our membership. I was told of a circumstance about him that made me restless the first few times I stayed there. The old gentleman was in the habit of praying with the entire family, coloured as well as white, and it was requisite to hold morning prayers as early as possible, so that the hands, at the proper time, could go to their work. A minister, of very high standing, spent a night there, and it so happened that he did not rise till the sun was marching on his course. When he descended from the bed-chamber, he was asked to breakfast. Said the minister, "We will, if you please, have a word of prayer first." Whereupon the good old gentleman replied, "I have had prayers, but if you don't think it was done well, you can do it over again." I did fear that I, too, might oversleep myself, and not be in time to join in the devotions of the family. But this was never the case in a single instance, and I had the pleasure of being chaplain to that house whenever it was my happy privilege to sojourn with them. In whatever other respects I may have been blameable, I feel a clear conscience in this respect throughout my itinerant life. Dear young brethren in the ministry, let us endeavour not to sleep at our post. Much is to be accomplished in the devotions of the families where we sojourn, if those devotions are performed at the proper time, and in the right way. And may I be permitted to suggest that the time thus spent is not lost, either to us or to the families in which we may officiate. Read God's holy Word, sing one of the songs of Zion, and devoutly pray. The effects will accompany us throughout the day. Every minister that faithfully carries out the directions here given, will, in my humble opinion, "cast bread upon the waters, and find it after many days."

On the island we frequently heard of Rev. Solomon Sharp, although many years had passed away since he laboured in that region. But there, as elsewhere, he "made his mark." Probably it will not be out of place to relate an incident that occurred on this island, and with which he was prominently connected. He preached at a private house on a certain day. Much divine influence attended the preaching. The congregation was, at the proper time, dismissed. One lady, who was powerfully wrought upon, remained in the greatest distress, and, writhing in agony of soul, her body was convulsed, her face the picture of despair. Rev. Solomon Sharp drew near to her. She exclaimed, in a sepulchral tone, "You are a pretty preacher of the Gospel!" This flaming minister of Christ, this "true successor of the apostles" who were empowered to cast out devils, said (for he believed it was Diabolus himself that uttered the words), "Yes, you know I am a preacher of the everlasting Gospel of God, and I command you to come out of her." And to the day of his death, he believed that it was the devil in her, that she was diabolically possessed, and that he plainly saw, with his bodily eyes, the evil one go out of her at his command; and as he passed out of the door, Mr. Sharp said, "Sneak off, to your native hell." The lady was truly happy, and "longing hopes and cheerful smiles sat undisturbed upon her brow."

I knew, when I travelled here, two venerable men that were boys at the time this occurred, and they were both present. They did not tell me that they saw the devil, but they did give me the other facts above related, and stated, that this minister of Christ was known all over the island and county as, "*Solomon Sharp, the devil-driver.*"

My first colleague, Rev. William Connelly, told me

that he often heard Father Sharp refer to this incident, and there are now many living witnesses to the fact, that he never wavered in his belief that this was a case of demoniacal possession, or that God gave him power on that occasion to carry out the command, "Cast out devils."

Mr. Sharp was, by no means, an ordinary preacher. He was a man of prominence. He filled the office of Presiding Elder for several years, and occupied some of the most important stations in the Philadelphia Conference. He was a very ready and rather witty man. I will, to illustrate this position, relate a circumstance connected with his leaving a certain appointment, the conference year having expired. Said he, when about closing the last sermon in that charge, "Brethren and sisters, this is the last sermon, in all probability, I shall ever preach for you." One in the congregation replied in an audible manner, "I am glad of it!" To which Mr. Sharp replied, "Yes, and so is your father, the devil, also glad of it." At an appointment on a Circuit he travelled, there was a class leader who was somewhat notorious for being timid relative to collecting class money. He believed in keeping the preacher poor, and seemed to think that this would keep him humble. And for these reasons, and also for fear of destroying the spirituality of the society, he seldom mentioned the subject of quarterage. Are there not some in our Israel too much like him? But this class leader was proverbial for praying for the preachers. Father Sharp was made acquainted with his character, and went to his first appointment, prepared to administer to him a reproof. At the close of the class the minister called on the leader to pray, and he very ardently proceeded in this good work. He soon began to invoke God's blessing upon the ministers; especially he prayed, "Lord bless Father Sharp, and give him many souls for his hire." To this petition this servant of God responded, "Amen! Amen!! Amen!!! but thou knowest, O Lord, that Father Sharp cannot live on human souls." So we see he was apostolic in this respect as well as in other particulars, and was ready to say, in relation to himself and his brethren in the work of the ministry, "If we have sown unto you spiritual things, is it a great thing if we should reap your carnal things?" I was credibly informed that the result was, that that class leader never failed afterwards to have his quarterage ready to go into the hands of the stewards at the proper time.

I heard him once preach when I was a very small boy, at a camp meeting. His dress was remarkably plain, his hair was long, and whitened by the frosts of many winters, and hung in ringlets down to his shoulders. His effort had a signal effect, and many fell under his powerful appeals. The ministers in the stand were greatly moved. I did not then comprehend these things. I saw persons borne off from the aisle apparently dead. I was then six or seven years of age, and my childish conclusion was, these men *have caught their souls;* and the first name I ever applied to Methodist ministers, and it was done sincerely, was, "Soul Catchers!" I did not miss in this matter greatly, for we must be "fishers of men." May we be Divinely assisted in our work, and "get the net on the right side of the ship," and catch a "great multitude of" souls.

> "They watch for souls for which the Lord
> Did heavenly bliss forego,
> For souls which must for ever live
> In raptures or in woe."

This ardent labourer in the vineyard of the Lord was ready to do good in every possible way. He heeded the rule, "See that each society is duly supplied with books." This is an excellent plan for accomplishing good in our circuits and stations, and it does not appear to my mind that this will, in the least degree, lower the dignity of the ministerial office, properly managed. I hope I may never be guilty of anything more incompatible with the spirit of the Gospel. As Paul said to young Timothy, "Give attendance to reading," so should we say to our people, especially to our young people, as by this means they would be able to "add to their faith knowledge."

For more than forty years Mr. Sharp was a travelling

preacher, starting when he was only twenty years of age. He died in his sixty-fifth year, at Smyrna, Delaware, on the 13th of March, 1836. His last sermon, a short time before his death, was upon Heb. iv. 9, on the rest that remains to the people of God. He was very happy, and was heard to say, "Now I feel as if my work was done." Only a little time elapsed before suddenly his soul fled to a Land of Spirits bright. He died of asthma.

Our quarterly camp meeting was held on this part of our Circuit, a gentleman of another church kindly furnishing us the ground gratis. May the Lord reward him! The meeting was a blessing to scores, I may say hundreds. We were favoured with the efficient services of Rev. Dr. Roberts, of Baltimore, and other strong men in Israel. As Rev. Dr. Roberts concluded one of his sermons, which was productive of the happiest results, among others pungently convicted was an aged, respectable gentleman. He shed tears freely. We all tried to induce him to yield to the powers of love, and consecrate himself that day unto the service of God. He hesitated. He was almost persuaded to become a Christian, but entreated us to excuse him on that occasion. The Doctor said, "That man of age, if he refuses this call, I fear seriously will go home and die, and never have another call." Those words were too true. In two weeks after my colleague and myself performed for him funeral services, and saw him lowered into the cold grave. He earnestly prayed on his dying bed, and enlisted all the help that he could. He had a faithful coloured servant, who plead earnestly at the throne of grace in behalf of his master, who was in the agonies of death. Many at that camp meeting heard their last sermon, received their last call from the sacred desk. The autumn that followed was very sickly, and deathly too. Seeing persons dying, in a few weeks after meeting them at such a place, led us to say, with deepest feeling, "If thou hadst known, even thou, in this thy day, the things that belong to thy peace! but now they are hid from thine eyes."

Rev. W. H. Elliot was with us at this deeply interesting camp. He was then, as he always has been since, and now is, a zealous, faithful minister of the Gospel. It is said, "A prophet is not without honour save in his own country." This worthy brother was raised here, he was at home, yet we found him acceptable among all the people, and his labours were owned of God. Among those who were awakened through his ministrations was a very aged person, who had fought in the Revolutionary War, under the immortal Washington. He was one of the few who live to be fourscore, and his faculties seemed perfect. He was a little trembling in his limbs, and when I saw him kneel at the altar, there were probably one hundred and fifty others, at the same time, bending the suppliant knee. I was afraid that this aged person would be trampled upon, and, the preaching being over, I had him removed up into the stand, where we tried properly to instruct him, and pray for him. It was not long before he obtained victory over the devil, and felt that he was set free by the Son of God, and was free indeed. Then, though at a late period in life, he enlisted in the "good fight." After we pass a certain age, earthly armies decline to receive us as soldiers. I am thankful that this regulation does not characterize the spiritual conflict, in which we may all engage—young and old—without respect to circumstances. But it is lamentably true that very few old persons avail themselves of this privilege. This is a rare case!

I desire to present to my readers the case of an interesting youth: his name was Frederick. He was seriously impressed on the subject of religion, but the time came for him to return to his home, which was some fifteen miles down the island. When he reached home, the family generally were absent, having also been in attendance at the camp meeting, and had not yet reached home. Home appeared to Frederick for the first time cheerless, and while he was reflecting and meditating on matters appertaining to the salvation of his soul, a voice, apparently proceeding from the barn, fell upon his ear, and reached, with great effect, his young and tender heart. The words that he supposed he heard were,

"Frederick! Frederick!! Frederick!!! go back, and seek religion this night." The sun had hid himself behind the western hills. Nevertheless, this youth felt that the call was from Heaven, and, like young Samuel, he was determined to hearken to it! He deliberately saddled his horse, and started for the meeting. He soon met his father and mother returning. The father said, "Where are you going, my boy?" With a heart swelling with emotion, and tears coursing down his cheeks, he replied, "I am going back to the camp ground, to try to get religion." He was young, yet his parents knew him too well to doubt his sincerity for a moment, and they bid him God-speed. Wisely did they act! How differently do parents—professing godliness, too—sometimes act towards their children, at times when their young hearts are deeply affected, and they have a desire to become pious. It is said to them, "You are too young; you do not know what you are about; wait till you get old enough to keep religion when you get it." This course, dear parents, may be ruinous to your children. Rather encourage them to "bear the yoke in their youth."

> "It saves us from a thousand snares,
> To mind religion young."

Frederick, being encouraged by his noble-hearted parents, prosecuted his journey, and, that night, while I was, with other soldiers, reconnoitering the spiritual battlefield, among the slain of the Lord, which were many, I saw, by the light of the camp fires, my young friend Frederick in agony. But soon the Heavenly Physician made the wounded whole. He joined the Church with many others, the morning the meeting closed, and every one could plainly discover that this youth had experienced a change of heart.

"Ye shall know them by their fruits."

I want my young friends particularly to look at the sequel of this case. In about two weeks after giving his young heart to God, sickness and death overtook him, and he had to leave all his earthly ties behind. But he had one tie in Heaven, that was more dear to his heart than every other, than all others: that tie was Jesus. And after exhorting his kind parents, brothers, and sisters, to love the Saviour, and telling them he was "Going Home to die no more," he could sing (my young friends, don't forget it),

"All hail the power of Jesu's name,
Let angels prostrate fall;
Bring forth the royal diadem,
And crown Him Lord of all."

At another point on this Circuit I used to put up with an excellent family. There was an indentured youth that resided there. He was treated kindly, and, to my certain knowledge, his religious culture was anxiously looked after by the gentleman to whom he was apprenticed. I used frequently to admonish him to become pious, but our united efforts seemed unavailing. On a certain Sabbath he was urged to go to preaching, but offered some excuse, did not go, but, instead of doing so, went to gather cherries. And, when in the top of the tree, the limb, on which he stood, breaking, he fell, and came in direct contact with a sharp fence stake, that pierced him through in a vital part, and the poor boy, aged about sixteen, was soon, almost instantly, senseless and dead! "Remember the Sabbath day to keep it holy." How much better it would have been for him to have gone to Sabbath School, and to Church! To-day he might be living, and useful in society.

In this county another sad event took place, that I feel anxious to introduce, hoping it may be of service in restraining the young from evil, and in inducing them to "Remember their Creator in the days of their youth." The young man, of whom I now speak, I knew intimately. Many a time I have urged him to serve the Lord. He was a regular attendant of Church, but procrastinated his salvation. He associated with some calculated to lead him away from the house of God. "Evil communications corrupt good manners." He became a gambler, a drunkard, and, under the influence of ardent spirits, with a weapon of death, murdered one of his fellow men! I visited him in the prison before he had his trial. He was a tender-hearted young man. He wept bitterly, and said, "Often have you urged me to embrace religion. O! that I had taken your advice! I should have been saved from this horrible place, and the guilty conscience that now abides with me by day and by night. But it is now too late. I am ruined for time, and, I fear, for eternity. I beg an interest in your prayers." He was sentenced to a long imprisonment in the Penitentiary. His amiability there won him many friends, and, it was thought, that he would have been reprieved by Executive clemency. But death terminated his career there prematurely. I hope he clung to the Gospel, the only hope of the guilty. Young readers, beware of the company you keep. "Blessed is the man that walketh not in the counsel of the ungodly, nor standeth in the way of sinners, nor sitteth in the seat of the scornful." "And look not upon the cup."

While I travelled this Circuit, I found that there was much kindness shown to the slave and colored population, generally. It is not my purpose to write an apology for the institution of slavery, but I will say, that great injustice, sometimes, is done to our people in the South relative to the treatment of their slaves. They had a place, and they were cordially welcome in this Circuit, in all our churches. I have frequently, of Saturday nights, preached for them in the churches of the whites, and never a murmur escaped from the lips of any person that I am aware of. I used to be pleased in family prayer to see the coloured part of the family brought in, and, after reading a portion of the Holy Scriptures, I used to give out some plain hymn, such as, "O that my load of sin were gone;" or, "When I can read my title clear," or some other familiar verses, and such singing I rarely ever heard. They would sing without restraint and pray fervently, and seemed as happy as they could live.

We had regular preaching in the Quarter at Major Massey's. When I travelled the Circuit, this appointment was still continued, although the good Major had deceased the year before in great peace, having a bright prospect of eternal life. His widow was anxious to carry out his wishes relative to the spiritual improvement of the coloured people. We used to hold meetings there with great comfort, and much good was done. The congregations were quite large. The people of colour would come from neighbouring farms. Many of the very best, and most intelligent members of our Church led class for them, and did not feel it beneath their dignity to do so. This being the case, many of this class were brought to a saving knowledge of the truth, and we had about five hundred communicants of this class of society, within the bounds of our Circuit.

I have already stated that it was very sickly and deathly in this Circuit this year, and we were often called upon to preach funerals. Amongst many others, I preached the funeral sermon of an estimable, wealthy citizen, on a Sabbath afternoon. He was a member of the Protestant Episcopal Church. A very large audience assembled together. It was a heavy cross for me to officiate, but I trusted in God, felt happy in trying to faithfully warn the people from "Prepare to meet thy God." After leaving the place, a very old Methodist, who felt much for me, and, no doubt, earnestly prayed for me, said to me, "Brother Manship, you did well at the funeral, but I think it is likely the devil has told you so before this." The old gentleman understood human nature very well, and was well acquainted with the wiles of Satan. Persons should be careful how they commend and flatter a minister to his face. We are but men. Still I am of opinion that a word of encouragement, occasionally, from judicious persons, is calculated to "Strengthen the weak hands, and confirm the feeble knees." And it may save the young minister from despondency for him to duly consider, and for discreet friends to "let him know" that he has been instrumental in "converting a sinner from the error of his way."

I formed the acquaintance of an elderly gentleman in this region, who attended our meetings, and was somewhat interested. He invited me to his house. He was remarkably clever in his way. He was brought up in the Protestant Episcopal Church. He told me I was the first Methodist preacher that had ever been in his house. I went home with him for the sole purpose of trying to promote his salvation. It was considerably out of my way, and in this region there was no scarcity of homes for the ministers. And the brethren deemed it a privilege to entertain us. I could hardly tell what means to adopt to win this elderly gentleman's affections more fully, and, by that agency, be likely to lead him on to the cross. Thinking of Paul's course, which was to become "all things to all men, that he might by all means save some," I felt disposed to adopt it in this case. I had not long been his guest before he asked me to "smoke with him." He presented me with a pipe. I supposed it might be the pipe of peace. He smoked, and I did likewise. I was not accustomed to it, or to the use of tobacco in any form whatever. He enjoyed it apparently very much. I soon lost my equilibrium, and almost my senses. For a short time I never was so sick. From that day till the present I have had "Neither part nor lot in this matter," and advise my readers, especially my young readers, to "Touch not, taste not, handle not" the article; for it paves the way for other unprofitable habits, and the issue may be most disastrous.

At the proper time I took my departure from my kind old friend's comfortable mansion, hoping (although I failed in my smoking operations, perhaps) that I was of some service to him and his family; for, in the last prayer I had with the family, we had a weeping time. He has gone to his long home. I hope his end was peaceful. But I assure my readers I never adopted this expedient again in trying to get a soul converted. But I have tried and hope still to try to "Be instant in season, out of season, reprove, rebuke, exhort with all long-suffering and doctrine."

We had during the year prosperity—many were added to the church, young and old, rich and poor, bond and free; and my beloved colleague and myself left this field of labour with much regret. We had the pleasure of seeing one new church completed and dedicated by my colleague to the worship of Almighty God. This was in the neighbourhood of Ruthsburg, and the church was called "Ebenezer," meaning, hitherto God hath helped us. He did help us there, and the little society increased considerably. For this enterprise the community was greatly indebted to Brother James Clark and Brother Joseph K. Cook, temporally and spiritually; for they not only mainly built the house, but they led class, one for the white society, and the other for the coloured. They met with considerable opposition in this work, and many discouragements; but, by the blessing of God, they were enabled to see their noble wishes realized. Those who are the means of accomplishing such a work, are public benefactors; and the amount of good that is thus accomplished, will not be known until that glorious day shall roll round, when many that we did not think of in that connexion, will "arise up and call us blessed."

This house was contiguous to the Alms House of the county; and, literally, by the erection of this place, "the poor had the gospel preached to them." The gentleman that kept this institution, at the time I travelled there, was a valuable member of the Church. I found this a most delightful home. The manner in which the house was kept and regulated, was a credit to the county. No one was, so far as I was capable of seeing, neglected. I often passed through the institution—visiting the sick and praying with them—in company with the kind-hearted overseer. And for the benefit of those who could not get to the church, we used occasionally to preach in the institution. And we there found many pious souls, and saw evidences that the poor could be truly happy. And from this place—Lazarus-like—there would be jewels, borne on the golden pinions of angels to Abraham's bosom; and though they are poor now, they will soon be rich. "For ye know the grace of our Lord Jesus Christ, that though he was rich, yet for your sakes he became poor, that ye through his poverty might be rich."

CHAPTER III.

Chestnut Hill made a distinct Charge—Not favourable to Union Churches—Kindness of a Presbyterian Family—New Methodist Episcopal Church commenced—Hold the Second Quarterly Meeting in a Grove—Night Meetings defended—School-House not accessible —Private House opened for Protracted Meeting Services—God prospers those who are faithful to his Cause—A wicked Man wanted me hung—Can't stop the Work of God—Hold another Woods Meeting near Dreshertown—The Character and Liberality of an aged German—Rev. Albert Barnes—Anecdote of General Jackson—God's Ambassadors truly honourable—Rough Fields of Labour profitable to the young Minister—Against making our own Appointments—The Petitioning System not the more excellent Way.

I WAS sent, in the spring of 1844, to Chestnut Hill. I left the Conference before it closed, a few days, not dreaming I was to come up. I passed on to spend a few days with my friends on the peninsula; and, when I was informed by some of the preachers that my appointment was to Chestnut Hill, I was very greatly surprised. I did not know there was such a place in the bounds of the Conference. But I soon found it, situated in the county of Philadelphia, then nine miles from the city, but now, since the Act of Consolidation was passed, a part of it. It was beautifully situated, a village set upon a hill. It had formerly been a part of Germantown charge; but it now became a distinct field of labour, and I was the first preacher appointed to it. But I was rather coldly received. The reason of the cool reception was mainly owing to the fear, on the part of the society, that they could not support a minister. At the first Quarterly Meeting, the funds amounted in all to about *two dollars!* I found some of the people distant; and, as I was a stranger in a strange land, it was calculated to depress my spirits. But there was a most happy change, ere long.

Our preaching place was a Union stone chapel. This edifice was built by a worthy gentleman, for the use of the different denominations. Much good was accomplished, and several churches had been built; and we were left, almost exclusively, as the occupants of the chapel, the Episcopalians and Presbyterians only occasionally occupying the house. I was not satisfied with this arrangement, and urged the society to arise and build, weak as they were; because, in the first place, the chapel was too contracted; in the second place, I was under the impression that each denomination would prosper more where they felt they had the entire control. And, while I profess to be in favour of *evangelic alliance*, and go in heartily for the sentiment of the Psalmist, "How good and how pleasant it is for brethren to dwell together in unity;" at the same time, I do not think favourably of the amalgamation of different denominations in one and the same edifice. While we agree upon the leading doctrines of salvation, there are matters of minor importance about which we disagree. Some work in one way, and some in another way, to accomplish the same end; and "behold how great a matter a little fire kindleth!" Therefore, I felt it my duty to use all diligence to get our society into the spirit of building a new, regular Methodist Episcopal Church. We were, to some extent, successful. A beautiful lot was procured. The spot was elevated, on a principal thoroughfare, and overlooking the whole surrounding country. The stone was on the ground, and a board of trustees were regularly organized. Some of the brethren from Germantown came up to our help, and none more effectively than Jacob Thomas, Esq., and Samuel Y. Harmer, a local preacher. The latter was the president of our board. The spirit and disposition to carry this enterprise through were becoming general, many of our Presbyterian friends also aiding us with their counsel and means. We had their co-operation, too, at our prayer meetings through the week. And one gentleman of this persuasion, who in this place had a fine summer residence, opened his house for a prayer meeting; and he and his excellent Christian lady took part in the public exercises.

When I first came to this place, there was but little to encourage; but, at the close of the year, I had a great desire to be returned, to see the plans carried out that had been devised for the erection of a new church. In this respect I was not gratified, but the work was committed to other and better hands; and, in due time, the end was accomplished. And now, for several years, Wesley Chapel, "beautiful for situation," has stood, as one of the ornaments of the place.

> "These temples of his grace,
> How beautiful they stand!
> The honours of our native place,
> And bulwarks of our land."

I had never, from experience or observation, known scarcely anything about a station. I could not, therefore, feel happy to confine myself to that point alone. I found that the surrounding country, so far as Methodism was concerned, was destitute of churches. There were other denominational organizations; and I may, with much truth, say, "as concerning this sect, everywhere it was spoken against." We succeeded, in August, in getting the use of a gentleman's woods, in the neighbourhood of Wrangletown, to hold our second Quarterly Meeting in. A large concourse assembled; and our venerable Presiding Elder, Rev. Solomon Higgins, preached to the vast mass of persons faithfully the unsearchable riches of Christ. The subject was the *disease and cure of Naaman the leper.* I was also, on that occasion, assisted by Rev. James Cunningham, pastor of Germantown Church. This meeting did much, in strengthening our weak cause, in this neighbourhood. Here we were permitted to use the school-house, at least on Sundays, during the day, but not at night. Some people have a horrid opinion of night meetings. I met with a man who said to me, "I had rather follow my daughter to the grave than know of her going to a *Methodist class meeting, or night meeting.*" I told him I hoped that neither he nor his daughter would ever get into a *worse place.* Some people "strain at a gnat and swallow a camel." We advocate night meetings, not because we are ashamed of the light of day, for we are willing to be "known and read of all men." But we have adopted them because we have much work to do, and there is not sufficient time during the day. And while we are anxious to get the wealthy converted, who have their time at their disposal, we also feel that "the poor" must "have the gospel preached unto them;" and hundreds and thousands of this large class, who cannot, from their situation, be present frequently in the day, can be at our evening meetings. The word of God encourages us to pray in the night season, as well as in the daytime. Jacob prayed all night; Paul preached till midnight, on a certain occasion; the Saviour spent whole nights in prayer. With such examples before us, we will "spend the day and share the night" in trying to accomplish the work which God has given us to do. And although I am in favour of closing our night meetings at a proper time, in general (and this is not only my theory, but my practice), yet there may be, and frequently is, sufficient reason for our continuing longer; and, like the poet, we feel it is right and proper to say,

> "With Thee all night I mean to stay,
> And wrestle till the break of day."

This we can do, and this we will do, if the exigencies of the case demand it; and, in our beloved free country, where religion generally is protected, there shall be none to molest or make us afraid. And, indeed, those sister denominations that used to be against night meetings, in theory and in practice, have found it necessary to recede a little as a *prudential regulation.* Now we are at it, and all at it; and, when we do all we can, we shall still be but "unprofitable servants," and many, it is to be feared, will not, after all, be saved.

Those who had the management of the school-house in this location, being inflexible in relation to our occupying it at night, the prospect being good, and we desiring to hold a protracted meeting, a poor man—but one of God's nobility—opened his house for this purpose. The community seemed amazed that he would, as he was not a member of the society, encourage this thing, and aid and abet this "constant singing, praying, shouting, and noisy preaching." The protracted meeting was held. It resulted in much good, and greatly contributed to establish in that neighbourhood a permanent place of worship, which was soon, by God's blessing, accomplished. And I want my readers to know, that this man, who opened his house for the worship of God, and for the entertainment of God's ministers and people, who some supposed would "eat him out of house and home," has greatly prospered, and now owns and lives on his own farm, increasing in goods, and, what is still better, happy in religion. He did not, though a sinner, despise God's infant church; and, consequently, God has not despised him. In this case we see the words of our Saviour fulfilled: "He that receiveth a prophet in the name of a prophet, shall receive a prophet's reward; and he that receiveth a righteous man in the name of a righteous man, shall receive a righteous man's reward."

Threatening remarks were made against me by a neighbour, who was wealthy. Two of his daughters embraced religion at our meetings. He seemed very desirous to get me out of the neighbourhood; and, in fact, judging from his remarks, out of the world too; for he said, "*I will buy the rope if any one will hang him!*" His daughters, happily converted, softened him down considerably. They took him our book of discipline also, with the view of convincing him that the Methodists were not the worst people in the world. But he had grown old in sin; he did not live long thereafter, yet we hope God was merciful to him. When his death was announced, I could not but think of the words of the Psalmist: "He hath also prepared for him the instruments of death, he ordaineth his arrows against the persecutors."

The work of religion prospered; and the more this infant society was opposed, the more it increased. I was greatly aided at this point by the family of Minnicks, Brothers Samuel, Joseph, and George, two of whom are living still, and are ministers of the gospel. Brother Joseph died in the city of Philadelphia some years since. And, as he lived, he died, a happy Christian, with a bright prospect of eternal life before him. We found, at this point, labourers to be few, and much opposition to encounter; nevertheless, the Lord brought us safely through by his love and power, and those who supposed they would nip this matter in its bud were disappointed. "Can a man stop the rolling tide? Can he retard the progress of the sun? The cause of God is in motion, and will crush every obstacle. Nor is this all. He makes opposition an advantage: his enemies intend one thing and he another, and they serve an interest they despise, and labour to repress; their schemes fulfil his plan; he turns them from their natural currents into secret channels, prepared to receive them, and in which they flow along, into the fulness of Him that filleth all in all."

We felt a desire to plant the tree of Methodism in the neighbourhood of Dreshertown, Montgomery county, about seven miles from Chestnut Hill. There were a few in this neighbourhood who wished to be in fellowship with us, and they were highly gratified with the idea of a woods meeting. This was new to the community. A beautiful place was offered to us; and, under those majestic oaks, we prepared for the accommodation of a large concourse. They came from every quarter, many, probably, for no good, but the Sabbath was well spent. God's word was faithfully preached, fervent prayers were offered for the revival of God's work, and songs of Zion were sung with the spirit, and the sacrament of the Lord's supper was then and there administered, for the first time among the Methodists, to about *twenty persons.* This was a small proportion of the great crowd; but the Lord was in our midst, and a few poor penitents that day were not ashamed to cry for mercy. While I beheld the great crowd who did not take a deep interest in this religious meeting, and the little band that were ready to shout out, "God forbid that I should glory, save in the cross of our Lord Jesus Christ," I could but think of the solemn words of our Great Teacher; "Enter ye in at the straight gate: for wide is the gate, and broad is the way that leadeth to destruction, and many there be which go in thereat: Because straight is the gate, and narrow is the way, which leadeth unto life, and few there be that find it."

I was highly favoured with ministerial help on this occasion. Rev. William McCombs, and Rev. Peter Isenbry were with me, and represented Methodism well. They were greatly assisted from on high that day, in the pulpit. I thought such preaching would take the world—plain, practical, powerful. The minister ought to feel. May we imitate the ancient preacher, who said, "Oh that my head were waters, and mine eyes a fountain of tears, that I might weep day and night for the slain of the daughter of my people."

In this neighbourhood we found a true friend in a gentleman by the name of Wiseman. He was a German, and entertained some singular notions that appeared to me very superstitious. I could not see the use of having so many horse-shoes about the premises; but I was told, "the object was to keep the witches away!" The old gentleman had a horse that he appeared to love fondly, and it was his custom, about midnight, to get up and feed him. I have known him, for fear of worrying the horse, to walk fifteen miles, and scarcely any load in the wagon. How different from many, who have no compassion on the dumb beast! but "a righteous man regardeth the life of his beast, but the tender mercies of the wicked are cruel."

This elderly gentleman was not only generous towards his noble animal, but he was kind and friendly towards God's people and cause. He allowed us to establish preaching in his house, and form a class there. Our preaching-room was his fine parlour. But it was soon evident that it was insufficient to hold the people that came to the meetings. He allowed us to have the wall that divided the parlour from the large dining-room removed. And soon literally this middle wall of partition was taken away, and folding-doors introduced in its place. By this arrangement, the two rooms could be brought into one, which afforded space for a considerable congregation. Here we preached, and the Lord owned his Word, and our society increased greatly, and it did seem to me to be a field that was "white to harvest." The venerable German joined the class with his companion, and they were both very desirous to have a regular church built. He presented to us, towards the close of the year, a fine lot for the church location, and burial purposes, and proffered to give all the stone requisite to build the house. I would not raise my voice against the episcopacy in their appointments; but I do firmly believe that I ought to have gone back, the second year, to that field of labour. I felt a very deep interest in this matter. The old German gentleman and myself were great friends, and I would have had some advantages that a stranger could not be expected to possess. The itinerancy made changes. This point was somewhat difficult of access. It was a long distance to walk, and there truly were barriers in the way. The matter was allowed to rest, the society there was feeble, and a few years only rolled around before my dear old German friend passed away! The lot was not taken and occupied according to his wishes at the time, and now this matter is in other hands, and the prospect vanishes. We ought not to neglect anything till to-morrow that should be done to-day. It would have been well for our cause could the old adage have been observed, "Strike while the iron is hot."

At Chestnut Hill, my principal appointment, the Rev. Albert Barnes, who stands at the head of the New School Presbyterian Church, in connexion with his family, spent his summers generally. And it is difficult to find a more healthy place. The air fresh and pure, and, very near the village, is the romantic Wissahickon, affording fine bathing facilities. Mr. Barnes was generous personally towards our new enterprise at this place. And from all I could see and hear, I am led to consider him one of the first men of the present day. There is one circumstance I want to mention. He declines titles. Many have them annexed to their names, I suppose not so learned as he, and not so meritorious. Not only do his sermons, but his voluminous writings, show him to be no ordinary man. But to be a minister of the everlasting Gospel, he may think, is high enough honour for him.

I feel at this point inclined to speak of an incident in regard to General Jackson, when President of the United States. An office was asked at his hands by a gentleman, who presented a strong recommendation to the old hero; and to make it doubly strong, as he supposed, urged that he was a minister of the Gospel. The President said, "Sir, this being the case, you hold a higher office, and more honourable station, than I or any other man can give you. My advice to you is to go home and make a faithful use of the very high commission you already have." He failed to accomplish his purpose, but that advice, perhaps, did him more service than any office would have done that the President had the power to confer.

Brethren in the ministry, let us call to mind the words of the Apostle: "Now then we are ambassadors for Christ, as though God did beseech you by us, we pray you in Christ's stead be ye reconciled to God." This being our high and honourable calling, why should we desire to "receive honour one of another, and seek not the honour that cometh from God only?" We will go forward as faithful representatives of the King of kings, and not "covet crowns, nor envy conquerors."

I went to the field of labour of which I have been treating, with a heavy heart. I had always lived in a portion of country mainly under the influence of Methodism, and in the South, where the people are remarkable for hospitality, and ministers, of our denomination in particular, were greatly esteemed. The change was great, but I shall always be thankful for the trials I experienced in this appointment. I here encountered some repulses, and, like the Master, sometimes had not a place to lay my head, and was led to cast, more than ever, my "care upon the Lord." We were here surrounded by almost an endless number of denominations, many of them efficient in the great harvest field, and others sowing seed that would produce a crop of noxious weeds; and it was requisite for me to be up and doing, and I felt the force of God's word, "Woe be unto them that are at ease in Zion." I here learned lessons I shall never forget, and a courage was imparted to me that I hope has to this day characterized my poor labours and operations as a Methodist preacher, and I trust ever will, enabling me to meet responsibilities and to triumph over difficulties in the name of the Lord. To my young brethren in the ministry I want to say, wherever our lot may be cast by those who have the rule over us, it will be the more excellent way for us cheerfully to go, even though the field is rough and uninviting, and though our enemies may be strong, our societies weak, and our support, judging from appearances, likely to be very meagre. Let us think of the hardships endured by our fathers, and joyfully move onward, singing as we go—

"We want no cowards in our bands,
That will their colours fly;
We call for valiant-hearted men,
That are not afraid to die.

The trumpets sound, the armies shout,
They drive the hosts of hell;
How dreadful is our God to adore,
The great Immanuel!"

Going forth under the most unfavourable circumstances, in the right spirit, we must conquer in every field of toil. "Now thanks be unto God, which always causeth us to triumph in Christ, and maketh manifest the savour of his knowledge by us in every place."

When I entered upon this year's work, from the force of circumstances I was powerfully tempted to give up, and go home; but, when the year closed, I felt an attachment to my charge that I had never before experienced. It was the first one where I had been without a colleague, and in charge; and, although it was so hard for me to go, and to stay after I did go, could I have had my choice, at the Conference that followed, I would have said, Give me for my next charge Chestnut Hill mission; and I thought I desired no better place till I should travel the Circuit of the skies. Experience and observation, however, have taught me that, with us as a denomination, it is far better that the ministers and membership of the Church should leave the appointing power where it was originally placed. Sacrifices by this arrangement must be made, both with the ministers and members; but are not the advantages far more weighty than the disadvantages? When we have nothing to do with making our appointments, then we can, in the severest trials, look with propriety to the Lord for support and deliverance; which we could not so fully do, if we controlled our own appointments, and used means to place ourselves in the position, where "storm after storm rises dark o'er the way." And I trust I shall ever feel willing to subscribe to the sentiment, on this point, presented by the prophet; "As the clay is in the potter's hand, so are ye in mine hand, O house of Israel!" And, if the people would (instead of taking this matter into their own hands, and rolling in upon the Bishop petition after petition for their favourites, thus manifesting a lack of confidence in the authorities of our beloved Church, and also in the Great Head of the Church), devoutly pray that labourers of the right stamp might be sent forth into the vineyard of the Lord, praying also for our chief ministers, and having confidence in their piety, judgment, and disposition to do the very best for both ministers and flocks, and resolving that whoever, in God's providence, comes, shall have a cordial welcome—they would find it the better way, and more for God's glory. He might not be the choice of some one, two, or three of the leading men of the church; yet often he is the very man for the place, and the sequel proves it; and, by God's blessing, he leads to Christ very many; and, among the rest, the children of those leading men, who felt that everything depended on some other one being appointed to the station or Circuit.

Dear readers, let us in this particular keep the rules. Bad results follow from petitioning. Several churches ask for the same person—all cannot be gratified—consequently, heart-burning is engendered towards the appointing power. I verily believe by it injury is done to the work, and preachers and people suffer by it. Out of the few known to the station or Circuit, the selection is made by the committee to whose care this matter is intrusted. The Bishop, assisted by the Presiding Elders—who travel over the entire work, and know all the ministers—could, it is reasonable to suppose, from the whole, make selections more advantageously and profitably to all parties than they. More brethren, by this means, will be brought into notice; and it will be better for them, and will place them more upon an equality with their brethren; and our stations will, by this arrangement, ascertain that there are men of the brightest genius, men of sterling worth, but, owing to the course pursued, never placed in positions to which their powers fully entitle them. In conclusion, let me humbly, but sincerely, urge upon both preachers and people to "ask for the old paths, where is the good way, and walk therein." But I am afraid some will be differently inclined, and say "we will not walk therein." I would not be understood to say our petitioning system is the only thing that keeps a man from being prominently brought forward. The fault is sometimes in ourselves. It may be we are neglectful in our studies, and we do not attend to the pastoral work, and we may not be as fully consecrated to the Lord as it is our privilege. In most cases, if a man is faithful in all respects, he will be "known and read of all men," and duly appreciated; and the appointing power will not be fearful in sending him anywhere. Some will urge that our system is despotic, and that the people should be permitted to choose their pastors. If the people have the privilege of choosing their preachers, the preachers should have the privilege of choosing their places. This would destroy our itinerancy, so signally owned of God, and so dreaded by Roman Catholics; for, with it, we can keep pace with them in carrying the gospel into new places, and with it, if our Church proves faithful in all respects, we will reach the farthest verge of the green earth, sooner or later. Under all the circumstances, for the good of the cause, we will, I trust, continue mutually to make sacrifices. And our people must never lose sight of the fact, that the pressure comes more heavily upon the ministers and their families than on any other person or persons. May the Lord give each one of us grace to enable us to say, in this glorious work, "Neither count I my life dear unto myself, so that I might finish my course with joy, and the ministry, which I have received of the Lord Jesus, to testify the gospel of the grace of God."

CHAPTER IV.

Trip to Conference in a Bay Craft—Happy Death—A little Bible Reader—Appearance of the Town—Kindness of the People—Rev. Henry White—Divine Influence at the Conference—First Quarterly Meeting a time of Revival—Be kind even to a Drunkard—Life Membership in the Missionary Society—Baptize a large number of coloured Children—Union Camp Meeting—The Church should work when God works—The Devil sometimes overleaps the Mark—Children may lead their Parents to Jesus—A Song of Victory—A deeply pious young Lady—A faithful Sunday School Labourer—Still among the Tombs—Preaching at Sunrise—Angels are interested in Revival Work—A sudden Death—Ministers should faithfully warn Sinners—A very startling Dream.

IN the spring of 1845, the Philadelphia Annual Conference was held in Milford, Delaware. When I arrived in Philadelphia, on my way to Conference, I met with a gentleman, Captain George Primrose, who invited me to take passage with him in his vessel. The invitation was accepted. The winds were favourable, and the trip every way pleasant. We had religious exercises on board, and felt that we were not only sailing for an earthly port, but for the Celestial City. Our captain since has effected an entrance into the heavenly harbour. His excellent Christian lady followed on to join his society, not long after. Her death was very triumphant. She had pious children; they could sing sweetly the songs of Zion, and, surrounding the couch where their mother, their best earthly friend, was dying, they were requested to sing the hymn beginning with

> "Joyfully, joyfully, onward I move,
> Bound for the land of bright spirits above;
> Angelic choristers sing as I come,
> Joyfully, joyfully, haste to thy home."

Ere this stirring hymn was concluded, her happy spirit fled to join those loved ones who watched her approaching the shore.

There was on board a little girl of the Episcopal Church, greatly absorbed in her Bible, which she read almost constantly, and she conducted herself like a Christian of much riper years. I found her heart was in the Sunday School cause. I felt that such a pious, dignified child was an honour to her parents. I thought the direction of the Holy Scriptures had been, in her case, adhered to: "Train up a child in the way he should go." When she becomes old, may she "not depart from it"

The town looked very inviting. It seemed to me that there had been a general renovation. Almost every house had been either painted or whitewashed. This is one of the largest and most business places in the state. There is a great amount of sociability in this place; and I suppose that the Conference was never more hospitably and liberally entertained. The different families all seemed to think they had the choice or best preachers, and the preachers generally seemed to be under the impression that they had the best homes. A person might say the treatment received during an Annual Conference, which may come perhaps to a given place only once in a lifetime, is not a sufficient test of the general character of the people for hospitality. It was my lot to remain in Milford, as junior preacher; and the opinion I formed during the session of the Conference, relative to their generosity, became strengthened with length of acquaintance. I am now going to say, what cannot be said of every place even on the Methodistic peninsula, that my greatest difficulty there, during the year, relative to homes, was that I could not go to the places to which I was invited in advance. If the people everywhere treated their young preachers as they did in Milford, there would be no necessity of boarding-house arrangements, which is rather a new thing in Methodism on our Circuits. And they would save their junior ministers from many an hour of sadness and anxiety relative to this matter, which, to them, is of momentous importance. Be kind to the homeless young itinerant. "I was a stranger, and ye took me in."

The Conference sermon on the first day was preached by the venerable and aged Rev. Henry White. The sermon was exceedingly plain, as always has been his manner throughout his long ministerial career. Some felt that Father White was too severe, especially on the young ministers; but, as a general thing, it was received in a proper spirit, and we felt that we would try to profit by it. "Faithful are the wounds of a friend." Not long after the close of the Conference his health failed, and from that day to the present, he has not been effective. He is quite feeble. A few years ago he had a severe attack of sickness, and it so happened that it was my privilege, in company with Bishop Waugh, to visit him. It is said, "Iron sharpeneth iron, so a man sharpeneth the countenance of his friend."

Although Father White had been somewhat gloomy, the sight of the senior Bishop, with whom he had often sat in council, caused him to revive. And, while the Bishop proceeded to inquire if the gospel which he had so long and faithfully preached to others now sustained and comforted him, with a heart gushing with love to God for the gift of his only begotten Son, he, with a tremulous but confiding voice, said, "Though he slay me, yet will I trust in him." An appropriate hymn was sung, and one of the most fervent prayers I ever listened to, was offered by the good Bishop, and the presence of God filled all the house. We parted with throbbing hearts, for we thought that we should "see his face no more." Eternity alone will disclose the myriads converted through his instrumentality. He was long a faithful Presiding Elder, which was the last appointment he ever filled. And, in the district where he was called upon to labour, I never heard a murmur against this office.

I am one who firmly believes in the utility of the Presiding Eldership, and I consider it requisite to the existence of the itinerancy. Great care and pains should be taken, however, to procure men of the right stamp. This done, and all will feel it is an indispensable arrangement of the Methodist Episcopal Church. This servant of God in this office, or elsewhere, did "speak and exhort, and rebuke with all authority." A little while before he failed, at a camp meeting, I listened to a powerful exhortation delivered by him. It reached many hearts. I saw a young man tremble; he made an effort to leave; he commenced running away from the place where the Holy Spirit was doing a great work. I whispered to Father White, told him the fact, and pointed out the person. He instantly exclaimed, "Young man, fly not from the Spirit, grieve not the Holy Ghost; come back and get converted, or you will be damned as sure as the devil is damned!" He turned instantly, retraced his steps, and was happily converted in a little while.

Many persons seemed to be greatly afraid of Father White; and I am frank to confess, until I formed his acquaintance intimately, this was my own feeling. The first camp meeting which I ever was at with him, a circumstance took place bearing on this point, which I will take the liberty to relate. The ministers at night had generally retired; I was the last one that sought for "nature's sweet restorer." The meeting was very interesting at the mourner's aisle, and I was rejoicing over the conversion of some dear friends until a late hour. When I entered the church, which was near the camp ground, and which was used as a lodging place for the ministers, each bed was occupied by two brethren, except the one where Father White was sweetly reposing. I quietly retired by his side, and felt I was highly honoured to sleep with such a venerable man. I took the position with a degree of fear and trembling, but did hope that all would be well. I soon fell asleep; but as I went to sleep happy, and in quite a rejoicing frame of mind, in my sleep I shouted too much for my venerable associate. Said he, "Brother, you shout and go on at such a rate I can't sleep. I wish you had finished this matter before you came to bed. There is time for all things." The stern manner in which he addressed me, caused me suddenly to make my escape, and I betook myself to the floor for the residue of the night, greatly annoyed in my mind at the idea that I had been the means of disturbing the repose of the faithful Presiding Elder of the district. But, notwithstanding this repulse, I loved him still. He is a diamond of the purest water. And, when the period shall come for him to leave the shores of mortality, it may well be said, "There is a prince and a great man fallen this day in Israel."

There was much power, not only in Father White's sermon at Conference, but the ministers generally were most happy in their pulpit performances, so much so that sinners were awakened and converted during the session. This was a primitive Conference in this respect; and I think that, at our sessions, we ought to labour for the conversion of souls. It is true there is other business to be adjusted, but is there not time for both? And is not getting people converted the most important business in the world? And there are many, a large majority of the Conference, not deeply immersed in business. May we all feel like praying, "O Lord revive thy work" at the sessions of our Conferences! Would not these occasions then be, to those places, where they are held, "the savour of life unto life?" The ministers, at this Conference, heartily entered into the work, not only of preaching, but exhortation, prayer, and praise. The singing was delightful. I never heard sweeter music than fell upon my ear and heart at that session. My brethren in the ministry will remember our worthy and deeply pious Spry. He appeared to be on Pisgah's top; and, while he did in almost angelic strains sing many pieces, the "Sonnet" was his favourite, beginning,

"When for eternal worlds I steer."

I noticed the lamented Pitman, then Secretary of the

Missionary Society of the Methodist Episcopal Church, listening with deepest interest, with tears coursing down his cheeks, at the music as it poured from lips touched with fire taken "from off the altar," and from hearts swelling with pure seraphic joy. Brother Pitman remarked, "I never heard the like before, and never shall perhaps again, until I listen to the choristers of glory!"

How solemn the thought that both Brother Pitman and Brother Spry, who were then in their prime, and bid fair to live and labour in the Church below many years, have been struck down in the midst of their great usefulness! With them

"The battle is fought, the race is won."

The revival, that commenced in Milford at the Conference, followed us at our first Quarterly Meeting, which was held in Mispillion Neck, in the month of May. Father White was with us, and preached Saturday and Sunday in great power. Unexpectedly a glorious revival broke out, that continued throughout the entire year at that place. A new class was here formed, and Jonathan Sipple, one of the best of men, now no more, was appointed leader. The revival influence moved the whole community, and the people came from every part of the Neck. And, among others, some of the votaries of Bacchus came; and, one night, I was led to quote, in my sermon, "No drunkard shall inherit the kingdom of God." A man in the gallery vociferated, "*That is a lie!*" with a horrible oath to it. The meeting was very much disturbed, and the official members of the church were prompt in removing him, and they were disposed to put the law in force against him. I interceded for him, and the brethren concluded, if he would never do so again, they would excuse him. The next night he was sober, and "in his right mind." He was that night the very first man who came to the altar as a penitent, and professed to be converted to God.

We held at this appointment a missionary meeting, which was something new for Mispillion Neck. The contributions were liberal, and, I want to say for their credit, that they, that day, paid respect to me, beyond what had ever been done up to that time anywhere, viz. by making me a life member of the Parent Missionary Society. The night of the afternoon that I held this missionary meeting, my esteemed colleague, Rev. James L. Houston, held a similar one in the town of Milford. I reached his meeting just awhile after he began to make his appeal for aid. The money seemed to come in rather slowly. I felt stirred to go on the platform, and made the following speech: "Christian friends, it is frequently said that Mispillion Neck is a wicked place, and it is sometimes called *Turkey!* owing to the fact that it has been a wicked place. All I have to say is, if you will here, in highly favoured Milford, do just as well, considering everything, for the missionary cause, as *Turkey*, this very afternoon, has done, I shall be abundantly satisfied, and the collection will be superior to anything ever known in this place for this glorious cause." Then I stated to them the amount, and told of the courtesy that they had shown to me. This had a good effect, and told favourably in the missionary collection that night.

The camp meeting held this year at Pratt's Branch did our Circuit much good, especially those appointments near it. The morning it broke up, at least thirty joined for different points on our circuit. At the Conference, held at Milford, I was ordained with others a deacon, which gave me authority to baptize. At this camp I was requested to baptize a few coloured children. I mentioned it to the preacher in charge of the Circuit. He requested me to comply with their wishes. There was a large number of coloured people in attendance, and the rising generation was well represented; and, before I stopped, *one hundred and twenty* coloured children were, in this way, dedicated to the Lord. I took the most of them in my arms. Some were rather too stout for this. I felt, when this service was finished, I was much fatigued. But if this tired me, what must have been the circumstances of John the Baptist, who baptized thousands in a short space of time, and some suppose that they were all adults, and that the mode was immersion? Although our Baptist friends ridicule the idea of baptizing children, we still feel authorized to do so, and expect in this work to persevere, for it is written, "Suffer the little children to come unto me, and forbid them not, for of such is the kingdom of God. And he took them up in his arms, and put his hands upon them, and blessed them." Thank God! "The promise is unto us, and unto our children."

There was held this season a very interesting union camp meeting, between our Circuit and Seaford, at Rosse's Woods, near Bridgeville. This is an old ground; it has become rather popular, and it is now a place of fashionable resort; nevertheless, many precious souls were this season happily converted. Bridgeville and Seaford, being near, were more especially benefited. Some other contiguous appointments, however, and also Milford, though somewhat remote, felt powerfully the influence of that meeting. A small proportion of our society were in attendance. They carried home with them the camp-fire, and it did swiftly run. A protracted meeting, from the force of heavenly influences, was immediately held, which resulted in the conversion of many precious souls. There was in consequence "great joy in that city," or town. It is better for us to hold extra meetings, even if it be in the summer time, when there is "a shaking among the dry bones," than to make our arrangements several weeks previously, and announce that we will hold such a meeting, and toil for days and weeks, and accomplish but little, if any good. Whenever God works we ought to be co-workers with him, and act on the word of the Lord, "Now is the accepted time, behold, now is the day of salvation."

The following circumstance illustrates the saying that the devil sometimes overshoots the mark:—There was in attendance at the camp meeting a young lady, much infatuated with this fashionable world. The work of conversion was gloriously progressing at the altar, in what we call the mourners' aisle. She was invited to go forward, and seek religion. She said positively, "before she would do that she would run the risk of being damned, or, in other words, of going to hell!" She was a lady of honour and feeling, and she was blessed with praying friends, and connected with one of the most influential families, and who were, some of them at least, among the first fruits of Methodism in the State of Delaware. The expressions which she uttered at the camp meeting tormented her, and, although it seemed to be a great deal for a young lady to say, still it proved to be the means of her salvation; for, immediately after the close of the camp meeting she humbly bowed at the foot of the cross in our protracted meeting at this point, in broad daylight, and was savingly converted. She followed the example of Naaman, who went away in a rage, when the prophet commanded him to "dip seven times in Jordan;" but, finally, he made the experiment, his proud heart and national pride yielded, and the effects were salutary. "His flesh came again as the flesh of a little child." So this young lady was cleansed in the blood of Jesus, and made happy in God.

At this protracted meeting there were some deeply-interesting cases of conversion. A very young and interesting female, about twelve years of age, meekly bowed at the foot of the cross, and remembered her Creator in the days of her youth. This had a most excellent effect on her parents. They did not act as some parents do, viz., oppose their child, and hedge up her way, but they encouraged her in deed and in truth, by likewise giving their hearts to God; and although they had not been trained in the Methodist, but another branch of the Church, yet they heartily said to their little daughter, who had joined the Methodists, "Thy people shall be my people, and thy God my God." I want my young readers not to forget that Sabbath School children can be converted, and can also lead their parents and friends to the loving arms of Jesus, and into the bosom of the Church. "A little child shall lead them." "Out of the mouth of babes and sucklings Thou hast perfected praise." The children shouted hosannah to the Son of David, when the chief priests owned him not, but despised and rejected him. I look to our Sabbath Schools as our strongest bulwark, and would urge our Sunday School labourers not to think for a moment that the work in which they are engaged is of small import. Those little ones must be converted. This being done, as in the case I have referred to, they will win others to the cross; their preaching is irresistible. I knew one to embrace religion who was very young. She instantly inquired, "Where is my father?" He was pointed out to her. She went to him in a run, fell upon his neck, and kissed him, and sweetly said, "O father! father! come to Jesus, just now." She led him herself to the altar. He had resisted many sermons and appeals from the sacred desk; but, with this influence brought to bear upon him, he was constrained to say—

"I yield, I yield, I can hold out no more."

A young man, the child of many prayers, was seen with the multitude, prostrate at the feet of Jesus. He was, after a hard struggle, set free from the bondage of sin. At the close of the meeting, many of us accompanied him to his paternal home. The venerable father and mother had retired to rest. They were aroused from their slumbers, ere we reached the house, by the singing of a sacred song of triumph, which we did heartily, all the way from the house of God to the home of this interesting young man. The chorus of which was—

"Victory, victory, when we've gained the victory,
O how happy we shall be,
When we've gained the victory."

9

The parents—the mother, particularly—(how strong is the affection of a Christian mother for a child, and especially a converted child!) forgot the gravity of age, and leaped, and praised God, and there were none to make her or any of us afraid; for the whole town felt the mighty influence of the Holy Ghost, more or less. Some, that were brought to God through that revival, which the Lord himself started and carried on in his own way, have, ere this, crossed Jordan's stream, which was to them narrowed down to a very small rivulet, so that they could, being bidden and comforted by Jesus, step over with but little difficulty. "Thanks be unto God, who giveth us the victory" over the king of terrors!

I must be permitted particularly to refer to an interesting young lady, Miss Fanny Darby. She in early life sustained the greatest earthly loss that mortals can sustain—I mean she was left without a mother. And who can fill the place of a mother? She grew up to womanhood, in a measure lost sight of the fact that she was an orphan, and was inclined to be gay and thoughtless. There were evidences, however, that she possessed rare qualities; even before her conversion to God she delighted to be employed in the work of a Sabbath School, in which she had been nurtured. No better place for an orphan to go to than a Sabbath School; for here we may appropriately say God has kings and queens, and they are to the orphan, and others placed under their care, "nursing fathers and nursing mothers."

When our revival in Milford broke out, we all desired that this much esteemed young lady should be consecrated fully to God's service. With much timidity, but deep emotion of heart and tear-bathed cheeks, she bowed at the altar and piteously asked an interest in our prayers, and entreated God to be merciful to her a sinner. She did not seek in vain, and from that glad hour in her history to the day of her death, she was eminently pious; her soul and body, her all was consecrated to the service of the Lord. A brighter example of Christian perfection, perhaps, I never saw. She desired all the help she could obtain from her Christian friends by Christian conference, and correspondence. In reply to a letter I addressed to this young Christian, she said, "I have ever esteemed it a privilege to correspond with a friend in whose Christian character I had confidence, and on whose Christian counsel I might with safety depend. Of all classes of individuals there are certainly none more capable of improving the mind and heart in the ways of truth than a faithful minister of the Gospel. Such a friend and minister I am sure I have a right to consider you." In the same letter she remarks, "To you I feel I owe a debt of untold gratitude, for the interest you have ever manifested in my spiritual welfare, especially when I was so blind and ignorant concerning everything that made for my eternal peace. Since that time, I trust, I have found a never-failing source of light, a star that will guide all who will fix their trusting eyes upon it, safe through this world of change and trial to a brighter and better above the skies."

Thus consecrated to God, in addition to her natural amiable spirit, which gave her influence, and made her a general favourite, she was calculated to do much good in the circles in which she moved. Her highest ambition was to be holy and useful. She took an active part in a revival, in the town of Milford, a very short period before her death, and had the pleasure of leading some of her young friends and associates to the blessed Saviour. She stated to me, in a letter relating to this revival, "You have no doubt heard of our interesting meeting, and of the many that are coming over to the Lord's side. Among the number are our friends, V. G., S. E. A., P. G., and others, all happily converted, and rejoicing in a Saviour's love."

The extracts I have made from her own writing, will show in what element this interesting young lady delighted to live. She saw the vanity of earthly things; she had tried them, having

"Sought round the verdant earth
For unfading joy."

But her experience taught her the lesson, that

"Each pleasure hath its poison, too,
And every sweet a snare."

In the service of the Lord, however, she found true happiness, and pleasure unalloyed. May I be permitted to suggest to my young female friends, that no earthly adornment will compare with the meek and quiet spirit that characterizes the true Christian; and that nothing will make them so useful in society as a holy heart and a spotless Christian life; and that nothing, save this, will cause them to shine in Heaven as the stars of the firmament.

In the month of October, 1848, she, after a very brief illness, at the residence of a relative in the town of Dover, found "the weary wheels of life to stand still." It was my privilege to see her for a short time, a few hours before her death, and, although she was insensible, she seemed to be contemplating heavenly things, and her countenance appeared to me to shine like the countenance of an angel.

In the spring of 1855, I visited Milford. Solitary and alone, I rambled through the "old churchyard," connected with our denomination, and, for a season, my "meditations were among the tombs." Among the first I observed minutely, was the one erected in memory of the Christian young lady of whom I am now writing, by a devoted friend. Her devotion to the cause of religion had deeply impressed this gay young friend's heart in favour of religion; and through her, he was "almost persuaded to be a Christian." He too has been struck down by death in the morning of his life. Family influence, honour, wealth, nor any other possession can ward off the blow of the king of terrors. It was my privilege, about two weeks before his death, to preach to him, no doubt, the last sermon he ever heard. I knew the natural goodness of his heart; I knew he had been impressed; and at the close of the sermon, I took up the cross before a large audience in the city of Wilmington, and urged him personally, to "seek the Lord while he might be found." How well I recollect his gentlemanly deportment on that occasion; and I saw the sparkling tear; but he said familiarly, "Not to-night, Brother Manship, but at some other time, I intend to be a Christian." In theory, both he and his talented father, Hon. J. M. C., were Christians. The latter, on all proper occasions, is ready to defend Christianity. He has read and studied the Bible closely; and his mother was a consistent member of the Methodist Episcopal Church. I once heard him say in a stage, "I have frequent controversies with infidels at Washington. I have read many works on the Evidences of Christianity; but there never was anything that so fully convinced me of the truth of the Christian religion, as the Lord's Prayer and the Sermon on the Mount." He has read also the words of our Saviour to Nicodemus: "Verily I say unto you, ye must be born again." My readers will perceive that my allusions are to Mr. Clayton of Delaware, long a prominent member of the United States Senate, and Secretary of State under General Taylor.

My eye, on this occasion, fell upon the spot where sleeps the dust of another esteemed friend, Miss R. A. Sipple, whose acquaintance I formed while I travelled Milford Circuit, and whose friendship I enjoyed as long as she lived. May it be renewed in Heaven! I believe in the recognition of friends in the Better Land.

She was the child of truly pious parents, and of many prayers. She came of a good old Methodist stock. Her father and mother were faithful members of the Church; they loved all her means of grace; particularly did her father, as this young friend has told me, appreciate camp meetings. He died some years before I travelled the Circuit; and this child of whom I am speaking, felt the necessity, especially after losing her earthly father, to cry to God, "My Father, thou art the guide of my youth." She also felt it a high privilege to worship the God of her father in the tented grove. But young as she was, disease of a fatal but slow character, in the form of consumption, took hold of her; and for a number of years before her death, she was not permitted, to any great extent, to be thus gratified. Her health, however, did not prevent her from being at her post in the public worship at God's house. In the class room she was generally present, and her experience was thrilling, and calculated to impress all that she had sat at the Master's feet, and learned of him. But this young friend shone with greater lustre perhaps in the Sunday School room, than anywhere else. She was in this department a "golden candlestick;" and, in connexion with kindred spirits, so radiated there, as to make the Sabbath School of that place one of the most interesting with which it has ever been my lot to be associated. Such a teacher could not fail to allure the tender children to the embrace of the religion of Jesus, of whom it is said by the Prophet: "He shall gather the lambs with his arm, and carry them in his bosom." The loss sustained by the Church in that place was great, when in this instance, "the silver cord was loosed, and the golden bowl broken," and the dust of that faithful Sunday School labourer "returned to the earth as it was." And, while looking upon the marble which marked the resting place of this pious friend, I felt that all the Church, and especially the Sabbath School, if called upon, would unite with me in exclaiming:

"Sister, thou wast mild and lovely,
Gentle as the summer breeze;
Pleasant as the air of evening,
When it floats among the trees.

"Peaceful be thy silent slumber,
Peaceful in the grave so low;

Thou no more wilt join our number—
Thou no more our songs shalt know.

"Yet again we hope to meet thee,
When the day of life is fled;
Then in Heaven with joy to greet thee,
Where no farewell tear is shed."

There, too, I glanced at the monument of undying maternal love, reared upon the spot of earth which conceals the mortal remains of a loved one, who now sweetly sleeps near the resting place of the two Christian females already named. "She was the only daughter of her mother, and she was a widow." I thought of the deprivation. Lovely, intelligent, pious; her mother's heart clung to this object of her affection especially, because all her near kindred "had passed on before," and this only daughter was the solace of her heart in her declining years. Many a time I have heard this aged mother eloquently refer to her blasted earthly hopes, and I have wept with those who wept. Doubtless it would have pierced one's heart to have beheld the tender mother, following the breathless corpse of her amiable and only child to her long home. While I stood and mused upon the scenes with which I was surrounded, in my imagination I saw my dear friend, who was about to bury her earthly hopes, drowned with tears and overwhelmed with sorrows—stand like a weeping statue. She wrings her hands, and floods pour from her eyes.

The obsequies are over; throughout their performance all hearts had melted, all eyes had overflowed; for she and hers were universally beloved. The heart-broken mother advances to the brink of the grave. All her soul is in her eyes. She fastens one more look upon the dear object before the pit shuts its mouth upon her; and, as she looks, she cries in broken accents: "farewell, my daughter! my daughter! my only beloved! would God I had died for thee! Farewell, my child! and farewell all my earthly happiness! I shall never more see good in the land of the living. Attempt not to comfort me. I will go mourning all my days, till my gray hairs come down with sorrow to the grave!"

But I thought, after the paroxysms of grief were over, my aged friend would, as doubtless she might, soliloquize in the manner following:—"I have cultivated her morals, and tried to secure her immortal interests. She in early life bowed to the sceptre of God's word, renounced the pomps and vanities of the world, and now basks in more than a mother's love." Indeed, to my certain knowledge, that once heart-broken mother feels that, although she has committed this last pledge of maternal affection to the dust (and how dear to a lonely widow is an only daughter, with the charms which she possessed), she has cheering hopes of receiving her again to her arms, "inexpressibly improved in every noble and endearing accomplishment."

From the time I travelled Milford Circuit, until I perambulated the solemn place of burial connected with the Methodist Episcopal Church in that place, nine years had passed away. And, with the flight of those years, my observation taught me that death had been doing his work, and that many, with whom I had spent happy hours and taken sweet counsel, were here embraced in the icy arms of death. I left that sacred spot greatly benefited, I trust, but ready to say, "Rest, then, ye precious relics, within this hospitable gloom. Rest in gentle slumbers, till the last trumpet shall give the welcome signal, and sound aloud through all your silent mansions: *Arise, shine; for your light is come, and the glory of the Lord is risen upon you.*"

> "These lively hopes we owe,
> Lord, to thy dying love;
> O may we bless thy grace below,
> And sing thy grace above."

Throughout our entire Circuit we had a good work; and as the people were kind, and my colleague, Rev. James L. Houston, pleasant, I may say a perfect gentleman and Christian, and an excellent minister, I felt a desire that I might be permitted to remain another year. But it was ordered otherwise, and this was, probably, the more excellent way. At my last appointment, at a small week-day preaching place, I gave out to the people four weeks previously, that when I came to preach my last time, I would preach the preceding evening also. It so happened an aged member died, some fourteen miles from this place; she was to be buried on Thursday morning, the very time I was to preach my last sermon, and it was her dying request that I should preach the funeral sermon. On Wednesday night, therefore, I stated the fact, and told them if I preached on Thursday morning, it must be on or before sunrise. We had at that hour a large congregation, a memorable season. What a delightful hour for the worship of Almighty God! The Psalmist was an early worshipper: "My voice shalt thou hear in the morning, O Lord; in the morning will I direct my prayer unto thee, and will look up." The great founder of Methodism, and the fathers, frequently at this hour, preached the Gospel to those who would give attention. How well, occasionally, would such a course prepare us for the duties, labours, and trials of the day! This to me was an unpremeditated, rather Providential service; but it was one I shall never forget, in time or in eternity. More such I hope to participate in before I go hence. With this humble people I had enjoyed much of the presence and power of God. We held here a very interesting meeting. The house was small, and very frail; I could see through the roof in some places. I tried to profit by this. The bright, glittering stars (for the nights were clear) shining down upon us, apparently dancing with joy, seemed to approbate our proceedings, and I was almost ready to construe them into angels' eyes, for angels are concerned in these things: "which things the angels desire to look into."

It became necessary to make a temporary enlargement, for the accommodation of the people. We procured a large canvass tent, and pitched it immediately in front of the little church, and by standing in the front door of the church we could make all present hear. No one will doubt this, when I relate the following fact. At that meeting a good old brother S. was praying one night in public, and he exclaimed, "God bless our young minister, make him strong to labour, and give him a voice like thunder! We thank thee that we heard him preach last night all the way to our house, which is about two miles." Thus ended his prayer in regard to myself. I had strong faith in my good old friend, and could not for a moment doubt his word, especially when he was on his knees; but I supposed that he must have been under a mistake; yet the thing was possible; the sound might have been heard afar off, the night being calm, and everything quiet. Would to God it had done execution! as in the case of Rev. F. Garretson, who, preaching once in Dover, Del., at an early period in Methodism, was the instrument, in God's hands, of converting a lady who was so prejudiced that she would not go to hear the Methodist, but hoisted her window to listen, half a mile off, and was reached and converted, and the conversion of the whole family followed. This is from a living witness.

Since taking my departure, in the spring of 1846, I have never met with those loving friends. I was pleased to learn that they had energetically gone to work, and built a neat house of worship. May it make that wilderness and solitary place glad, and "the glory of this latter house be greater than that of the former."

Before closing this chapter, I desire to speak for the edification of any one who has been led to procrastinate his return to the Saviour, from whom he has, ever since he crossed the line of accountability, been wandering. We commenced a protracted meeting in Onins' Chapel, in the lower part of the Circuit, towards the close of the Conference year. It commenced on Friday night; the great snow-storm prevented it from going on; but on Friday night we did our utmost to get souls converted. There was one there that night, among others, pressingly urged to arise and come to his Father. He thought some other time would do as well, and declined. He reached home about ten o'clock, and suddenly he fell prostrate on the floor, a lifeless corpse. I preached his funeral sermon on the following Sunday. I felt deeply solemn, and was led to ask myself the question, "Did I do my duty towards this fellow-being, who was in attendance at God's house, and heard me preach on the Friday night preceding, a few moments only before his death?" What an awful thing it will be if the blood of perishing sinners be required at the hands of ministers! But if I warned this person, and if we, as watchmen on Zion's walls, warn every man, and they "turn not from their wickedness, nor their wicked way, they shall die in their iniquity," but we "have delivered our souls." "Take heed to the ministry which thou hast received in the Lord, that thou fulfil it." It is possible, after we have preached to others, that we ourselves may be cast-aways. I will, in this connexion, hoping it may do good to myself and others, present a remarkable dream. I take it from the Life of Mr. W. Bramwell. It was related by the late Rev. R. Bowden, of Darwen, who committed it to writing from the lips of the person to whom the dream happened, on the evening of May 30, 1813. It is as follows:—

"A gospel minister, of evangelical principles, whose name, from the circumstances that occurred, it will be necessary to conceal, being much fatigued at the conclusion of the afternoon service, retired to his apartment, in order to take a little rest. He had not long reclined upon his couch before he fell asleep, and began to dream. He dreamed that, on walking into his garden, he entered a bower that had been erected in it, where he sat down to read and meditate. While thus employed, he thought he heard some person enter the garden; and, leaving his bower, he immediately hastened toward the spot whence the sound seemed to come, in order to discover who it was that had entered. He had not proceeded far before he discerned a particular friend of his, a Gospel minister of considerable talents, who had rendered himself very popular by his zealous and unwearied exertions in the cause of Christ. On approaching his friend, he was surprised to find that his countenance was covered with a gloom which it had not been accustomed to wear, and that it strongly indicated a violent agitation of mind, apparently arising from conscious remorse. After the usual salutations had passed, his friend asked the relater the time of the day; to which he replied, "twenty-five minutes after four." On hearing this the stranger said, "It is only one hour since I died, and now I am damned." "Damned! for what?" inquired the dreaming minister. "It is not," said he, "because I have not preached the gospel, neither is it because I have not been rendered useful, for I have now many seals to my ministry, who can bear testimony to the truth as it is in Jesus, which they have received from my lips; but it is because I have been accumulating to myself the applause of men more than the honour which cometh from above; and verily I have my reward." Having uttered these expressions he hastily disappeared, and was seen no more.

The minister awakening shortly afterward, with the

contents of this dream deeply engraven on his memory, proceeded, overwhelmed with serious reflections, towards his chapel, in order to conduct the evening service. On his way thither he was accosted by a friend, who inquired whether he had heard of the severe loss the Church had sustained in the death of that able minister, ———. He replied "No:" but being much affected at this singular intelligence, he inquired of him the day, and the time of the day when his departure took place. To this his friend replied, "This afternoon, at twenty-five minutes after three o'clock."

"O popular applause! What heart of man
Is proof against thy sweet seducing charms?
The wisest and the best feel urgent need
Of all their caution in thy gentlest gales;
But swelled into a gust—Who then, alas!
With all his canvass set, and inexpert,
And therefore heedless, can withstand thy power?
Praise from the rivell'd lips of toothless, bald
Decrepitude, and in the looks of lean
And craving poverty, and in the bow
Respectful of the smutch'd artificer,
Is oft too welcome, and may much disturb
The bias of the purpose. How much more,
Poured forth by beauty splendid and polite,
In language soft as adoration breathes?
Ah, spare your idol! think him human still.
Charms he may have, but he has frailties too!
Dote not too much, nor spoil what ye admire."

Some of the brightest stars have set in gloom, and it is possible, notwithstanding we have prophesied in the name of the Lord, at last it may be said, "I never knew you."

CHAPTER V.

Conferences more interesting in small Towns—Though Churches are embarrassed, they must not be abandoned—Rev. William A. Wiggins —First Church in Lancaster—Father Benedict—Preachers' Meeting —Singing does good in more ways than one—Coloured People gave freely—Aunt Lottey a shouting Methodist—Wrong meaning given to the word "Niggardly"—Better to dedicate Churches on Week Days—The shout of Glory, and not the cry of Murder—What's a name—Rev. George Lacey—A dying Girl clings to her Bible—"We won't give up the Bible."

THE Conference was held, in the spring of 1846, in Union Church, Philadelphia. The city of Philadelphia is more central than almost any other point, and there are some advantages to the ministers arising from our sessions being held in the city of Brotherly Love; yet it is my decided conviction that more real good is done by their being held in different and smaller places; and, as our system is itinerant, I think it proper to carry it out in this respect also. By adopting this method, in the course of time we reach, with our annual sessions, all the neighbourhoods in our geographical boundaries; and, although we have sometimes gone to small places, there never has been any difficulty in procuring accommodations for all concerned. In the small towns there is, to a greater extent, an interest awakened, and a reciprocity of feeling with preachers and people; and, actually, we all feel the day of Pentecost has fully come, and continuing "daily with one accord in the temple, and breaking bread from house to house, we eat our meat with gladness and singleness of heart, praising God and having favour with all the people." The departure too of the ministers makes a deep impression, and causes a sadness and a regret among the people, which is not to be looked for in a large bustling city, where we are scattered in every direction, and have not, consequently, an opportunity to form those friendly associations, which it is our privilege to form when we meet in smaller towns.

At this Conference my appointment was announced for Lancaster, with the Rev. William A. Wiggins, who was, of course, the principal pastor. The church at this place was deeply involved in pecuniary embarrassment at the time, so that there was a probability of its being sold. The Conference vigorously took hold of this matter, passing resolutions commending it to the friends of Methodism in and out of our bounds. The preceding year Rev. N. Heston was appointed, and this year myself, to do what we could in saving that noble building from the sheriff's hammer. Both Brother Heston and myself however found, from experience, that it was much more difficult to obtain funds, than it was for our brethren of the Conference to pass resolutions appertaining to the matter. In this crisis the preacher in charge, Rev. William A. Wiggins, worked diligently, visited a number of points, plead for the church in eloquent strains, and did not plead in vain. At the time I was associated with him, his health was feeble; nevertheless, he had a large share of vivacity and energy, and, so far as I could learn his character, he generally looked upon the bright side of everything. He was a happy man. And who will say that he was not a useful man? Many years he was the secretary of the Philadelphia Annual Conference, and performed the duties of that arduous office with satisfaction to all. Eternity alone can disclose the seals to his ministry. After finishing his two years in Lancaster, he was appointed to the city of Reading. It was in this place he triumphantly finished his course on Thursday evening, October 21st, 1847, in the fifty-first year of his age, and twenty-fifth of his ministry.

> "He fell like a martyr,
> He died at his post."

His dying testimony was as follows: "I am a great sufferer, but I must suffer to glorify God, and through suffering be made perfect." He said to his children, "O my dear children, your mother (his first wife) expressed her belief, on her dying bed, that God would bring us an unbroken family to heaven. You will live awhile in affliction, perhaps in poverty, but what are the riches of this world? We brought nothing into it, and we can carry nothing out. But let me see you not only within the gates of heaven, but with us about the throne." His devoted wife asked him just before he quit the world, if he knew her. "Yes," he answered, "dear Elizabeth, I am going to leave you; but we shall have a happy meeting in heaven; farewell." His children sung, "On Jordan's stormy banks I stand." He joined in the singing as well as he could. His last words were, "Triumph! Triumph!"

His remains were brought to Philadelphia and interred in the St. Paul's Methodist Episcopal Church burying ground. And, as an evidence that this man of God was appreciated, thousands attended the funeral. The spacious church did not accommodate the great concourse, though it was filled to its utmost capacity. During the services wailings came up from many a heart, and tears gushed from many an eye. As it was said of Barnabas, so may it be said of Rev. William A. Wiggins: "For he was a good man, and full of the Holy Ghost, and of faith: and much people was added unto the Lord." Lancaster was, and every other appointment he filled, made better by his labours among them.

The original Methodist Episcopal Church in the city of Lancaster, was opened for worship in 1809. Rev. Ezekiel Cooper and Rev. Dr. Sargent, officiated at the dedication. Too much credit cannot be given to Father Benedict, who still lingers on the shores of mortality, for the interest he took in the introduction of Methodism into this place. The first class was formed in his house, consisting of four or five, including himself and wife. His house was the preaching place for two years, until the church was built, which was done mainly through Brother Benedict's agency. He had very hard work to get a piece of ground on which to locate the church; for, at that day, "this sect was everywhere spoken against" in Lancaster.

When we contrast the condition and influence of Methodism then with what we found it in the spring of 1855, at which time the Philadelphia Annual Conference held its Annual Session there, we are ready to cry out: God hath wrought wonders! For, at the beginning, there was scarcely a home for the way-worn Itinerant; now, there are homes of the best quality for over *two hundred ministers.* At the time of the beginning, not only were the people ready to cry out "away with them!" but ministers of the older churches, were ready to denounce them as false prophets. In this respect, a happy change has taken place; for their houses, pulpits, and hearts, all appear to be open; and they all said to us at our late session: "Is thine heart right, as my heart is with thy heart? If it be, give me thine hand."

The small structure, which was opened for divine worship in 1809, after being the birthplace of many precious souls, and "strengthening the things which were weak," has given place to a very large and beautiful temple, second to but few, for neatness and appropriateness, anywhere in this country, of our own or any other denomination. But this achievement has cost the brethren of the laity in that city much toil, and the ministers have had a heavy share of the care to rest on them. Together we have struggled, and, by mutual effort, success has been the glorious result.

I felt mine was, in the spring of 1846, in this connexion, an unenviable field, when I ascertained that my chief work was to *raise money*—to go from place to place, and deliver what I supposed would be an unwelcome message. But I found my brother ministers everywhere sympathizing; and, generally, when I entered their fields of labour, they bid me welcome; and the people were more generous than, under the circumstances, I had any reason to expect.

The first effort I made was in the Preachers' meeting in Philadelphia. They manifested a deep solicitude; and, they not only loved this object in word, but, as they generally do, in deed also, for almost every man gave to the object, in that meeting, the sum of *five dollars.*

I found the Presiding Elders of several Districts exceedingly anxious to assist in carrying this project to a successful issue. Rev. L. Scott, who then had charge of the district in which Lancaster was located, would encourage me in the time of temptation. And I found it no small privilege to travel with him around the district, and he aided me much in presenting this matter to the public. I was with him at one of his quarterly meetings where my mission was made known. Some of the people seemed not to approbate the object, especially one influential lady, the wife of the principal man of the society; she was very much offended because her husband contributed to it. But before I left that place, I paid a visit to the house, in company with the Presiding Elder and the pastor; and, while there, I was called upon by the ministers to sing a very sweet hymn, that was then new. I did it in the spirit; and, to my surprise, the dear old lady, that had treated the cause with so much indifference, became very happy while the song of Zion was being sung; and with the activity of a young girl, she ran to her bureau, and procured a respectable amount, and put it into my hands, bidding me God speed in the work in which I was engaged. That morning we had a time not to be forgotten; not only was the old lady blessed, but we all had our spiritual strength renewed.

When I visited Port Deposit, in Cecil county, Maryland, I had much to encourage me. The preacher, Rev. William H. Elliott, and the people, endorsed the enterprise. After preaching in Port Deposit in the morning, I rode, accompanied by Brother Elliott, some four or five miles in the country, and I preached to a fine congregation of coloured people. Even the coloured people at this point contributed to the object. We returned, and I tried again to preach at night in the town. This was a very warm day; the labour was hard; but I felt I was "in the spirit on the Lord's day."

During the camp meeting season I was principally on the peninsula, and travelled with Rev. J. T. Hazzard, the Presiding Elder of the Easton District, from camp meeting to camp meeting. At nearly all of those meetings, I asked the privilege to preach at eight o'clock on Sunday mornings to the coloured people. They seemed to appreciate highly this arrangement. Much good I hope was done. And my readers will be almost startled, when I tell them that the coloured people, at the different camps, contributed that summer about *one hundred dollars* towards saving this church.

I attended a deeply interesting camp meeting at Ennal's Springs, in Dorchester county, Maryland. This has been one of the most celebrated places on the peninsula for camp meetings. The woods here, a thousand times, have been made vocal with ascriptions of praise to God, coming up from new-born souls. I recollect my travelling companion at the time, Rev. J. T. Hazzard, was preaching at the stand, with an unction for which he is proverbial; and, suddenly, clouds gathered over the encampment, the thunder roared, the lightnings flashed, and the rain came down in torrents. I ventured, from the impulse of the moment, while the people were flying for shelter, to start the little chorus:

"Stand the storm, it won't be long,
We'll anchor by and by."

It seemed to be very appropriate, and to do good; and, although the preaching was stopped, the work of conversion gloriously went forward.

When I presented the cause to this warm-hearted people, the response was very generous; it seemed, indeed, to be a privilege for them to contribute. Had our church been sold from us, it was generally supposed, it would have fallen into the hands of the Roman Catholics. I mentioned this circumstance on this occasion; it made a deep impression on the heart of an aged Christian lady, known all through that country favourably, and generally called Aunt Lottey! She had long been a shouting Methodist, and on this occasion, she was powerfully blessed, and

"Her glad soul mounted higher
In a chariot of fire,
And the moon was under her feet."

And while she leaped and praised God, we heard her exclaim: "Glory to God, the Roman Catholics shall never have that church." Again I heard her remark: "I wish I had a plenty of money." Just at that juncture of time, a wealthy brother, appreciating highly Aunt Lottey, placed in her hands a bank-note; and, forthwith, she shouted up to the stand, and gave it to me with the greatest cheerfulness and enthusiasm.

In regard to this mother in Israel, I may remark to my readers, that she continued to the day of her death to obey the command, "Cry out and shout, thou inhabitant of Zion, for great is the Holy One of Israel in the midst of thee." And, when the hour for her departure arrived, she was ready; and could still shout and sing,

"On Jordan's stormy banks I stand,
And cast a wishful eye
To Canaan's fair and happy land,
Where my possessions lie."

If I am privileged to reach the better land, I shall expect to see Aunt Lottey there, close by the throne, shouting in nobler strains, "Alleluiah: salvation, and glory, and honour, and power, unto the Lord our God."

I met with Rev. Mr. Cross at the next camp I

attended, who was pleading for the seamen—and he was an efficient speaker. As my turn came after him, I was apprehensive that I should entirely fail; but the generous-hearted Marylanders "do not weary in well-doing." Brother Cross, in presenting his cause, used the word "*niggardly*," which was unfortunate for him with the coloured people. They were highly incensed at the minister; the interpretation which they gave to the expression was, "*he is calling us niggers.*" I plainly saw that his cause, with them at least, would not receive any sympathy; and after the white people were through with their liberal donations, I took it upon myself to explain to them that Brother Cross was misunderstood. I told them what was meant by the word niggardly; and, immediately, they endorsed his cause, by adding to his collection at least *ten dollars*.

From the camp meeting referred to, in company with my travelling companion, I went to the town of Cambridge, to witness the dedication of the new and beautiful Methodist Episcopal Church, built through the perseverance and energy—in a great degree at least—of Rev. John D. Onins, who was the preacher in charge at the time. It was on a week-day, which I think far more appropriate for such occasions than Sunday. The ministers and people, from surrounding churches, can then have the opportunity of uniting in the interesting exercises. Bishop Janes officiated, morning and afternoon, and Brother Cross at night. Since that day I have been present at many dedications; but it is rare to have more of the Divine presence than we were favoured with at that time and place. The new house was paid for; and the temple, on the first day of its occupancy, was filled with God's glory. Rev. Mr. Cazier, a local minister of Talbot, who was blessed with this world's goods, was very liberal that day in aiding the Cambridge friends, and seemed to act on the principle, as they had received of his carnal things, he would have a large share of spiritual things; and he shouted up and down the aisles of the church, and appeared to be perfectly at home, and to feel "where the Spirit of the Lord is there is liberty." He has since gone to his reward in Heaven.

We all spent the night at the residence of our worthy friend, Rev. Dr. Thompson. At a late hour we were aroused from our slumbers, and considerably alarmed by a very great noise. At first it seemed to us to be the noise of distress, and we did not know but that somebody was being murdered. We listened attentively, and heard the words, "Hallelujah! Glory!! Glory!!!" It was the power of God amongst the Doctor's coloured people in the Quarter, a short distance from where we were lodging. "At midnight they prayed and sang praises unto God, and we heard them." Our fears were allayed, and we were led to cry out while we listened to their shouts:

"In every land begin the song,
To every land the strains belong,
In cheerful songs *all* voices raise,
And *fill* the world with sounding praise."

After I finished my camp meeting tour, it was my privilege to spend very pleasantly the month of September in the city of Lancaster, at the house principally of my friend, Mr. Adam Wolf. I spent also, in connexion with Bishop Scott, my time with this family at the Annual Conference in the spring of 1855, and I shall not soon forget their hospitality and *lamb-like!* disposition towards me. No man took a deeper interest in relieving the Lancaster church, in the days of darkness, than Brother Wolf.

During the residue of the fall and winter I was mainly occupied in the churches in the city of Philadelphia. I preached, as well as I could, in each one, large and small. And although I had much financiering to do, I was not all the time thus occupied. I participated with our brethren in the ministry in their protracted meetings. And at different points I had the gratification of seeing good accomplished. That year I formed many acquaintances that I should not in the ordinary way ever have formed. I place a high estimate on my circle of friends. No class of ministers have the facilities that we have for forming acquaintances and making friends; and our friends are a fortune to us. I recollect that Rev. Dr. Lacey, in Philadelphia, with whom I resided, said to me on a certain occasion, "Brother M., you are now eating your white bread." And it is a fact, notwithstanding I had to *beg money!* I so managed, I trust, as to keep myself in the love of God. And associated as I was in Philadelphia, with one of the most amiable families, with plenty of work to do, I could not be otherwise than happy. And neither rolling years nor the vicissitudes of life can ever efface from my recollection the generous manner in which I was always treated, not only by Rev. George Lacey, but by every member of the family.

I feel sorry that the failure of Brother Lacey's health made it necessary for him to retire from the effective ranks. His labours were owned of God. In his present pursuit, however, I cannot see any good reason why he may not be eminently useful both to the souls and bodies of his fellow-men. How important it is for physicians to be men of God! so that when their medicines fail to produce the desired effect, they may tell their dying patients "there is balm in Gilead, there is a physician there," and direct them to look to Him who has a panacea for the miseries of the world—

> "A sovereign balm for every wound,
> A cordial for every fear."

Since my connexion with this household, a gloom has been cast over that happy family, not only by the failure of Brother Lacey's health, but by the premature death of their only child. She was tenderly raised, she was watched over with an angel's care, and those devoted parents heeded the injunction, "Take this child and nurse it for me, and I will give thee thy wages." She was educated at home, under the superintending care of her mother, whose heart was much fixed upon her, and I do not wonder; for Emma Lacey was a perfect model of amiability. She was just blooming into womanhood when God, in his providence, transplanted her into a more congenial soil, where she will "flourish in immortal youth." From a child Emma "knew the Scriptures:" she read them regularly. This bright candle of the Lord,—

> "Star of Eternity! the only star
> By which the bark of man could navigate
> The sea of life, and gain the coast of bliss
> Securely,"

pointed this young girl's eye to the eternal hills, and enabled her courageously to sail across the river of death, fearing no evil. So much was this young lady attached to the Book of God, that she not only clung to it in death, but at her desire, as I suppose, this, her favourite book, was buried with her. So, upon that young heart, in the grave, rests the book, whose teachings gave ease in life, and victory in death, and inspired the hope of a glorious resurrection:—

> "Of resurrection at the promised morn,
> And meetings then which ne'er shall part again."

Before closing this chapter, I want especially to urge my young readers to follow in the footsteps of Emma Lacey, particularly in regard to the Bible. If young persons are believers in and lovers of the Word of God, while it brings other blessings, it will give them character in the business world. A youth of this description, who was left without a father, and whose mother was poor, found it necessary to go out into the world to seek his fortune. He entered a city, and applied at a merchant's establishment for a clerkship. And the prospect was not encouraging by any means; but he persevered, and from his carpet-bag drew one recommendation after another, all from respectable sources. The merchant still gave a negative answer. While, however, the youth was ransacking his carpet-bag for other favourable testimonials, his Bible rolled out, and fell upon the floor. The merchant asked, "What is that?" The youth replied, "That is the Bible which my mother gave me, and I promised her to read a portion of it every day." That was enough; the youth was employed without further testimonials.

We will say, then, to all who hate the Bible, and would tear it from us, if they could—

"We won't give up the Bible,
God's holy book of truth,
The staff of hoary age,
And guide of early youth."

CHAPTER VI.

Bishop Hamline—Ordained an Elder—Rev. Ezekiel Cooper's Funeral—One Soul worth twenty years' labour—Young Ministers should not marry prematurely—Sent to Bethlehem Station—"He repented and went"—A Minister's Son converted, and becomes a Preacher—Death by Hydrophobia—Dancing down to Hell—Lutheran Minister's Heart "strangely warmed"—Affecting circumstance in Prison—The reception of Soldiers returned from the Mexican War—Determined to be a Soldier of the Cross—Mothers, pray for your loved ones.

THE Annual Conference, in the spring of 1847, convened in Wilmington, Delaware, which is a very convenient place for the session of the Philadelphia Conference, being about the centre of our territorial bounds. Bishop Hamline, who was elected Bishop in 1844, for the first time, was with us. He professes the great blessing of sanctification, and I doubt not but that he enjoys it. He seemed to be constantly under heavenly influence, generally arranged for each session to be preceded by a prayer meeting. I never saw a Conference where there was more harmony among the ministers. The Bishop's health was feeble; yet he passed through his arduous labours without special difficulty, and, on the Sabbath morning of the Conference, preached a sermon of great power, from Romans xii. 1; after which followed the Ordination of Elders, and I, with the class, was solemnly set apart to the full work of the ministry. May I be divinely assisted to pay the vows which I have made to God and the Church! Bishop Hamline's health afterwards so failed, that it became requisite for him to retire from the episcopacy. He felt that he was unable to do the work; therefore he would give place to some other one more able to bear the labours of the superintendency. The General Conference of 1852 accepted his resignation, showing that our views of episcopacy are different from some others. We do not hold to the doctrine "once a bishop always a bishop." We do not consider it an order in the ministry, but an office. Mr. Wesley's mind, indeed, was abused in relation to Bishop Asbury, and he made some unkind remarks to that humble man, under that influence, relative to the title of Bishop, &c. But the true state of the case is, that the views of our Church on this point are purely Wesleyan. We consider *presbyter* and *bishop* one and the same order, and we have done nothing, on this great matter, unauthorized by the Founder of Methodism.

When the colonies became independent he gave us the forms of ordination, and felt himself providentially moved to provide, in this way, for his sheep in the wilderness. We think our episcopacy not only Wesleyan, but also that our polity in general is as nearly in accordance with the original Church of Christ as any in existence.

By a vote of the Conference, Rev. Bishop Morris was requested to preach the funeral sermon of the venerable Ezekiel Cooper, during the session of the body. Father Cooper had deceased the preceding winter. He was the oldest minister at his death, perhaps, of our Church in this country, if not in the world. He entered the work in 1785; was present when Rev. Dr. Coke and Rev. Francis Asbury had their first meeting at Barratt's Chapel, in Delaware. Rev. Nathan Bangs, his old and long-tried friend, preached his funeral sermon at the time of his burial, at St. George's Methodist Episcopal Church, in Philadelphia. His remains were buried in front of the church, and a plain marble slab marks the spot of his repose. A slab is also erected against the wall of the church, in front, with an appropriate inscription. Rev. Ezekiel Cooper never had many if any colabourers in the ministry that were blessed with greater talent. He was known, in his day, throughout the length and breadth of the land as a strong man, competent for controversy, or any emergency.

His funeral sermon, in compliance with the request of the Conference, was re-preached at St. Paul's Methodist Episcopal Church, in Wilmington, by Bishop Morris. The Bishop, on that occasion, related an incident in the way of encouraging ministers, that made a deep impression on my mind. Said the Bishop, "There were two brothers, who were both Methodist preachers; one was a great revivalist, very popular, and successful wherever he went. The other was a very solid preacher, but never seemed to have much fruit. The popular one said to the other, at a certain time, 'Brother, you have been preaching now twenty years, and I know of but one soul that you were ever instrumental in getting converted; and, if I were in your place, I would retire from the work.' Said he to his popular brother—'Do you think I have been the means of getting one soul converted?' 'I have no doubt of that,' was the reply. 'Then,' said the brother who did not despise the day of small things, 'here goes for twenty years' more hard toil for the sake of getting another one converted to God.'"

Having passed through the course of Conference study, and having been ordained Elder, it was impressed upon my mind that I could with propriety think of changing my situation in life. I did, after much thought and prayer, resolve to offer my heart and hand to the friend of my youth. And this matter thus commenced, was consummated some eighteen months thereafter. I felt it my duty, however, to keep aloof from all matrimonial engagements until I had, at least, graduated to Elder's orders. I do not take the ground that God's word requires this of ministers; for Paul says, "Let the *deacons* be the husbands of one wife, ruling their children and their own houses well." But I think many reasons can be given why, as a general thing, this course would be better for Methodist ministers. 1. Mostly, we are young, and have much to learn, when we first start in the work; and, for several years, it is as much as we can reasonably expect of the Church to provide for us, without the encumbrance of a family. 2. We do injustice to ourselves; for it is impossible for us, with the cares of a family, to devote as much time to study, and other important duties, as the exigencies of the case absolutely require; and, consequently, we cannot rise in the esteem of the Church as we otherwise might. 3. It is unfair towards our married brethren who are recommended to the Conference. Men of power, and capable, in many instances, of taking charge of Circuits at once, are not—owing to the fact that they have families—received; and the preference is given to single men, exclusively owing to this consideration. Therefore, fair dealing requires that we should not prematurely marry, and bring a family upon the Church, the very thing that led to the failure of the married man's application. 4. Is it respectful to the Conference to marry in one, two, or even three years, when it expects us to remain single at least four years? 5. By being premature, can we place our families in situations of comfort?

It would be well for us, young brethren in the ministry, to deliberate upon this matter. Perhaps some will say: "Have we not power to lead about a sister, a wife, as well as other apostles, and as the brethren of the Lord and Cephas?" We have a right; and, at the proper time, we shall be perhaps to blame, and we shall perhaps do ourselves and the Church injury, if we do not go according to our right. But let us marry in the Lord; then we shall experience that "Whoso findeth a wife, findeth a good thing, and obtaineth favour of the Lord."

At this Conference, I was appointed to Bethlehem station, in the city of Philadelphia. This church was built in 1843, under the supervision of the North City Home Mission. Rev. John Street was, at the time, the missionary; and, through his efficient services, this work was greatly advanced. This brother has a mind for the work, and has been a blessing to many. He will not lose his reward. The occupancy of this church in Callowhill street, superseded the Fairmount church; this being a more desirable location, they all flocked to the standard planted by this pioneer society. Many souls, however, had been converted; and a goodly number had, through the efforts of the Fairmount church, joined the

Church triumphant in Heaven. I found this an interesting appointment, and our house was much too small. One evening when there was a great crowd of persons, during the prayer meeting which followed the preaching, the north-west corner of the church sunk down some two feet. The meeting at the time was very lively. Some were shouting, and others were seeking religion at the altar. The accident was hardly observed. Had the greatest catastrophe come upon us then, we were happy in God, and the probability is, we should have shouted on. The breach was healed, and the house ready for occupancy the next evening.

I remained with this church two years, and had a great desire to see a larger edifice erected; but, in this respect, it was not my privilege to see the salvation of God. The society continued to worship in the same humble place till 1852; when Bethlehem was razed to the ground, and, on the same lot, a large and a more beautiful temple was put up, under the pastorship of Rev. William L. Gray, who remained another year to preach, in this delightful structure, the unsearchable riches of Christ. The new house was called "Emory Methodist Episcopal Church," in honour of Bishop Emory. Many, however, clung to the name of Bethlehem—interesting name, as it was the place where the Saviour was born! This church compromised this matter of name, by putting the stone originally inserted, bearing the name of

"Bethlehem," &c., in the north end of the church. On Callowhill street, the church fronts, and the modern name appears. I like this spirit of compromise. But, above every name, may God's name be therein recorded! This name is high over all, in hell, or earth, or sky.

The Lord favoured us in this charge with an interesting revival. Many were added to the Church. The Sunday School here was a great acquisition to us; it was well conducted. In reviewing the persons I received into society in that charge, I find at least two who are engaged as itinerant ministers. I recollect, in one case, when I accosted the young man on the subject of religion, he was disposed to treat me and the cause with considerable disdain; but I do not consider this a bad omen in all cases. He was like a young man, in the gospel, who said, when called upon to work in the vineyard, "I will not; but afterwards he repented, and went."

While labouring in this charge, it was necessary, on a certain occasion, to make a strong financial effort. Our brethren desired the services of Rev. Henry G. King, one of our most valuable living ministers, and now among the fathers in the Philadelphia Conference. His services on such occasions are greatly appreciated, and justly so. On this occasion, he did well, and all that was asked for was obtained. At the time he was serving us, he was pastor of the Frankford Methodist

Episcopal Church. The arrangement was for me to preach in his pulpit the Sunday night of that day. I did the best I could; and, although there was no protracted meeting, and I had to return to the city that night—a distance of six or seven miles—I felt impressed that it was my duty to hold a prayer meeting, and try to get some one converted. I told the audience my feeling, and pressingly invited mourners forward. There was, instantly, almost, a youth who presented himself, greatly distressed; he used a holy violence, and seemed determined to enter into the kingdom of God. The mother of the penitent said to me, with emphasis, as I was passing up and down the aisle: "Brother Manship, that's my James; pray for him, do pray for him!" We all rallied around the youth; and it was not long before the shout of the new-born soul was heard. I believe my readers will be greatly pleased when I tell them that that youth was the son of Rev. Henry G. King; and they will be still more pleased when I tell them that God has called him to the work of the ministry, and that he is now a promising young minister, travelling in the Philadelphia Conference.

The height of my ambition was realized—a soul was converted! I went into the city in a shouting mood, and bore the news to the father that night, late as it was. "When the Lord turned again the captivity of Zion, we were like them that dream." I was able joyfully to testify that this was not a dream, but a glorious reality. How it must cheer the heart of the aged, faithful minister, who is passing downwards to the tomb, to have a son coming forward to do battle for the Lord of Hosts! It is a beautiful sight to see the son walking in the footsteps of his sire. How grandly does the prophet speak of the legate of the skies! "How beautiful upon the mountains are the feet of him that bringeth good tidings, that publisheth peace; that bringeth good tidings of good, that publisheth salvation, that saith unto Zion, Thy God reigneth!"

I should perhaps treat the trustees and the society of Bethlehem charge with want of gratitude, if I did not mention a little incident, which occurred towards the end of my term with them. As an expression of their esteem they presented me with a valuable watch, which I shall carry near my heart, perhaps till the day of my death. The kind friends offered me a gold watch. It was beautiful and very tempting to the eye; but, in view of my position, the teachings of the Scriptures, and our general rules, which forbid "the putting on of gold and costly apparel," I could not conscientiously accept the offer, and told the committee that a good silver one would be preferable. My wishes were gratified. There was a difference in the cost of some forty dollars; but that society, unexpected to myself, generously gave me the difference in money. The watch that I have is just as good as it regards keeping time. There are many in the ministry who carry gold watches, better Christians than I am, and I do not wish to be considered censorious, and I endorse the doctrine of Paul: "Let every man be fully persuaded in his own mind." Such a present is valuable in more ways than one. May it not have a spiritual bearing? It admonishes us of the flight of time, and we should be impressed with the vast amount of work there is to be done by us ministers, and the short time there is for the accomplishment of the work.

> "Time, like an ever rolling stream,
> Bears all its sons away;
> They fly forgotten, as a dream
> Dies at the opening day."

I was called upon in this neighbourhood to visit a man who had been bitten by his pet dog, and was supposed to have the hydrophobia. It was a trial to go; and yet I felt it my duty. Of course, under such circumstances we should be discreet. But, as a general thing, ministers should feel like saying in the time of danger in the language of Nehemiah, "Shall such a man as I flee?" I found the man, who was in this sad condition, to be the head of a family, in the meridian of life, and of the most respectable standing in society. But, awful to tell, he had neglected to prepare to meet God, and it seemed now too late (there being no hope, according to the opinions of physicians present, that he could live over a very few hours) to do the work of a lifetime. I tried to pray with him. Afterwards, at his request, I sat down with him at the tea-table. He could neither eat nor drink. Wildly he would exclaim, "This is the last supper! this is the last supper!!" He was an object of pity, the picture of despair, even in his best mood, while I was present. A fit came on, and he was a perfect demoniac, foaming at the mouth, and with the fury of a tiger, the effect of the disease. He rushed upon the company, who had met at the house under the awful circumstances; and I am frank to confess, I went out with more velocity than I went into the house! Again, under the influence of this distemper, he broke through the back door: Samson-like, he was powerful and carried everything before him. At this crisis orders were given to have him bound, for the safety of others. Bound down with cords, this strong man soon died in the greatest agony. His pet dog cost him his life.

On returning to my boarding-house at the close of an evening meeting where we had a season of rejoicing, I passed a hotel, where there was a ball going on, and the parties seemed happy in their way. How late it lasted I know not. Many are ready to censure the Methodists, if they should happen, from the force of circumstances, to continue their meetings till ten o'clock, or a little after, especially if they should be constrained to shout the praises of the Lord; and yet they will allow a ball to go forward with impunity, even though the parties should ever so much annoy the surrounding neighbourhood: there is no spécial verdict brought in against them! But there is a "*handwriting*" against such revellings and bacchanalian feasts. It was literally so in this case; for a prominent actor in this carousal, intoxicated and overcome by strong drink, at midnight's hour fell headlong down stairs, and broke his neck. I was reliably informed this man had been religiously educated and trained; but alas! he was "suddenly destroyed." I would, through this medium, admonish all our readers to beware of the cotillion party, shun the decent ball. Who ever reflected on a dying bed with pleasure upon the hours spent in a ball-room? Who would like to be transferred from the dancing hall to the grave, and thence to the judgment seat of Christ? Yet with all that may be said against dancing, there are those who entertain the idea that their sons and daughters are not fully educated without this acccomplishment, and their great desire to have them learn politeness, induces them to place them under the dancing master. Is he such a character as you would have your children to associate with for moral and mental improvement? I am astonished when I find sometimes professors of religion winking at this practice, and aiding and abetting this means, among many others, which the devil resorts to, in order to lead the children of men "captive at his will." Who can dance and at the same time obey the precept, "Be ye sober and watch unto prayer?"

During my last protracted meeting in this charge, we were favoured on a Sunday evening occasion with a sermon from a young Lutheran minister, who had been trained at Gettysburg, and had not long been a regular minister. He read his sermon; it was a very creditable production; it did not, however, cut like a two-edged sword, as we could have desired. I followed with an exhortation, in which I tried to arouse the slumbering energies of the congregation. The minister looked on with considerable amazement. Penitents presented themselves at the altar, and plead in plaintive strains: "God be merciful to us sinners." I invited the young minister to labour with the mourners; he had not been in the habit of seeing it on this wise, and was ready to say, no doubt, "We have seen strange things to-day." At our urgent request, however, he went to work, and, while labouring in this, to him, strange manner, his heart was, as Mr. Wesley said, "*strangely warmed.*" The next day he paid me a visit at my residence, spent an hour conversing on Christian experience, and we prayed together, and our hearts burned within us. He told me that he *experienced last night what he never before felt!* "I thanked God and took courage." I have not seen that young minister since; I hope to meet him on that bright shore

"Where parting sounds will pass our lips no more."

Several of my members were employed in the Eastern Penitentiary, and, among the number, the brother with whom I boarded. I was kindly invited to go there and preach, which I did, occasionally. Frequently I visited that place in company with friends. The unfortunate ones there are well cared for; and, I presume, there is no place in this nation where greater pains are taken, and more money expended, to make the institutions of this character comfortable, than in Philadelphia. But how withering the thought, I am an inmate of the state's prison! And how few do such institutions reform, comparatively! I want, in this connexion, to present my readers with a most touching incident. A fine-looking young man was sentenced to the Penitentiary. Before he was assigned his place, the Superintendent kindly conversed with him, and asked him many questions. He replied promptly to them, displaying no special feeling. He at length proposed this question to him: "Have you a mother?" His countenance changed instantly, tears stood in his eyes, and he exclaimed, "My God! sir, mention not that name to me!" Overcome with emotion, he sank down into an arm-chair, and wept aloud. His mother, perhaps, had taught him to pray, "Our Father who art in Heaven," and had admonished him to sobriety and religion; but he had disregarded her counsel. Although she was, perhaps, cold in death, and could not watch over him—he could not hear her friendly voice nor see her bosom heaving with solicitude for him, and he had been overcome and brought to this doleful place—still, he had not forgotten his mother, and could not bear to hear her name mentioned.

While connected with this charge, I spoke at the funerals of several returned volunteers in the Mexican war. When that war terminated, and our heroic soldiers came home, there were some most affecting scenes. They were received by a delighted city; never did I see Philadelphia present a more cheerful appearance. The stars and the stripes were seen in every direction; the firing of cannon was almost constantly heard. Flowers strewed the pathway, now and then, of the careworn but victorious soldiers. "Music sweet, music soft," was heard from almost every band in this city. In golden letters the beholder could see inscribed, in prominent places, "Welcome home!" They appreciated it all; and, could they have spoken, I imagine they would have exclaimed, in substance,

"Home is sweet, home is sweet,
From a foreign shore;
And oh! it fills my soul with joy
To meet my friends once more."

As the procession passed through one of the streets, there was seen the delicate form of a female. Her countenance was sad. Her son had been in the war, and news had, some months previously, been brought to her that he had fallen in battle; she therefore never expected to see him again. He however yet lived, and was one of those who, by God's blessing, had the privilege of treading again his native soil. He was aware that his mother was under the impression that he was dead; and, when he caught a glimpse of his grieving parent, he exclaimed, making signs so that she might recognise him, "*Mother, here's John; he is safe at home!*"

The Lord was better to that lady than she expected; and she could say, "the Lord delivered me from all my fears." Joy filled her; it was to her like one rising from the dead.

While I gazed upon the scenes of this day, I thought of the sacramental host; I thought of the last battle being fought with the enemies of King Jesus; I thought of the victory that we should gain. The passage rushed upon my mind: "The ransomed of the Lord shall return and come to Zion with songs and everlasting joy upon their heads: they shall obtain joy and gladness, and sorrow and sighing shall flee away."

And, indeed, my readers, I was so happy and overjoyed, I could scarcely contain myself. I felt the force and spirit of the poet:—

> "It sets my heart all in a flame,
> A soldier for to be;
> I will enlist, gird on my arms,
> And fight for liberty.
>
> "To see our armies on parade,
> How martial they appear!
> All armed and dressed in uniform,
> They look like men of war.
>
> "Sinners, enlist with Jesus Christ,
> The eternal Son of God;
> And march with us to Canaan's land,
> Beyond the swelling flood.
>
> "Lift up your heads, ye soldiers bold,
> Redemption's drawing nigh;
> We soon shall hear the trumpet's sound
> That shakes the earth and sky."

I would most devoutly pray that our own and other nations should be so brought under the influence of the Christian religion as "not to lift up sword against nation, neither learn war any more." But with holy enthusiasm I would admonish my fellow-soldiers to endure hardness, and march forward under our glorious standard-bearer, the Lord Jesus Christ, under whom alone we can fight in security, and by whom alone we shall triumph gloriously. Soldiers! after all your fighting here, though doomed to hardship and many a battle, there is a rest, a glorious rest! "And in that day there shall be a root of Jesse which shall stand for an ensign of the people, to it shall the Gentiles seek: and his rest shall be glorious."

"When that illustrious day shall rise,
And all thy armies shine
In robes of victory through the skies,
The glory shall be thine."

Christian mothers, think of the transport of that mother—who was under the apprehension that her son would never return, but that his bones would bleach on the sun-burnt shores of Mexico—when she saw, to her great surprise, with the returned volunteers, that form so dear to her, and heard his exclamation, "Mother, here's John; he is safe at home!" and, while you think of this, hope for your prodigal son. You have a thousand times remembered him in your prayers: "Rachel has wept for her children." Suppose those prayers and tears should apparently prove unavailing; that, when you lie on the bed of death, that callous-hearted youth should refuse—hesitate to make to his dying mother even the promise to join her society on Canaan's peaceful shore. Yet those prayers will follow him, your dying admonitions he cannot forget. He will see the old family Bible which lies on the stand, its pages marked by the delicate hand and bedewed with the tears of his mother, and may resolve to be again united never more to sever; and, when the "ransomed host shall shout, We are come," led on by our all-victorious Captain through that City whose walls are jasper and whose streets are gold,

> "Triumphant there, in bliss complete,
> And cast our crowns before his feet,
> In endless day,"

think what the transport will be when you shall see this son, that you feared would be for ever lost, amid the sacramental host, and hear him shout, thus dispelling all doubt, "Mother, here's John; he is safe at home!" Cease not, fond mothers, to pray for your loved ones; "for the promise is unto you and your children."

CHAPTER VII.

Sent to Easton—Rev. Joseph Hartley—Changed to another Field in two Weeks—Reasons for the Change—Reflections on this Matter—Receive a valuable Letter—All for the best—Methodism in New Castle—Churches should be eligibly located—Thomas Challenger, Sr.—High Sheriff converted, and dies happy—Preach his Funeral Sermon—"Preach to Spirits in Prison"—The Gospel the Hope of the Hopeless—Perform the Marriage Ceremony in Jail—A Man wanted to be unmarried!—Rev. John D. Long—Persecution not to be tolerated—The Word of the Lord the highest Authority—The Midnight Cry—Rev. Nicholas Ridgley—Happy Day; several seeking Religion in a Parlour—Camp Meeting well conducted—The efficiency of Sunday Schools—We all should take an Interest in them.

IN the spring of 1849, somewhat to my surprise, my appointment was read out by the Bishop for Easton, Maryland. Into this place, Methodism was early introduced. My readers may be interested by calling their attention to Rev. Joseph Hartley, a man of great zeal and faithfulness, who was one of the first travelling preachers in that part of the work, and, like his contemporaries, met with great persecution in preaching the everlasting gospel. When in the adjoining county of Queen Ann's, he was apprehended for this work and labour of love, and had to give bonds and security to appear for trial at the next Court. When forbidden to preach, he attended his appointments, and, after singing and prayer, *stood upon his knees!* and exhorted the people. From this point, he was led into Talbot county; where he was actually seized and committed to jail for preaching Jesus and him crucified! This by no means silenced him; his imprisonment brought the people together at the prison, and, through the grates, he lifted up his voice like a trumpet. Many who heard the word were pungently convicted, and began earnestly to seek the Lord. This man of God was in a degree bound, but his word was not bound; it had "free course, and was glorified." This state of things created a great panic amongst the enemies of religion, and led them to say: "Unless Hartley is released from prison, he will convert the whole town of Easton." He was released, sure enough, as a matter of policy; but a powerful revival followed, and a society was established. And this rod, which our Aaron "threw down, has swallowed up all the other rods."

When I, more than seventy years afterwards, had the privilege of being appointed to the charge of that field of labour, I found Methodism wielding a tremendous influence, not only in the town of Easton, but throughout the beautiful county of Talbot. As an evidence of the estimate that is placed upon Methodism and Methodist preachers in that town—although it is a comparatively small place, not exceeding in population fifteen hundred —yet, in the spring of 1848, the Philadelphia Annual Conference was held there; and, had there been many more connected with the Conference, they could have been entertained nobly and with the greatest ease; for the people there have hearts!

After the close of the Conference, I delayed no time in getting on to the field which had been assigned me. There are many reasons, I think, why a preacher should, as soon as possible, reach his new appointment. Our first preaching was in the town of Easton. The text I took was, "He that goeth forth and weepeth, bearing precious seed, shall doubtless come again with rejoicing, bringing his sheaves with him." The text, it would seem, was ominous in my case about that time, as my readers will presently see. My colleague was Rev. Charles I. Thompson, who had been on the Circuit the preceding year, and who lived greatly in the hearts of the people. We were both comparatively young men, and we thought we had a disposition to do with our might whatsoever our hands should find to do. We began together to visit from house to house. We found the people affectionate, and in words and looks they told us *we were welcome*. We found a gracious revival had been going on, both among the white and coloured. It was still progressing among the people of colour. I preached once for them in their church, and a happier set of people I never saw. We were arranging, in our intercourse together, our plans for the year. Brother Thompson thought that one or two churches on the Circuit could be built, if we could begin in time. I told him I was ready to do my part. I was greatly pleased with the Circuit, and felt myself highly honoured to be sent to it; and I was deeply interested in my associate in the glorious work, and felt that what I might lack he could supply. The month of April, however, had not passed away, before I was apprised, by the powers that be, that my appointment was changed! This was an unexpected arrangement to me, and it was not any less so to the people of Easton, who had, unworthy as I was, received me kindly. And, to prevent any from concluding that the change was made by their seeking, at their first Quarterly Meeting a preamble and resolutions were unanimously passed, clearly stating their satisfaction with my appointment among them, and "that I should have been cordially and gladly retained, but for the change made by the proper authorities." And this loyal Quarterly Meeting Conference, composed of intelligent and pious men—though they had not, any more than myself, been consulted relative to the change—determined that they would receive the minister who was to take my place, and rally around him. I exhorted them, publicly and privately, so to do. I thought this was the best, under the circumstances.

The inquiry will be started, Why was this change necessary? I answer, it grew out of the refusal, on the part of one of our stations, to receive the minister who was that spring appointed to them. With all due deference to the places that pursue a course of this kind, I feel, from a sense of duty, compelled to say, it is a pity that the practice of refusing an appointed preacher should ever have been allowed. Unless very speedily stopped, it must ruin the itinerancy. There is but little hope of continuing it, if the people are permitted absolutely to nullify a regular appointment. It would be far better that several churches and congregations should be given up, than that this great principle should cease to operate. Let the people remonstrate by giving reasons, where they exist, for a change; but *never*, *never* should a church be allowed to *refuse* to receive one sent them. Independently of the importance of the principle, no change can be effected, ordinarily, without inflicting an injury *somewhere*.

In this revolution of "the great iron wheel," as our system has been called, I had more to suffer than any one else. The affliction was severe; and yet I have not one word of censure to offer to the *appointing power* of the Methodist Episcopal Church. I know that the Bishop and his council are fallible, and may err, and may also be *imposed upon*. Nevertheless, I say, from my heart, I want Methodism to remain as it is, and stand

"As she ever hath stood,
And brightly her builder display,
And flame with the glory of God."

In the end of this unusual arrangement, I found myself safely moored in the quiet harbour of New Castle, Delaware, an old town, laid out by William Penn at an early period in the history of our country. It is actually an older town than Philadelphia; and Penn's design was, there to locate his city. But, after taking steps to this effect, he found it better to go farther up the beautiful Delaware, and fix his city in another location.

A dear friend, of high standing in the Church, writing to me, says: "Providence may have a hand in this whole matter, to an extent which we cannot now discover. The events of the year may develop it. It may be that you are the very man whom God has chosen, and thus mysteriously directed, to put Methodism on a right foundation in New Castle, a place which seems to have defied, to a great extent, all our previous labours. And, then, it is a healthy position; and the change may be the preservation of your life, and that of your wife, for future and yet more important labours. So, cheer up, Brother M.! you have not forgotten that beautiful passage: 'All things work together,' &c.—you know it." In this very encouraging letter from a valuable friend, there was a message also from Bishop J. "Tell Brother M. he has our sympathies and prayers; and tell him to go to work in New Castle like a good fellow—it will do him no harm in the end." Much good is accomplished by Christian correspondence.

This point reached, I tried to dismiss from my mind the events of the past, put the best construction on everything, and "rejoice evermore, pray without ceasing, and in everything give thanks." That spring (1849) this station had not been supplied, and there was a vacancy. The design was, for New Castle to be connected with Delaware City; to this, New Castle objected, and desired still to be a distinct station. Therefore, in this respect, there seemed to be a Providence; and not only in this particular, but in many others, I think I was able to see the hand of Providence plainly. Neither in time, nor while eternity shall roll its solemn rounds, shall I have occasion to regret that I was mysteriously placed over the church of our denomination in that place. And, after remaining one year, such was my contentment, and such was the heavenly feeling that pervaded both the hearts of the people and pastor, that I should have been highly gratified to have been re-appointed in the spring of 1850. But my poor services seemed to be required in another direction, as my readers will see by and by; and I was under the necessity of giving to this loving society and congregation the parting hand, and my connexion as pastor was dissolved; but our affection, I trust, has not, and never will be.

In New Castle the Methodist Church is not the strongest. Our Episcopalian and Presbyterian friends are older: both the Episcopal and Presbyterian churches have been established more *than a hundred years!* Their antiquity gives them strength. Moreover, in the town of New Castle there is a greater amount of aristocracy than in any town in which it ever has been my lot to labour; and our Church is not so well suited to the aristocracy of this country as some others. This gives our sister denominations in this place an advantage over us. I will venture another reason why our church has not been more efficient in this town. When our fathers erected churches, for some cause the plan of putting them in the outskirts of the town was adopted; no doubt the fathers supposed they had sufficient reasons for pursuing this course. And the brethren, thirty years ago, when they first built a house of worship in this place, fell into this error. In my opinion, no circumstance has clogged our wheels more than this. In the town of New Castle the church is not conveniently located.

At the present day, we pursue in this matter a different course, and, I think, "a more excellent way." We try to secure the best and most prominent sites for our church edifices in our towns and cities. And we feel it is right, "not to keep our light under a bushel," but to act on the suggestion of the evangelical prophet: "O Zion, that bringest good tidings, get thee up into the high mountain." Take a conspicuous place. We are not to be intimidated by any class of community. And while our mission is to the poor and humble of earth, we are to follow in the footsteps of the Master, and preach salvation to lawyers and doctors; and, Paul-like, we must penetrate into the very heart of Athens. On this point again hear the prophet: "O Jerusalem, that bringest good tidings, lift up thy voice with strength; lift it up, *be not afraid.*"

I hope to live to see the day, when this teaching will be practically carried out in the town of New Castle among our people. A church of the right size and quality, in the very heart of the town, would place Methodism where she ought to stand in that place. I would not be considered as inclined to undervalue what has been accomplished in this place for the last thirty years. If we could, for a little while, "walk the plains of light," and be made acquainted with the redeemed there, and find out from "whence came they," doubtless we should ascertain that a considerable number came from this place, directly through the instrumentality of Methodism. And this day numerically her number is the largest of any one denomination in that place. In connexion with the establishment of our church in this place, too much credit cannot be given to Thomas Challenger, Sr., formerly from the land of the Wesleys. He has watered the grain of mustard seed with his tears, and though he has not seen all he could desire, yet, to a great extent, he has seen the seed which he and his few co-labourers planted, "shooting out great branches, so that the fowls of the air may lodge under the shadow of it." He still lives the same faithful Christian, to see his "labour in the Lord has not been in vain." A few such men would have saved Sodom and Gomorrah from destruction.

While in this station, I formed the acquaintance of the high sheriff of the county. His wife was a faithful member of our church. The sheriff was not religious. God laid upon him his afflicting hand, and it was sanctified to his good. I often visited him, and conversed with him on the subject of a preparation for death, and he became deeply concerned, sought and found peace with God through our Lord Jesus Christ. There is mercy even for the politician, who will hate his sins, repent, and believe the gospel. I took him into our church, and he was faithful unto death, which overtook him before his term of office expired. I was removed to the city of Wilmington before he died, yet I often visited him, and was with him a short time before he left the world. I found him waiting joyfully his change. His funeral sermon was preached by myself at the request of himself and that of the family, to a very large concourse of people. He was a man much esteemed by all who knew him. His last days were his best and happiest days.

Being intimate with the sheriff and family, who had charge of the jail, I frequently visited "and preached to the spirits in prison." The poor unfortunate creatures did very greatly excite my compassion. The prisoner ought to be visited: "I was in prison, and ye came unto me." I think we should take the gospel to them, for, while there may be no hope for their reputation, their family may have no hope in them, and they may have no hope of release from the stern arm of the law, which they have violated, still the minister of God, whose business it is to "proclaim liberty to the captives, and the opening of the prison to them that are bound," with God's Holy Word in his hand, which is the hope of the hopeless, may say to those immured in their cells or dungeons, "Turn you to the strong hold, ye *prisoners of hope;* even to-day do I declare that I will render double unto thee."

In the jail, on a certain occasion, I had to perform for a couple the marriage ceremony. Their term of imprisonment was at an end; and I suppose that they thought it would be well to perpetuate their friendship; and they obtained a legal license, and, in the presence of the sheriff and several others, I united them together in the silken bonds of matrimony. I was almost overcome that day, notwithstanding the sacredness of the institution. When I commenced, "Wilt thou have this woman to thy wedded wife?"—he prematurely exclaimed, "Yes, sir." Again I proceeded with the ceremony:—"Wilt thou love her?"—and before I could say any more, he replied, "*Yes*, sir—yes, sir." My readers may imagine how unpleasant my situation must have been; the persons present could not refrain from a hearty laugh. When I turned to the bride, she conducted herself very properly, and, in a moment or two, the happy twain were one. To do justice to the groom, I should say, notwithstanding the unfavourable circumstances, he did not fail to hand to the parson a *respectable fee.* This I did not expect; but sometimes, when ministers have reason *from appearances* to expect much, they feel the force of the old adage, "A bird in the hand is worth two in the bush." I never heard of that couple from that day till the present time. I was struck, however, with the anxiety which seemed to characterize the bride and groom to be wedded, especially the groom. I hope they have lived happily together; but I had my fears. I have often thought of that man, and wondered to myself whether the case had any resemblance to a wedding that once took place in the lower part of Delaware. Rev. Mr. Davis, a very popular local preacher, long since gone to heaven, was the officiating minister. The groom did not give the minister any compensation: nothing was said at the time. However, not long afterwards, the minister met the groom and pleasantly remarked to him: "You did not think to present me with anything for the service I rendered you the other day?" The groom replied with considerable emotion: "Mr. Davis, if you will only *unmarry* me, I will pay you both bills." Poor fellow! it is presumable he had a dear bargain, notwithstanding the fee was not paid; and it is very likely he felt the force of the Scripture: "It is better to dwell in a corner of a housetop, than with a brawling woman, and in a wide house."

Rev. John D. Long was supernumerary at this time in New Castle. His health was so feeble that he was not many years able to do effective service. He had formerly been pastor of the church in this place, and God made him a blessing, and he will not be forgotten. I think I should present my readers with one remarkable case of conversion and addition to the Church in this place, while he was the pastor. It was a young woman from the Emerald Isle. She had been brought up a strict Catholic, and had never known any other religion, until God in his providence led her to the Methodist Church in this place. Her eyes were opened to see: She saw "men as trees walking." Here she learned to feel and sing,

> "Jesus, thy blood, thy blood alone
> Hath power sufficient to atone."

After her conversion she joined the Church, which created a great commotion, and her Roman Catholic relations actually threatened to do her injury—they "took counsel to kill" her. How thoughtless, and how wicked! She found an asylum in a good Methodist family, and no threats which were made, moved her from her purpose; she was "steadfast, unmovable:" and when I laboured in that station, she was "abounding in the work of the Lord." She is now the head of a family, settled in life. I met her recently at a camp meeting in the state of Maryland, and found her rooted and grounded in the faith of the "glorious gospel." In this "Land of the free, and home of the brave," Popery must not be so violent as she is in some other countries. If she is, the American Eagle will pounce down upon her fiercely, and strike her with his talons to the heart. I am opposed to forcible measures either among Protestants or Catholics, but let truth be presented, and let every one have the opportunity of "choosing" whom he or she "will serve." The Bible, I insist, should be read. It is a sufficient rule for our faith and practice. This is God's book, and not man's. It is the basis, bulwark, and boast of our free institutions, and points out the way to heaven. Then let *all* "Search the Scriptures; for in them ye think ye have eternal life: and they are they which testify of me." These are the words of Jesus; and however great councils, cardinals, and popes may be, their words and commands are insignificant, when contrasted with His who "spake as never man spake."

One Sabbath evening I was endeavouring, while pastor of the New Castle Church, to preach from the parable of the Wise and Foolish Virgins. The subject was solemn, I felt deeply so myself. But there were some young persons a little inclined to levity, and to disturb those near them. In explaining my subject as well as I could, I insisted that while other things were meant by the midnight cry, death was also comprehended, and at midnight literally, the cry would be made, and some one present would have to go. And who knows, I asked, but it may be one of those who are inclined to annoy the meeting? Not many days elapsed, before one was taken ill: his sickness was unto death. I was called up late at night to pray for him. I cheerfully went, and tried to encourage him to have faith in the Lamb of God. He did the best he could under the circumstances, in the way of praying. The body was weak, and the mind somewhat flighty. As the town clock dolefully struck *twelve*, we were all upon our knees, calling upon a merciful God in his behalf. Before the last stroke of the clock was heard, we saw plainly death had struck the fatal blow. "At midnight," in this case, "the cry was made, Behold, the bridegroom cometh." Readers, let us have our vessels filled with oil, our lamps trimmed and burning brightly, that when the call shall be made by the Lord, we shall have the privilege of entering in to the marriage supper of the Lamb. "Watch therefore, for ye know neither the day, nor the hour, wherein the Son of Man cometh."

Rev. Nicholas N. Ridgley was, in the spring of 1844,

stationed in this place. I would not for a moment undervalue other brethren who have laboured in this field. From what I know, however, I feel compelled to say, that none of us, before or since his day, have here exerted a more wholesome influence in favour of Methodism, and it would, in my estimation, have been very judicious for him to have remained another year. He was always exceedingly moral. He was blessed with a pious mother, a member of the Protestant Episcopal Church. She instructed him in the great truths and principles of the gospel. So earnestly and so early did she attend to this that he says, in his Journal: "I cannot recollect the period in my life at which I had not as clear a conception of the utter corruption of my heart—my absolute dependence on the atonement of Christ even for natural life, and much more for salvation, and of the exposure of all men to the wrath of a justly offended God, and indeed of all the essential features of the gospel, as I have since had; though, of course, these truths were not as much realized in my experience as they were when I was converted." This event took place in 1839, and, in the fall of that year, he felt that it was requisite to his happiness that he should be united to the Church. The Protestant Episcopal Church was the communion of his family. But he felt, if he joined it, he would have no privileges, for there was no regular ministry within many miles of Dover, where he resided.

Having for some time previously been connected with the Sunday School of the Methodist Episcopal Church, as a teacher, he was led, in a great measure, through that instrumentality *to seek the kingdom of God.* While teaching others he felt the force of the passage, "Physician, heal thyself." He attended several class meetings, from which he derived much benefit. The Methodists, he says, "took me by the hand and led me on. So on the 8th of October, 1839, I joined this Church." He was one of her brightest ornaments, without reproach and above suspicion. In this Church he lived, and in her died happy in God. In relation to the benefits of class meetings, so much dreaded by some, he says: "I verily believe I should have returned to the world an open apostate in one year, but for their influence." His love for class meetings never abated after he became a travelling minister in the Philadelphia Conference of the Methodist Episcopal Church, in the spring of 1842. He was inclined towards the ministry of the Protestant Episcopal Church, not that he believed that Church any more apostolic, but it was the Church of his family, and he thought his father would more readily consent to his becoming a minister in this Church. But in this respect he was most agreeably disappointed, for he was rather more favourably inclined to the Methodist Episcopal Church, asking his son, "Why he thought of the Protestant Episcopal Church rather than the Methodist

Episcopal Church?" From what I have heard my friend say, and from his Journal, I should conclude his most prominent reason was, he thought his sight, which was defective, would not allow him to do the work of an Itinerant. His interviews with Bishop Onderdonk and Rev. Mr. Presstman, "were not satisfactory, there was too much exclusiveness in their views." He sought advice, prayed and thought much on the subject, until the spring of 1842, when he felt it was according to God's holy will that he should join the Itinerancy, which he did, and was appointed to the Caroline Circuit, on the Eastern Shore of Maryland. Here he remained two years with Rev. John Bayne. They were happy and very successful years. Very many were added to the Church, and, although his sight was poor, he did all the work faithfully of a Methodist preacher; and I suppose Caroline Circuit will ever consider that they

"Ne'er will see his like again."

From that point he came to New Castle, then went to Haddington, then to Phœnixville, then to Twelfth street Station, Philadelphia. This was the last charge he filled. Here his health so gave way that it was necessary for him to leave the effective ranks. He fixed his residence thereafter in the city of Wilmington, where, December 1st, 1849, he triumphantly shouted victory over death. His life had been so blameless, we expected in his death that the king of terrors would be swallowed up in victory, and our expectations were more than met. I was with him in his last illness. Never shall I forget his sweet language. While he thanked God for all blessings, he seemed to be particularly thankful that he had been favoured with a pious mother. He said, "I shall soon be with her, my mother, that first taught me to pray." Readers, if you have pious mothers, you are highly favoured.

I was intimately associated with him in the work of the Itinerancy, while he was on his first Circuit. I shall never forget a day we spent together in the month of August, 1842. The camp meeting for Denton Circuit closed on the day I allude to. Many were converted—among the rest our friend Miss Marietta T., most powerfully. She resided with some dear relatives of hers, in the neighbourhood. We accompanied them home. Miss T. was remarkably happy, she praised God aloud, and shouted all over the yard and through the house. Her friends were not religious, but by no means unfriendly. A deep impression was made on their hearts by the conversion and happy frame of mind of their relative. After dinner, we went to prayer, and, in their parlour, my friend Brother Ridgley led the devotions, and the power of God was felt by all present without an exception, and those who were not rejoicing, "leaping and praising God," were crying for mercy.

At least three of the family were on their knees earnestly praying. The whole afternoon was spent in this delightful work. Late in the afternoon, the devoted cousin of our happy sister was most sweetly converted. This gave new life to our friend Miss T., and there was great joy in that family. All was love, and the mistress of the house being converted, the servants were glad, and she did not feel it at all out of place to throw her arms of affection around those whom she met. Brother Ridgley, speaking of this day in his Journal, remarks simply: "Very happy day." A year after I was with him at a camp meeting on his Circuit. In consequence of affliction in the family of his colleague, Rev. J. Bayne, the management of the camp devolved upon him. I never saw a meeting more judiciously managed, and, considering its size, I rarely ever saw a meeting that was productive of more good than was the one held by my friend R. in Tilghman's Woods. "He had an old man's head on a young man's shoulders." Had he lived, and could he have enjoyed health, he had talent and piety sufficient to lead us to conclude that the day would come when he would fill any Church, or office in the Church, with dignity. The Church would have delighted to honour him, and, from my knowledge of that worthy brother, I verily believe he never would have betrayed any trust committed to his care. But just as the Church began to see he was no ordinary man, God in his providence called him from labour to reward. The Church was thus, to human view, prematurely deprived of a pure-minded, talented, influential minister of the gospel. None felt his loss so keenly as his partner in life, with her little ones. But "a father of the fatherless, and a judge of the widows, is God in his holy habitation."

In the foregoing remarks relative to Rev. N. Ridgley, we see another evidence of the utility of the Sunday School cause. This young student of law was mysteriously led to the little Sunday School of the Methodist Episcopal Church, in the town where he resided, and, although the piety of his mother did much in leading him to a profession of religion, perhaps no circumstance did as much in bringing this young man into the enjoyment of religion as the influences did which were brought to bear upon him in the Sunday School, and he loved this cause to the end. I would not detract from our ministers, who were not brought into the Church through this agency; still I will venture to assert that many of our most enterprising, useful labourers in the ministry, are those who have grown up with this institution. It is dear to their hearts; it affords them great pleasure to commingle with the schools of their station, or Circuit. They do not consider it "a cause of small import," but feel, however talented they may be, there is room for that talent to be exercised. If a minister is ardently attached to, and faithfully labours in this cause, it is to be expected that he will be ready for every good word and work; and, if he feels no interest in this direction, and considers this a matter of minor importance, it is apt to be the case that he is inefficient everywhere. "These my words ye shall teach them your children." "But those things which are revealed belong unto us, and our children for ever." God reiterated this matter of caring for the children to his ancient people. "And I will make them hear my words, that they may learn to fear me all the days that they shall live upon the earth, and that they may teach their children." Our Discipline makes it obligatory upon us as ministers to instruct the little ones: "Catechize the children in the Sunday School, and at special meetings appointed for that purpose." In our ordination vows, we covenant to labour in this important department. And, so far as my knowledge extends, what is thus made our duty by God's Word, and the Discipline of our Church, is performed with great pleasure by our ministers generally. "Take heed that ye despise not one of these little ones; for I say unto you, that in Heaven their angels do always behold the face of my Father which is in Heaven." Christ set a high value upon children. It cannot be beneath our dignity as ministers, if Jesus and the angels take such an interest in them. The latter, I verily believe, hover round the well-conducted Sunday School, and as one has said, viz. Summerfield, its "hum is music in an angel's ear—there they are, in numbers."

CHAPTER VIII.

Sent to Union Church, Wilmington, Delaware—Rev. Edward Kennard —A good Site for the new Church—Corner-stone laid with Masonic Ceremonies—Shepherd smitten, and Sheep scattered—Females efficient in the Work—No Society to begin with—Interesting public Meeting to revive this Church—Places opened in various parts of the City for purposes of Salvation—Church and Theatre together—The Press—Rev. Levi Storks—Shouting out a Subscription—An Apology, and its Effects—"Give, and it shall be given to you again"—Agree to raise Funds from home to finish the Basement—Leave of the Odd Fellows' Hall—Dedication and Conversion—The main part of the Church opened.

IN the spring of 1850 I was sent to Wilmington, to do the best I could to complete the third regular Methodist Episcopal Church, which the preceding year had been commenced, under the pastoral care of Rev. Henry S. Atmore. When he went on in 1849, he found a considerable society, which was to be the nucleus for the third church, mainly gathered together through the indefatigable labours of Rev. Edward Kennard, who had, with the view purely of extending Methodism, purchased the church of the Protestant Methodists, in Orange Street. This plant does not seem to have grown in that soil.

In this house Brother Kennard, being thus instructed by Rev. Daniel Lambdin, Presiding Elder of the Wilmington District, faithfully preached the Word, and was in this, as he had been in many other places, instrumental in the salvation of souls. The vigour of this brother's days was spent in the work of the Itinerancy. He had been some years, before he asked a location, a supernumerary in the Philadelphia Conference, and in this sphere did much good, labouring as much as his strength would allow. Under very powerful temptation, in the spring of 1850, at the Conference held in Smyrna, Delaware, he asked for and obtained a location. I did think at the time the Conference should have held on to this brother, and shown their appreciation of him, by not granting his request. This, I am sure, in the end would have been very conciliatory both to him and to his friends. At the time of his location the Conference acted, I am sure, for the best, and thought they were conferring a favour. But deliberative bodies as well as individuals may err; but such was the kind feeling towards this brother, at the ensuing session, had proper steps been taken, he would, I have no doubt, have been reinstated.

The society in Orange Street, with Rev. Henry S. Atmore as their leader, determined to abandon that location, and fixed upon a very suitable lot, I think, in Second Street, near Washington. It was remote from any church, with a very considerable population, and greatly increasing. How we fail, frequently, in sites for our churches! In this respect we should do well to take knowledge of the Roman Catholics. The building of the church was contracted for, and the work commenced early in the Conference year. The corner-stone was laid with Masonic ceremonies. This was to the people generally a new thing under the sun, and it was not, of course, acceptable to all. And I know, as well as and other person, it is hard work to please everybody, and I know the respectability of this ancient order, and that many of the greatest and best men of our nation are associated with it, and I am the last man to oppose anything that is good; still I think this arrangement had not a wholesome effect on that church; and this, among other things, led to a failure, and created a prejudice that was very hard to overcome. One of this order in that city, and second to no man there, either in Church or State, for noble deeds, said to me, "With this movement I was greatly displeased. I went to the corner-stone laying to give, but when I saw the state of things, I went away with my money in my pocket." On such occasions, the more simple and spiritual the better. Let me quote Paul, who said once, "Wherefore, if meat make my brother to offend, I will eat no flesh while the world standeth, lest I make my brother to offend." So, readers, when we may have such a matter in hand (however excellent this order may be, and I have seen instances of great generosity connected therewith), let us adhere to the old-fashioned way, and not transfer these matters into other hands, "lest I make my brother to offend."

In the autumn of the year, the brick work having been finished, the work ceased, owing to the want of funds. The minister was much discouraged. At his request he was removed. The little flock were without a shepherd. The classes met in private houses, and for awhile kept their prayer meetings moving, but having no head, they dwindled. "Smite the shepherd, and the sheep shall be scattered."

I should fail to do justice to this account, if I omitted to state that there were a few Christian ladies who, seeing the church roofless, and believing that the walls would by the storms of winter be ruined in their exposed condition, vigorously went to work, and secured a sufficiency of funds to roof the house. This was a good work, and frequently, when we fail, if we would call in the co-operation of Christian females, they would accomplish what we cannot. Their influence, brought to bear upon the Christian enterprises of the day, is almost omnipotent.

I would not be understood to advocate *women's rights*, as some in modern times do. But I am firmly fixed in the opinion that pious women have in them the elements for great usefulness in the Christian Church, and I think, in an appropriate way, they ought to be encouraged to improve their talents. We find they were inclined, when the disciples fled, to linger around the cross: "And many women were there which followed Jesus from Galilee, ministering unto him." And we find also they were first at the sepulchre, "with spices and ointments." And they were the first human beings to publish the glorious doctrine of the resurrection of Christ. We should feel like bidding our sisters God-speed, from the conviction that their piety is of a deep-toned character. We come to this conclusion from the information we have of them in the Scriptures, and from their valorous conduct in more recent times, in suffering and dying cheerfully as martyrs for the truth. They can greatly aid us in carrying out the spirit of the prophet's advice to the Church: "Enlarge the place of thy tent, and let them stretch forth the curtain of thy habitations; spare not, lengthen thy cords, and strengthen thy stakes."

When I reached my appointment in person, and entered upon the work, I found a most unhealthy state of things to exist. On the church, in its unfinished state, there was an indebtedness of *twenty-six hundred dollars*, and confidence was forfeited. In fact, it was regarded in the light of a swindling concern by some of those who had claims.

'I found there was no place to preach in, for the church was nothing but a hull, of course not ready for occupancy. And this was not all, for there was not *a member in society!* The society which had existed was disbanded; some had joined with other churches, some had backslidden. My heart was considerably discouraged. Popular opinion was unfavourable to the idea that the enterprise could, under the circumstances, be resuscitated, and succeed. We were all ready to ask the question, "Can these bones live?" for we plainly saw "they were very dry." I was sent to this discouraging field, and commanded to "prophesy upon these bones, and say unto them, O, ye dry bones, hear the Word of the Lord!"

When Methodism first began to operate in this city, it was very small. The building, used as a preaching place, at the corner of King and Third Streets, was a one-story small brick house, perhaps twenty by forty feet, which to this day stands in the same location. In this city, as early as 1775, the great pioneer of Methodism on this continent, Rev. Francis Asbury, preached the everlasting gospel. The first regular church was built here in 1789, and bears the name of that excellent man, "Asbury," who perilled his life for the sake of those who "sat in the region and shadow of death." The original Methodist church had been from time to time enlarged, until it had become a very spacious edifice, with one of the largest memberships and congregations in our connexion. From this church there had emanated the nucleus of the St. Paul's Methodist Episcopal Church, in Market Street, which was built during the pastorship of Rev. J. Kennaday, D.D., a man of indomitable zeal in the praiseworthy, glorious cause of church extension. This edifice, which is an ornament to the city, and a credit to our society, and wields a wholesome influence, was much needed, but was not carried to perfection till 1846.

As has been already stated, the appointment was discouraging, yet I came to the conclusion what had been done could be done again. And as other churches through difficulties had been carried triumphantly through, I resolved "we will rejoice in this salvation, and in the name of our God we will set up our banners." I entered into a contract with the managers of the Odd Fellows' Hall, endorsed by my friend, Edward Moore, Esq., and we were permitted to occupy this beautiful and large saloon each Sabbath, for five dollars a day. It was a delightful place, seated with settees, and at night illuminated splendidly. In this place we formed our society. The first Sunday we had twelve to say, "Thy people shall be my people, and thy God my God."

Our congregations were full, and the basket collections ample to pay the expenses. And Sabbath after Sabbath our membership increased gradually, which was well calculated to cheer our hearts. In order to produce a more general interest, a meeting was called, very early in the Conference year, in the St. Paul's Methodist Episcopal Church, which meeting was attended by all the ministers of our denomination in Wilmington. The venerable Bishop Waugh made his arrangements to attend this meeting. He delivered an appropriate and soul-stirring address, which was like "apples of gold in pictures of silver."

This meeting did great good to the enterprise; the good bishop's fears, and the fears of all the community fled like chaff before the wind.

With renewed energy we proceeded in the task assigned us. I was well convinced, however, in order to succeed we must be active, "not slothful in business; fervent in spirit; serving the Lord." We felt it was expedient to have more than one rallying point. It is true, our head quarters were at the Odd Fellows' Hall. This was our only place of worship on Sundays. Here the gospel was proclaimed—here we organized the Sunday School, which was truly interesting, and promised much to our infant Church; but, in different parts of the city, we had private dwellings and school-houses opened for singing, prayer, exhortation, and class meeting purposes. In addition to these, we had granted us free of expense, by the kind-hearted St. Paul's trustees, which was endorsed by their entire Church, the use of their lecture room two evenings each week, so long as our circumstances required it. We acted, our readers will say, on the spirit of the text, "The kingdom of Heaven suffereth violence, and the violent take it by force." Our different places during the week evenings were filled to their utmost capacity, and, in our prayer meetings, our leading theme was, "O Lord, I have heard thy speech and was afraid; O Lord, revive thy work in the midst of the years, in the midst of the years make known; in wrath remember mercy." The cry, "Come over into Macedonia and help us," was heeded, and soldier after soldier joined our division of the army, and rallied under our ensign, until the enemy had to reluctantly beat a retreat, and exclaim in utter dismay, "Who is she that looketh forth as the morning, fair as the moon, clear as the sun, and terrible as an army with banners."

In the month of May, of our first year, 1850, our newly elected board of trustees generously took upon themselves the preceding indebtedness of the property. In the business community, confidence was restored, and in a short time thereafter, a bargain was made for the completion of the church, of which it might truly have been said, "Behold, your house is left unto you desolate."

But, as has been before intimated, the Odd Fellows' Hall was our church until we could occupy the new regular Union Methodist Episcopal Church. We only had the use of this building on the Sabbath, and it was occupied for other very different purposes during the week, as my readers will readily see when I inform them that there was a theatre carried on in this same room during the week. While I cannot convey in words an adequate idea of the injury that theatres do, in my judgment, to society, there are those in every community who are ready to patronize and encourage them greatly in preference to a place "where prayer is wont to be made." These nurseries of vice, which have led many of both sexes to ruin, are very adroitly managed in modern times. We find religious things dramatized. Thus the managers of those infamous places emphatically "steal the livery of Heaven to serve the devil in." And the passage is fulfilled, "For Satan himself is transformed into an angel of light." Dear Christian reader, whatever may be played, however sacred the subject, say firmly, "O my soul, come thou not into their secret: unto their assembly, mine honour, be not thou united." The pulpit here was, and in every place ought to be, arrayed against this evil. And be it spoken to the credit of the city of Wilmington, there is so little interest manifested by the people in theatrical performances, that there is not a building here (and I pray God there never may be), appropriated exclusively to such amusements and diversions. And the temporary one, that was contemporary with us there, after awhile "departed out of our coast." Thus in this place, in this particular at least, virtue triumphed over vice, God and Christianity over the devil and infidelity.

The Lord deigned to meet his people, and for some five or six months we remained in this large fine hall, where we preached, prayed, sung, shouted, and had the sacraments administered. And last, though not least, souls in this place were converted from the error of their ways. Persons passing would often make sarcastic remarks; and now and then, a newspaper would indulge in a little pleasantry at our expense. We did not think any the less of them for that; for on a certain article of this description we levied a tax, and, when we would make an appeal to a congregation, this piece, which I had cut from the paper and put in my collecting book, I used as a text. It brought us many a dollar. It related to the amalgamation of light and darkness. And this church operation and theatrical performances, blended in the same building, reminded the editor of some verses composed upon a place of worship on the second floor, with a tavern below. Had I the verses, I would give them to my readers. I am happy to say, as a general thing, the Wilmington papers paid great respect to religion and sound morals. And the press in no place in the land could be more generous than there, in supplying the different clergymen with their issues, free of charge. The press, properly managed, is an engine of much good.

In the spring of 1850, Rev. Levi Storks's health failed him so much that it was deemed proper for him to ask for a supernumerary relation. He determined to live in the city of Wilmington, and, by his own request, he was appointed in this relation by Bishop Waugh, to Union Church. In the providence of God, his health, early in the Conference year, recruited, greatly to his surprise and joy, and he did much in building up this charge. We found him always ready to co-operate with us in every department of the work. This dear servant of God was more than ordinarily pious. He enjoyed the great blessing of sanctification, he professed it openly, and lived it daily, and this, with other things, made him an eminently useful man. He was a plain but excellent preacher. He was also one of the few who, to the last, held on to the primitive Methodistic style of dress. Although he was made effective in 1851 again, he did not live long to labour in his Master's vineyard. While on North East Circuit, October 1st, 1853, he finished his earthly career, after an illness of five days. The Sabbath before his death he preached powerfully three times; he ran to the end of the race, and won his crown. Among his last expressions, the following fell from his lips: "Perhaps after a little I shall not be able to speak; tell all who inquire, it is well with me." I knew Brother Storks from my boyhood. Few walked more closely with God than he. Those dear ones he has left behind, may safely feel their loss is his gain.

In my zeal for the success of this work, I subscribed the sum of *five hundred dollars.* I told the trustees I would pay every cent of it, but, in order that I might, they must release me a few weeks during the camp meeting season. I left all matters at home in care of Brother Storks, and laboured joyfully among my brethren, and, wherever I asked for aid financially, I obtained a noble response.

The first effort of this sort was made at the Red Lion camp meeting, in New Castle county, Delaware. It was the last day of the meeting. Much begging had been done, and the prospect for us did not appear very flattering. But the Lord that day helped me to present the subject in such a light as to command respect, and so baptized the audience with the spirit, that they did give and shout, and shout and give. Surrounding circumstances led me to say, If any one gives a dollar, he or she shall be fully authorized to come to the new church and shout it out. Whereupon, one dear brother readily agreed to this, paid the money in advance, with this express understanding, and kept in mind the covenant; and, during our protracted meeting, the following winter at the new church, we were a little surprised and delighted, one Sabbath morning, to see him in the congregation. He spent "the day and shared the night" in our midst, and it appeared to us that he, like Paul, was so happy he could hardly tell whether he was "in the body or out of the body." He was successful in labours at the altar, and four or five precious souls, through his instrumentality, were enabled to rejoice in a sin-pardoning God. Over such an achievement we could not blame him for shouting. And throughout the day, he did it manfully; and I am inclined to think he felt the truth of the Psalmist's words, "For a day in thy courts is better than a thousand; I had rather be a doorkeeper in the house of my God, than to dwell in the tents of wickedness."

After the close of the meeting at night, he started for his home, which was a distance of at least twenty-five miles, ready, I doubt not, to give again towards building a house for the worship of God, especially with the understanding that he could have the privilege of *shouting it out.*

Our financial effort at Red Lion resulted very favourably to our cause. At least two hundred dollars was found to be in the collection. I venture to say that the spirituality of the meeting was not interfered with in the least. Both ministers and members seemed highly gratified with this effort. "And his banner over" us "was love."

An apology demanded.

I attended a series of camp meetings as I have before intimated. An account of one other at least will be given. I reached the meeting on a Saturday. It was to close on the following Monday. My aim was to leave on Saturday night at the latest, to be present at another meeting, thirty or forty miles distant, on the Sabbath. But a heavy storm prevented me from prosecuting my design, and consequently I had to remain over Sunday. Thinking I should leave Saturday evening, and anxious to do a little for our cause, after the preaching was over in the forenoon, and with the permission of the preacher in charge, I stated the case to an attentive audience. And, be it spoken to their credit, quite a number walked up to the stand, and contributed at least forty or fifty dollars. I supposed all was right, but was officially informed that I had placed the managers of the camp in a most awkward and very unpleasant situation, for they had promised the public that there should be *no begging* on the ground, beyond simply taking the Quarterly Meeting collection. A public collection should not be made even to defray the expenses of the camp meeting, but the amount should be raised privately. And, said these worthy managers, "Brother, you have, notwithstanding, come all the way from Wilmington, and plunged us into this serious difficulty, and we *demand* that you should make a due apology before the whole congregation, and take the *whole responsibility* upon your own shoulders."

I cheerfully acquiesced with the wishes of the managers, and let them roll the ponderous weight that seemed to be pressing them, upon my shoulders. Sabbath afternoon, when there would be a large congregation present, was fixed upon for this apology. Rev. G. D. Carrow preached on *The cure of Naaman the leper.* He also presented to us the character of Elisha the Prophet. I followed with the apology and exhortation. Everybody was attentive, anxious to see what turn the *intruder* would take. The speech was commenced by saying, "It seems that I have violated the rules of this encampment, and given offence to the people, by presenting yesterday the condition of the church of which I am pastor. I did not know that the rules were like the laws of the Medes and Persians, unchangeable. It would appear that my situation is very unpleasant. I am one of the last men designedly to give offence to any man or set of men; and to give offence to such a people as this; 'tell it not in Gath, publish it not in the streets of Askelon.' No, brethren, I hope I am incapable of such a discourteous act; and I now must throw myself upon your sympathies, and from the bottom of a warm heart say,

> "Show pity, *brothers!* O *sisters!* forgive,
> Let a repenting *Methodist preacher* live."

At this point there was a rustling amongst "the trees of righteousness, the planting of the Lord;" or, to be

The apology concluded.

more plain, there was a shout in the camp. I heard the words vociferously uttered, "Amen! Hallelujah!! Glory to God!!! God bless Brother Manship!" I began to think, I am safe, all will be well; and the passage in the prophet was suggested to my mind, "For ye shall go out with joy, and be led forth with peace; the mountains and hills shall break forth before you into singing, and all the trees of the field shall clap their hands." I thought it was time now to conclude my apology, and did so by saying: "Dear friends, after having made this apology, and taken this responsibility from the shoulders of the managers to my own, if any of you feel like coming to me, as Naaman the leper (of whom we have heard to-day) came to Elisha the prophet, and should beseech me to take a blessing, though I admire greatly the character of the good prophet (and may his mantle fall on me, and on all these dear ministers in the stand), yet in this *one respect* I shall differ from him, and receive whatever the liberality of this audience prompts them to bestow." So the dear people poured it in upon me copiously, and emphatically "rendered double unto us." I suppose the collection was increased at least one hundred per cent., and the managers and all the people appeared happy over this result, and I had certainly no occasion to be otherwise than pleased.

I hope not to weary the patience of my readers, but

I must be permitted to refer to another camp, where I gained access to the people, though with considerable effort; for the managers thought they had so much on hand in the way of church improvement on the Circuit, that they would have to give me a negative answer. I told them that that would never do, as I was then in my native county, and had not been refused among strangers. Perseverance led the friends to yield. I told them when I made the statement, that I only wanted them to give me fifty dollars. I also assured them, that I should not injure the religious tone of feeling that was then being enjoyed. After I was through with my address, bearing on this struggling church, I told the audience I would sing the hymn, the chorus of which is,

> "And to begging I will go—
> Home to glory I will go."

This hymn was not half finished before I had reason to believe the amount asked for was handed up to the stand. If I had allowed the giving to have gone on, which was done with the greatest cheerfulness, I could have had as much more. But I wanted to keep my word, and therefore I had to say to this liberal people, "Stop, you have done all I asked you to do." The flood-gates were suddenly shut down, the stream dammed, and the windows of heaven were opened, and streams of salvation flowed, so that we could appropriately sing, and did sing—

"It's flowing from the fountain,
It's running like a stream."

And that day, notwithstanding the financial business, many souls were converted. It was remarkable to witness, the moment after the money matters were attended to, at least *fifty persons* earnestly seeking that which is "better than gold and silver." Some persons give to the cause of religion, and in the same meeting give their hearts to God. And I have seen them soundly converted, realizing the truth of God's immutable word, "Give, and it shall be given unto you, good measure, pressed down and shaken together, and running over."

More fully to illustrate the passage quoted above, I will relate an incident or two in my own experience. While I was pastor of this church, and my prospect for support was not overly flattering, in the market one morning early I met with a case that interested me deeply. I gave however the sum of ten dollars, and it left me rather destitute. I scarcely had money enough left to purchase my marketing. On my journey home I stopped in the post-office. There was a letter for me containing checks to the amount of *one hundred and twenty-five dollars!* This was placed in my hands as a donation entirely unexpected. I was ready to say, "The Lord hath dealt bountifully with me." Brethren in the ministry, let us give. However, it is not requisite to exhort you to this course. As a general thing, I don't believe there is a more liberal set of men in the world. But perhaps the devil will tempt us that we shall come to want, and lead us to inquire, who will take care of our wives and children when we are gone? We will remember the passage, "There is that scattereth, and yet increaseth; and there is that withholdeth more than is meet, but it tendeth to poverty." I was connected with an infant church at a certain period in my itinerant life. We needed the sum of five hundred dollars. The Sunday was fixed upon for a financial effort, the society was rather feeble, and about that time I was not very flush in the way of means. I remarked to the audience, "I am hardly able, but here goes five dollars to this cause;" parting at that moment with the last five dollar bill I had. I remarked, I give this with a pure motive, and I give it in faith in God's promise. Before the afternoon service, in an unexpected way, the five dollar note was replaced in the shape of five dollars in gold. I mentioned this in the financiering of the afternoon. A gentleman remarked pleasantly, "Suppose you try it again, brother." I replied, "I will most cheerfully if you will do likewise." This agreement was made. Before the evening service was ended, I was requested to come to my residence in haste. I went—not knowing but some one was sick. My heart was sad, but I returned to the church with a light heart and a heavy pocket. In an unlooked for manner I had received five dollars in silver. The money matters were carried through the evening as well as the morning and afternoon services. I mentioned the goodness of God to me, in suddenly restoring me all I had given to his cause. I was challenged to try this experiment once more. I suppose my friend thought I would decline. I accepted in the fear of God. And by this means that day gave fifteen dollars. The very next day, Monday, two other couple, that I had no claims upon whatever, came to my residence *to be married*, making in all four couple from remote points, each party giving me five dollars. After all, I had five dollars left. The several weddings took place in less than twenty-four hours from the time the money was given.

The camp meeting tour at an end, I resumed my work in the Odd Fellows' Hall, where I laboured on the Sabbath, and, through the week, at the school-houses, private houses, and St. Paul's Lecture Room. In the month of September I made another pledge to our trustees, who did not contemplate finishing the basement. I told them that would never do, because for Sunday School and class meeting purposes the basement was absolutely necessary. And furthermore, if they would go forward and complete it, I would obligate myself to raise the necessary amount beyond the city of Wilmington. This proposition was accepted, and I turned my eyes and heart towards Philadelphia, and obtained a generous collection from Union, Ebenezer, Kensington, and Wharton Street Methodist Episcopal Churches. These amounts, with a few private donations, enabled me to fulfil my promise. And the trustees nobly fulfilled theirs. The basement was completed and ready for occupancy in the month of October of the first year of my connexion with them. We bade farewell to the Hall after occupying it nearly six months advantageously to our cause, and comfortably to our souls and bodies. We had every convenience we could ask. It was an imposing spectacle to see our Sunday School emerging from this place, on the afternoon of the day of our dedication, two and two, led on by the superintendents and teachers, to take possession of the home that had been provided for them. The school did well in the hall, doubtless better in the church. "They go from strength to strength." "Out of the mouth of babes and sucklings hast thou ordained strength."

The day of dedication was a bright one, and it was so arranged that we were not to have any special collection, as the greater dedication was close at hand. It was a day of great religious enjoyment. I tried to preach morning and evening to a crowded auditory. Never did a people feel more like fulfilling the direction of the Psalmist, "Sing aloud unto God our strength: make a joyful noise unto the God of Jacob." Not only did the people of God rejoice, but penitents in the even-

17

ing meeting cried for mercy; and one interesting young lady, while we were dedicating the house to God's worship, dedicated her soul, body, her all to the Saviour. She was accepted; and she was the honoured one first to be converted in this newly erected temple. No circumstance that occurred during the day was more pleasing to us than the conversion of this soul. We took this as an evidence that the Great Head of the Church would ever let his "eyes be open upon this house day and night, upon the place whereof thou hast said that thou wouldst put thy name there." We took this as a token that souls would from time to time here be born again. This is the great object to be had in view in erecting houses of prayer. They are not to be used for scientific or secular purposes: "For my house shall be called a house of prayer for all people."

This part of the house was not sufficiently capacious to accommodate the many that came, and, from the force of circumstances, we had to urge the completion of the upper part of the Church, which was done in the latter part of the month of November, and on Thursday, the 25th day of that month, it was opened for service. Bishop Janes preached the opening sermon. It was appropriate, and will long be remembered as a masterly pulpit effort. In the afternoon and evening the audience was addressed by Rev. Henry Slicer, who, on such occasions, is surpassed by few, if any, in our connexion. He is a

Methodist preacher of the primitive stamp, nevertheless popular, commanding respect in high as well as humble places. For many years he has served as chaplain to the United States Senate, and has filled with credit many of the important appointments in the Baltimore Conference, and is now a Presiding Elder in that Conference. May he live long to preach in simplicity and power the "unsearchable riches of Christ!" We were, as it regards ministerial help, highly favoured on this dedication occasion. The amount obtained that day surpassed our expectations. This, in addition to what had previously been done, left our circumstances quite manageable. Our society did nobly in this respect. Our expectations were high for a general revival, and we were all ready to say, "For Zion's sake I will not hold my peace, and for Jerusalem's sake I will not rest, until the righteousness thereof go forth as brightness, and the salvation thereof as a lamp that burneth."

CHAPTER IX.

The Prodigal Son coming Home—The vilest Sinner may return—A Visit from a supposed Jesuit—The Virgin Mary's Name called upon —Misbehaviour in Church reprehensible—Taken for a Roman Catholic Priest—Why object to Missionary Appropriations at Home—Good done in our new "Union" Camp Meeting Tent—A Blood-vessel supposed to be ruptured—The Sinner sometimes suddenly destroyed—The last Sabbath with the "Union" Church—Bishop Waugh—Invite Penitents generally—Do not make too free with the Benediction—Judge Hall—Will not the Prayers of the Children help Ministers?—Must feel deeply for our Relations—Old-fashioned Shout by a Presbyterian Lady—Rev. Jonas Bissey—Rev. James Smith.

AFTER we took posession of the new church, which was not only filled with people to overflowing, but with the presence of God, which did not prove to be a momentary affair. It abided with us, while I was permitted to remain, and has been realized by my worthy successors. We had many interesting cases of conversion. When this new church was opened, a gentleman commenced attending the meetings to the surprise of everybody. He was a man of good family, had inherited considerable property, which however he had squandered, was a prodigal son, and so alienated from God and religion, that scarcely any one supposed he would ever become religious. No one, however, was more regular in his attendance at our new house than he, and, hearing the gospel preached, and seeing the grace of God in the conversion of souls, and seeing there also one of his old companions in sin of every grade (such as fighting, horse-racing, drinking, &c.), "clothed and in his right mind," and labouring around the altar with mourners, and being invited by his old comrade to go with him to heaven, this man, whose heart was callous, and considered by the community a hopeless case, melted like wax before the fire. He came to the conclusion, "As we have been companions in wickedness, we will be companions in the service of the Lord." He reasoned thus, "If my friend has found pardon and mercy, then I may hope for salvation." And this athletic man, while we were singing,

> "The dying thief rejoiced to see
> That fountain in his day;
> And there may I, though vile as he,
> Wash all my sins away,"

came forward to the altar, to the astonishment of perhaps angels, men, and devils. Here he struggled for two weeks. Day and night, he was seeking, at the church and at his home. Finally deliverance came; the father met this long lost-son, and "we began to be merry;" we shouted over this "brand plucked from the burning." The news flew through our city; the people could not believe it to be possible. I remember the next day to have met the venerable Joseph Whitington, long a minister of high standing among the people of colour. Said he to me, "They tell me Mr. —— is converted; that he obtained religion last night at your church; is it so?" I remarked, I have not a doubt of it. "Well," said the old gentlemen, "if he is converted, then the devil himself can get converted." And we both rejoiced over the event, because we felt additional encouragement to preach the gospel to the very chief of sinners, and despair of the salvation of no man while he is above ground, and never give a bill of sale to the devil of the most hardened sinner this side of hell; and we determined we would preach and sing,

"While the lamp holds out to burn,
The vilest sinner may return."

I may farther remark that as it was in the case of Saul, who before his conversion was so desperate, so it was in regard to the person described. "And when Saul was come to Jerusalem, he essayed to join himself to the disciples; but they were all afraid of him, and believed not that he was a disciple." But the fears of the primitive Church were soon banished relative to Saul; and, by "ceasing to do evil and learning to do well," the dear brother referred to, has convinced all long ago that the gospel in his case has been "the power of God unto salvation."

The revival reached some of the Roman Catholic

friends, which caused a little uneasiness at *head quarters.* I came to this conclusion from the fact that I was visited one day by a person; whose name was not given, of very respectable appearance. He reported to me "that some in distress of mind, who had attended my meetings, and he amongst the rest, had gone to the priest for some counsel, and that he had been sent by the priest to request me to meet him at a given point, where he would convince me and his young friends concerned, that he had power to give absolution to penitents; and that he, in a word, would prove the infallibility of the Roman Catholic Church—that it was right, and that Protestants were wrong." I said to this individual, who declined giving his name, "Here are Kirwan's letters to Archbishop Hughes. Read them; they will throw more light on the subjects you *profess* to want light upon, than any controversy could that might take place between your priest and myself. Controversy is not very profitable; and please tell him I am doing a great work, so that I cannot come down; why should the work cease while I leave it, and come down to you?"

I heard no more from this quarter. I never saw afterwards the man that called upon me, and I never saw Kirwan's letters. The book was not returned, and I thought probably it was considered to be a *heretic* and burnt. Many heretics have been punished in this way.

Shortly after this interview, while our meeting was

going forward most gloriously, there were some ill-disposed persons who attended; two or three sons of the Emerald Isle especially, who were, I presume, a little intoxicated, notwithstanding they appeared to belong to *the Mother Church.* And such was their course, that our brethren were compelled to have them arrested. They were quite uproarious. We heard them say, in substance, "They converted S——, and we would like for them to undertake to convert us. We belong to the true Church; and, in the name of the Holy Virgin, we can whip any man that puts his hands upon us." Although high relationship sometimes screens a man from suffering the penalty of the law, in this case the associations with the Virgin did not exonerate them from being taken that night before the Mayor of the city, and committed to the city prison. They were dealt with as every such desperado ought to be, whether Catholic or Protestant, native born or otherwise. Disturbing a religious meeting is a most reprehensible thing. And when any one feels disposed to misbehave in a place of worship, it would be well if that heedless individual could have whispered in his ears the words of Solomon: "Keep thy foot, when thou goest to the house of God, and be more ready to hear than to give the sacrifice of fools."

The new priest who came to St. Peter's Church, in this city, during my connexion with this place, resided next door to me, and, so far as I know, was a gentleman; and, whether I looked like him or not, I was taken for him by a female, one morning in a grocery store. The circumstances were as follows. It was a frosty morning; I found my cloak to be necessary. It was rather long, as men of this order generally wear them. I came from the same locality, and the priest had not long been stationed at St. Peter's, and I think the lady was a new-comer. Said this female when we met, "Plase your reverence, did Mary Mc—— die last night?" I answered, "I did not know such a person." She replied, "*Sir*, you are the *praist*, and you were there last night, and administered the rites of the Church to her." I replied, "I am not the priest, but an humble Methodist preacher, living next door to the priest;" and added, "You have not been here long, and you are yet unacquainted with your minister and the country, and I trust you may do well and be happy. The Irish people are warm-hearted, and I like them when they walk uprightly;" and I also said to her, "I have been taken for an Irishman before to-day." She quickly said, "Yes, and God knows you can't deny it *aither*, you are the *praist*." I left her unconvinced.

At the Conference which was held in Smyrna, Delaware, in 1851, I was again appointed to labour in the Union Church, Wilmington. This infant church, during its first year, grew so rapidly "in favour with God and man," that it was considered unnecessary to make to it a missionary appropriation. In fact, we took to Conference the very first year nearly *sixty dollars!* And from that day till now it has contributed, and will continue to contribute to the missionary treasury, and also to sustain its own ministry generously.

I feel like asking the question, Why should there be objections to appropriations made to domestic missions? It comes back a hundred fold; it is a clear financial gain. Help the weak places, they will soon help themselves and help others. If a point needs a strong man, even if his family be large and the membership weak, send him, even if it cost the missionary treasury for the first year or two several hundred dollars. What is money in comparison with souls? But as I have already intimated, if the proper arrangements be made, the harvest spiritually and temporally will be reaped, and that too at no distant day.

From the Conference of 1851, till camp meeting season, with the ordinary means of grace, we frequently were permitted to see souls converted to God. But in our new large camp meeting tent at Red Lion, in August, we were specially revived again. At that meeting many were blessed under our new canvass church in the wilderness. One night there were twenty converted in our tent: one man nearly eighty years of age. We went home determined to scatter the *camp fire.* The work went victoriously on without much, if any, intermission, till the Conference of 1852. The labours were very arduous, and I thought one Sunday evening all was over with me. The house, galleries, vestibule, aisles, all were filled. I was inspired by surrounding circumstances, and preaching earnestly, suddenly, upon pressing against the breastwork of the pulpit, I found something had given way, and in an instant I saw dark spots on the fair pages of the Holy Bible before me, resembling blood. The first impression on my mind was, I have broken a blood-vessel, and in a moment I shall fall dead in the stand! This was a trying instant. My apprehensions were allayed by grinding under my feet something which appeared like glass. This reminded me that I had suffered greatly from the toothache, and I was that night fortified with a phial of medicine, which I carried in my waistcoat pocket. The phial coming in contact with the breastwork of the pulpit it had broken asunder, and its contents had gushed out. This was no more blood than the *coloured matter* which the magicians of Egypt brought about to imitate the miracle of turning the water of the river into blood. I doubt not but the devil had a hand in both transactions. It is true my case might be considered insignificant in comparison with the other; yet, if he could have driven me from my position that night, he would gladly have done it. He, the devil, knew well that God in his miracle-working power would be there. The conversion of every sinner is a miracle. He wanted to thwart the work by trying to make me believe that I had actually ruptured a blood-vessel. This circumstance caused me to press on in the work with greater vigour. I did not die, but to God be all the glory, that night many did die, in the sense of the apostle—"Sin revived," and they "died." But they lived again. May they live for ever! Ere that meeting closed, some of them could joyfully say in substance, "I am crucified with Christ: nevertheless I live; yet not I, but Christ liveth in me: and the life which I now live in the flesh, I live by the faith of the Son of God, who loved me and gave himself for me."

About this time a most solemn circumstance occurred. A man attended the revival who had not been much in the habit of frequenting such places. The Spirit operated powerfully upon his heart, he was urged to "yield to love's resistless power." But, like many others, he supposed another time would suffice. He had that night a restless time. He slept with a member of the church, who boarded about the same house. He talked much on the subject of religion, and expressed regret that he did not accept the invitation that was so cordially given him that night in the Union Church. It *was his very last call!* For, Monday morning, after taking his breakfast as usual, he stepped into the yard, and expected in a moment or two to be at the place of his business; but death struck him, he fell a victim to the king of terrors, in sight of the place of prayer where he had the preceding evening been entreated to be reconciled to God. Reader, "be ye also ready." Take warning from this case!

The two years spent in this charge were busy ones; but in reviewing them I felt an assurance that they were not spent in vain. There were received, all told, during the two years, about *four hundred and fifty*, into this church.

The last Sunday before Conference was a memorable day. The love feast, in the afternoon of the day, was one of great power. That meeting commenced at three o'clock P. M., and never closed till ten o'clock at night. We only spent the disciplinary time in speaking, *one hour and a half*. Then followed a deeply-interesting meeting, in which several souls were converted. We did not think about the evening shades beginning to prevail until we saw the gas-lights burning. The thought of supper escaped many a mind that evening. I preached, at the proper evening hour, my last sermon as their pastor. The next evening we were favoured with the presence and labours of Bishop Waugh, on his way to the Philadelphia Conference. He saw a very different state of things from what was before his eyes in the spring of 1850, at which time this good man did much to "strengthen the things which were weak, and ready to die." The congregation, to hear him on this occasion, was overflowing. Scores and hundreds had, in the mean time, been brought into the Church. And with much propriety it might be said, that "when he came, and had seen the grace of God, he was glad, and exhorted them all that with purpose of heart they would cleave unto the Lord."

The sermon was listened to with the most profound interest. It was well calculated to establish young converts, and confirm them in the faith of the gospel. It was about nine o'clock when the sermon was closed. I took the Conference collection, which was an excellent one, and then proceeded to exhort. I remarked, "Perhaps some of you" (for we had persons from all the churches to hear the Bishop) "will think it passing strange that Brother Manship should dare to deliver an exhortation of this character in the presence of the Bishop. But I know what manner of spirit he is of. He is at home around the altar, bending over the penitent, at our camp and protracted meetings. I doubt not but he would be greatly pleased this night to see a soul converted." Said the venerable man, "I should like to see it, brother." I replied, "Bless God, sir," (for I felt strong in faith,) "you shall see, this night, his salvation in the conversion of souls!" Some of the people felt that my remarks were too positive, and thought how badly Brother Manship would feel if none should come forward. And they feared, as it was late, and as there had been begging for a good Conference collection, and as the people came to hear the Bishop, that I should be disappointed in my calculations. To my great delight, as soon as the invitation was given, at least *thirty* or *forty* came forward promptly. And no meeting, that had ever been held in this church, was more marked by the presence and power of God. The Bishop took an active part in the altar work, thus setting an example to *younger ministers worthy of imitation!* When ten o'clock came, I said to the Bishop, "We will now close, if you think it proper, and retire to our rest." He was my guest at the time. He replied, "Here are some penitents that are in such a good way, we had better continue a little longer, Brother Manship." And, sure enough, the Bishop had the pleasure of seeing several converted, and among the number an old lady that had been keeping a *dance-house!* Her daughter was also converted. A great change took place in the family, and religious meetings were held in her house, instead of dances and frolics. The daughter soon fell away, and being led by some young persons, took a pleasure trip on the Christiana. The boat capsized, and this poor backsliding child was drowned, and brought home to her distressed mother a corpse. This would not have been the case had she continued faithful, and "remembered the Sabbath day to keep it holy." This sad affair occurred on the Lord's day.

Dear young reader, let us "stand fast, therefore, in the liberty wherewith Christ hath made us free, and be not entangled again with the yoke of bondage." Some that were converted that night are still in the way, and feel thankful that they had the privilege of hearing that venerable man. And, although it was unexpected to them, under the circumstances, they rejoice that the *invitation was given to approach the altar.* Are not good impressions and perhaps immortal souls *lost*, by a failure to invite mourners to the altar, after a powerful sermon has been delivered? Who has not heard it said, by the unconverted," I felt like seeking religion to-day. If there had been an opportunity offered I would have sought the Lord." I maintain it is in order always to get a soul converted. I once, on a very warm night, preached on a Circuit that I had previously travelled; the crowd was great, both inside and outside of the house; there was considerable feeling. Some shouted aloud for joy, others were pensive, and freely shed tears, and gave signs of true penitence. The junior minister of the Circuit followed me with a fervent prayer, sung the doxology, and dismissed with the benediction. The people manifested a disposition to remain longer; a spiritual, zealous member of the church started a lively tune, and it "swiftly ran." The circumstances led me to venture to invite penitents to the altar. Several came, and some were that night converted to God, one of whom has since gone to his grave. Another young man that was set at liberty that happy hour, is still travelling the celestial road. He has since occupied a public position in civil office, and is now a successful practitioner of medicine, but the vows he made that night he has ever endeavoured to pay. I received recently a letter from him, in which he says: "I would be very happy to do anything in my power for you. I hope you will not think I am flattering you when I say that I have more than an ordinary respect for you, and feel a greater degree of Christian love and affection than for any other minister of the gospel of my acquaintance, probably occasioned by the great interest you always seemed to manifest in my behalf. I am still trying to serve the Lord. I never can forget that happy, happy night!" My course, that night, to some might appear presumptuous. After the minister dismissed the meeting, prudence would seem to require that I should not have dared to invite penitents forward. But I adhered then, as I do now, to the principle that *it is always in order to get a soul converted.* It was somewhat amusing to hear one of the warm-hearted coloured friends, after the meeting was over, descanting upon the circumstance. He remarked, "I am much pleased with our junior minister, but I think he made entirely too free, last night, with the '*diction!*" I hope I shall never, when there is a likelihood of winning a soul to Christ, "make too free with the *benedic-*

tion!" O, how important is the salvation of one soul! "The cry of a believing penitent is sufficient to stop the most merciful Jesus, were he going to make a new heaven and new earth; for what is all the *irrational* part of God's creation worth when compared with the value of one immortal soul?"

I found Judge Hall, of this city, a Presbyterian gentleman of high standing in Church and State, formerly a member of Congress, and now Judge of the United States' Court for the District of Delaware, ready for every good word and work. I have frequently been associated with him in Sunday School extension. He will plead for this cause anywhere, and at any time. Many a youth in that city, in the Sabbath School, has he directed to Calvary, and instructed in God's Word. The Bible cause lies near his heart. He has been President of the "Delaware Bible Society" for many years. The Judge is by no means sectarian; he is a great friend to the Itinerancy, and Methodism generally. I have shed tears of joy, in different places in that city, while I have listened to his views, and seen him treading in the footsteps of Robert Raikes, labouring assiduously to save the poor children. I had the honour, several times, of following the Judge in advocating this cause. On a certain occasion there had been a one-story school room erected in a neglected part of the city. One leading object was to reach the children through Sunday School labour. The Judge finished his eloquent speech by taking out of his pocket a twenty dollar note, and saying, "Mr. Manship, you are to follow, and one object you will have in view will be to try to get this school room paid for. Take this, to begin with." This good beginning (and this was his manner) inspired me for my work. The amount asked for was received, and the good done in that one place will not be revealed in this world. Such men as Honourable Judge Hall are rare. I have not only met with him at the places referred to, but in the market, several times a week, generally. He always does his own marketing, though advanced in life. I have also taken sweet counsel with him in his study, and never had an interview but I felt I was improved both in my head and heart. He is exceedingly plain in his appearance, and no less so in his manners, and a stranger would not suppose there was anything in him remarkable. At the bar, in the halls of legislation, on the bench, labouring in the Bible cause, in the cause of education, temperance, and Sunday School work, he has purchased to himself "a good degree." But this humble Christian gentleman is ready to exclaim, doubtless, "By the grace of God I am what I am."

In my book, I very much desire to interest the children. I therefore venture to record here a circumstance that will, I trust, entertain them and be serviceable in other directions. I changed appointments, when

I was in Callowhill Street at "Bethlehem" church, with a young Itinerant, who at the time travelled one of our Circuits. He wished to spend a Sabbath with his mother, who resided in Philadelphia. I put up with an interesting Christian family, near where I was to preach the following morning. On Saturday night, it was remarkably pleasant to sit by a country fire, while the winds of winter were whistling, and everything without was in a state of frigidity. But there had been at the church in the neighbourhood a thawing glorious revival, and religion was the theme. There was but little else talked about; and, in our circle that night, the children were absorbed in the topic. How sweetly did they sing! I thought of the hymn,

> "People and realms of every tongue
> Dwell on his love with sweetest song,
> And infant voices shall proclaim
> Their early blessings on his name."

After I retired to my room for the night, I heard, it appeared to me, the sweetest song to which I ever listened, led by a happy little girl about six years of age. The chorus was to me then perfectly new. I was charmed with it. I was drawn down stairs, in order to have it repeated. I wanted to learn the tune as well as the words. They were as follows:—

"We will cross the river of Jordan,
Happy, happy,
We will cross the river of Jordan,
Happy in the Lord."

Since that day, when my hope of Heaven has been bright, I have very often sung that little song of Zion, which I learned from the lips of that little saint. The entire family of children won on my feelings very much; but particularly was I interested in this juvenile sweet singer in Israel. When I parted with the family, not to meet again soon, if ever, as I had noticed the children particularly they seemed affected at parting. I said to them, "Pray for Brother Manship, that he may be a faithful minister of the gospel." Years rolled round; and, while I was labouring in the city of Wilmington, one day I met Brother G., the father of these children. I inquired for the family in general, and the little songster in particular. I saw the tear start in his eye. He remarked: "She, poor thing, is dead; but she died happy. And I want to tell you, Brother Manship, from the time you were at our house until death, she regularly prayed for you night and morning; and she did not forget you in the closing scene; and the last words she distinctly uttered were *Lord bless Brother Manship!*" I was deeply affected, and could weep with those who wept. Brethren in the ministry, this circumstance has been a blessing to my soul. Shall we not be aided greatly in our work, if we can enlist the prayers of the children of our charges?

Readers, we all think it would be an excellent thing to have Romanists converted. Do we not sometimes adopt wrong means to accomplish this desirable end? I have a case to which I want to call particular attention. Through kindness a bigoted young Irish woman was led to a Methodist church in the neighbourhood of the city of Wilmington, where, in the providence of God, I was to preach. Rev. John B. Maddux had charge of the meeting. By a persuasive manner, this young woman was led to the mourners' bench, and was enabled to trust solely upon the blood of Jesus for salvation. We made the way as plain to her as we could. When she experienced the blessing, it made her so happy, she thought, how glad she would be could she tell it to her family connexions in Ireland. She deeply pitied them. She plainly saw they were in darkness. She resolved to use her best endeavours to be faithful. She joined the Union Church in Wilmington. The condition of her sisters pressed heavily upon her heart, and though she was poor, she was very industrious, and soon saved enough of her wages to import her sister Eliza. And soon after Eliza landed there, the Red Lion camp meeting was held. She was there one day, and that was much longer than she wanted to stay. Pungent conviction seized her in the forenoon, and during the afternoon, my wife has informed me, she was in the back part of our family tent, weeping and sobbing greatly. My wife asked her "why she cried." She replied, "I am sick." That sickness was not unto death. In a few months afterwards, the deep conviction she experienced there, was followed by a powerful conversion, in the basement of St. Paul's Methodist Episcopal Church. Her sickness was cured by the Heavenly Physician. This encouraged Mary (for that is the name of the first convert) to send as soon as she could for another sister. And Margaret came, and had not been with her sisters in their adopted country but a little while ere she felt the efficacy of the blood of Jesus. The third sister was sent for. She was older, and more confirmed in her Romanism, than the others; but they are all praying for her, and, although they find it a most difficult case, they expect to succeed. If they do not, *they have resolved to send her back.* But I have not the least doubt they will. For the last time I heard from them, this unyielding one had been a few times with them to the Sabbath School. How kind the Irish people are one to another! How remarkably affectionate has Mary R—— been to her sisters, since her conversion! However good a person may be without religion, with it they are a great deal better. And we can do for ourselves, for others, and for Christ, what a person in an unconverted state cannot do; for it is written, "I can do all things through Christ, which strengtheneth me."

Although I had a plenty of work to do at home, I sometimes found it remarkably pleasant to accept invitations from my dear brethren in the ministry to attend protracted, corner-stone laying, and dedication meetings. In the fall of 1851, a deeply interesting meeting was arranged and held by Rev. Joseph S. Cook, in the neighbourhood of Goshen, Lancaster county, Pa. There was a corner-stone of a new Church laid. This enterprising brother had seats in an adjacent grove, and a stand prepared, where all the services preparatory to the laying of the corner-stone took place. Several brethren in the ministry, Rev. Pennel Combe, Rev. William L. Gray, and others, participated. I was greatly assisted by the prayers and rejoicing of the people in my speech on finance. I saw there that day a lady, while I was speaking, in the rear portion of the congregation, leaping and praising God. It made no little stir in the audience. The preacher of the Circuit said to me in a low tone, "Brother Manship, that is a Presbyterian lady!" I was doubly pleased on receiving this information. I do maintain that the Christian, whatever may be his denominational connexions, has a right to shout. And if a person feels like *leaping*, from my heart I say, Amen!

"Hear him, ye deaf; his praise, ye dumb,
Your loosened tongues employ;
Ye blind, behold your Saviour come,
And leap, ye lame, for joy."

Especially when the life is right. I had good evidence that it was so in this case. For no sooner was the call made for contributions than this lady and her husband came forward and gave to this noble cause, although they were members of another communion. As it was at the dedication of Solomon's Temple, so it seemed to be among the hosts of Israel this day. "It came even to pass as the trumpeters and singers were as one to make one sound to be heard in praising and thanking the Lord." The congregation was mixed, several denominations were represented, but we "were as one."

On the first day of January, 1852, New Year's day, an excellent brick Methodist Episcopal Church was dedicated by Rev. Francis Hodson, D.D., with whom I was associated in the labours of the occasion, in Oxford, a beautiful village in Chester county, Pa. This place has for many years been under Presbyterian influence, and their religious training has been according to the usages of that Church. Methodism there was "small and feeble," and I am frank to confess I was surprised to see such a large and respectable church edifice, under the circumstances. Too much praise cannot be awarded to Rev. John Thompson. Though a young man, he wisely carried

19

this enterprise to a happy completion. He met with barriers, but trusted in God and moved onward, reading in his Bible, "Be strong and courageous; be not afraid nor dismayed." The day was a memorable and deeply interesting one. We there met with the widow and daughter of the lamented Rev. Jonas Bissey, and I should be derelict to duty if I did not, in connexion with the founding of this Church, refer to him. It was this faithful man that first conceived the idea of building a Methodist Church in Oxford. It was this brother who selected the lot, and bought it for the Church with his own means, humble as they were. And not only at this point of the Circuit, but all through this region of country, he was instrumental in converting souls to God, by scores and hundreds. The name of Jonas Bissey is written on many hearts, and rolling years cannot efface it. There never was a minister of our denomination or any other that had more weight of character than this burning and shining light in that part of the country. My readers will say, how mysterious is Providence, when I tell them that just as this ambassador of the skies was closing a sermon from "But to do good and communicate forget not; for with such sacrifices God is well pleased," and while a storm was raging, the muttering thunder and the vivid lightning's glare being heard and seen by the agitated congregation, to their utter dismay they saw their beloved minister *fall dead before them in the sacred desk!!* A ball of fire or electricity entered the building just over the pulpit, and this flash of lightning or thunderbolt did quickly the work of death. I might truly say that the God, who answers prayer sometimes by fire, saw fit "to send a despatch for him, and telegraphed him home to the skies."

He fell in the midst of his spiritual children and warm friends, in the New London Cross Roads Methodist Episcopal Church, which he had been the means of rearing, literally and spiritually. It was my privilege to attend his funeral, which was the largest one I ever witnessed in any country place in my entire life. The spacious parlours of Mr. Seal's Hotel were thrown open; and there was the manly form, just as natural as when I saw him, a few weeks before that, at a camp meeting, and heard him preach a powerful sermon, from "Ye must be born again." Both Mr. and Mrs. Seal had been brought to God through his instrumentality. This, in a measure, accounted for their great kindness. How strongly are we attached to those who have led us to the Saviour!

Rev. James Smith, Presiding Elder of the Wilmington District at that time, now no more, delivered a very excellent and appropriate sermon. Never did I see more tears shed on an occasion of the kind. This event, though to me rather incomprehensible, I firmly believed at the time would be the means of bringing many to God whom ordinary means would not reach. It was said of Samson, "So the dead which he slew at his death were more than they which he slew in his life." Doubtless, the death of this good man, under such circumstances, has accomplished and will accomplish glorious results.

Rev. Jonas Bissey had in Rev. James Smith a strong friend. I have often heard the latter speak in strong terms of commendation of the former; and he believed that he was the most efficient labourer he had on his district. When he heard of his death, and while preaching his funeral sermon, his eyes were a fountain of tears. He was then advanced in life, yet the circumstances inspired him. I never heard such a sermon from Brother Smith. And the hundreds, if not thousands who were there, will remember, at the close of the sermon, how sweetly he sung his favourite hymn:—

"We speak of the realms of the blest,
Of a country so bright and so fair,
And oft are its glories confessed;
But what must it be to be there!

"Do thou, Lord, midst pleasure or woe,
For Heaven our spirits prepare;
And shortly we also shall know—
Shall feel what it is to be there."

How true, in his case! During the succeeding winter,

his health failed; and, the following Conference, the mournful intelligence was brought to the Conference-room that Rev. James Smith was dead! He soon followed his friend, to whom allusion has been made, and in whose death he took such a deep interest. It may truly be said, "they were lovely and pleasant in their lives, and in their deaths they were not greatly divided." They have experienced "what it is to be there." It was my privilege to be in the sick-room of Brother Smith. His faith was strong in the atonement. The last time I visited him and prayed with him, confiding in Christ, he was happy. I left his room never expecting to see him alive again. I also left ready to endorse the sentiment of Young:—

> "The chamber where the good man meets his fate,
> Is privileged beyond the common walk of virtuous life—
> Quite on the verge of Heaven."

He died March 28, 1852. His funeral discourse was delivered by Rev. Francis Hodson, D. D., others participating. The Annual Conference, being in session, attended in a body, and saw their aged fellow-labourer consigned to the tomb in Ebenezer graveyard, Philadelphia. We sorrowed, but not as those who have no hope. We had "hope in his death." Some of his last expressions were, "Hallelujah!" "Hallelujah!!" Glory!" "Glory!" He had said those words in ecstasy a thousand times in life, and it will be encouraging to his friends to know that he could from a full heart repeat them in death. "Yea, though I walk through the valley of the shadow of death, I will fear no evil: for thou art with me; thy rod and thy staff they comfort me."

"Death is the crown of life;
Death wounds to cure! we fall, we rise, we reign!"

CHAPTER X.

"Wesleyan Collegiate Institute"—A great Disappointment—Professor Thomas E. Sudler—President Loomis—A Visit to Boston—Respect shown to General Conference by the City Authorities—Honourable Daniel Webster—Infidels sometimes hypocritical—"What hath God wrought?"—Rev. Jesse Lee—Old Elm Tree—Senate Chamber—Bunker Hill—Conflict with a Pugilist—Enter into every open Door—"Tormented before the Time"—Rev. Joshua Thomas, of Tangier Island—Matilda B.—"Do justly"—Do not bear false witness against thy Neighbour—Captain A. perishes at Sea—A Female publicly financiering—Churches ought to improve as well as other Things.

IN the spring of 1852, my appointment was to the Agency of "The Wesleyan Female Collegiate Institute," in the city of Wilmington; therefore I was permitted to remain another year in this exceedingly pleasant place. It will doubtless be borne in mind by some of my readers, that this Institute was originally established by Rev. Soloman Prettyman, in 1839; and that he, by his great energy, made it one of the first seminaries of the kind in the land. Students, from every state in the Union almost, poured into it. Many graduated there, who are now among the first ladies for intelligence and respectability in our country.

Mr. Prettyman, for a series of years, was a great acquisition to the city of Wilmington, and did as much as any other man, in raising the standard of female education in the Methodist Episcopal Church; and practically demonstrated that woman is competent for high mental acquirements. He was a native of Delaware, and, in the way of enterprise, one of her noblest sons. He bent his energies, not only to advance the cause of education, but to improve the lower counties in their agricultural and business relations. This he did by originating and mainly establishing a steamboat line between Lewistown, in Sussex county, and Philadelphia. This being done, the advantages to that part of the state are great. A market for all kinds of produce is brought to their doors; sources of improvement to their lands, placed in their hands; and otherwise, the results have been greatly beneficial. To this gentleman, consequently, the community owes a lasting debt of gratitude. While, however, he befriended others (and this must indeed afford to him no little satisfaction), it is to be deeply regretted, that, in his own circumstances, he was greatly injured. This is not, however, as history and observation demonstrate, unfrequent with those who nobly act as benefactors to their fellow men.

In the year 1852, Mr. Prettyman's embarrassments became so great, that he had to part with the "Wesleyan Female Collegiate Institute," the alma mater of so many interesting young ladies. Notwithstanding his strenuous efforts to prevent it, it was sold under the sheriff's hammer. I was present at the sale, and, although I am not in the habit of being in bar-rooms, that day I was anxiously looking on, to see into whose hands the Institute would fall. It was generally rumoured that the Roman Catholics would be the purchasers, and convert it into a nunnery, orphans' asylum, or something else. Mr. Prettyman himself was apprehensive that this would be the result. The bidding commenced; many of the creditors were there, anxiously looking on; now and then, fearing and trembling, they would bid a little more. They were in a strait betwixt two; they wanted it run up as high as possible, but greatly feared it would be struck off to them. There was a large fine-looking man present, who was observed occasionally to make a bid. Many asked "who is he?" Some supposed he was some dignitary of the Roman Catholic Church; some entertained one idea, and some another. Finally the sheriff, without knowing who he was, declared him to be the purchaser, he having given the highest bid. Rev. S. P., with tears, said to his friends, and to me amongst the rest, "The Catholics have bought it, it is gone for ever." And some of that denomination who were present, seemed much pleased that they were about to take possession of a *Methodist Institution*. Their eyes were soon opened, however, and their ears were made to tingle when they heard that this fine priestly-looking man was the representative of the Methodist Episcopal Church! Having been connected with the sheriff's office, in the city and county of Philadelphia, he was deemed a proper person to attend to this sale, and purchase. He did his duty faithfully. This friend was Amos Phillips, Esquire.

Professor Sudler was at once placed at the head of the Institute. The professor was a graduate of West Point; occupied a professor's chair for a number of years in St. John's College at Annapolis, and, at an earlier period of life, represented his native county in the state legislature, honourably to himself, and to his constituents. He came to the presidency of the Institute directly from Dickinson College. For many years he had filled the position of professor there; and as he was an excellent scholar, a gentleman of the highest style, and a faithful Christian, the board of council felt sanguine, that he would make them and the Church an efficient principal. He served one year; it was doubtless *the most difficult year* of the existence of the institution—a time that tried men's souls. In addition to other discouragements, the president lost an amiable, accomplished daughter, which was a great stroke to him. She was the light of his life. He bore up, however, under all like a Christian hero; and, when the Annual Commencement rolled round, there never was, in those "classic halls," more interest. There was one who that night graduated and took the honours of her class, who, while she had other accomplishments to adorn her, surpassed in instrumental and vocal music. Miss Bodine sang, I will say, now that she sleeps beneath the sward of earth, more like an angel than a human being. She died happy. How mysterious are the ways of Providence!

At the close of this deeply-interesting Commencement, when the diplomas were awarded to the graduating class, Mr. Sudler delivered one of the most eloquent and touching addresses to which it has ever been my privilege to listen. Many a tear spontaneously bedewed the cheeks of almost all in attendance. He remarked to the students whom he was leaving: "My sun is setting; yours is rising." With burning words he closed his address. I hesitate not to say, taking everything into consideration, that no one could have done better for the institution the first, which was the most difficult, year—the crisis in the history of the Wesleyan Female Collegiate Institute—than Thomas E. Sudler, A. M.

Rev. George Loomis, A. M., was chosen as his successor, a graduate of "Wesleyan University." For some years he was President of the "Genesee Wesleyan Seminary," at Lima, New York, and late Chaplain of the "American Seamen's Friend Society," in Canton, China. As a minister he is competent to fill any of the pulpits of the land, and as a scholar adequate to stand at the head of any of our colleges. This gentleman, though a stranger in our midst, soon won for himself universal esteem among the ministry of our Church; and, although he speaks among his pupils as "one having authority," his urbane manner towards them, and parental solicitude for their welfare, cause the young ladies to be strongly attached to him. Having at its head such a man, and being assisted by highly accomplished teachers, the "Wesleyan Female College" has become second to none in the country; and the public show their appreciation of it by filling it with their daughters.

The Philadelphia Annual Conference has taken an interest in the prosperity of this institution in various ways. For two successive years, agents were appointed. I was first placed in this position, and continued for one year. I did not, indeed, accomplish as much as I could have desired; and yet, under the circumstances, I did the best I could, and have the satisfaction to know that the year was not entirely a blank.

In the month of May, I visited the city of Boston. I went there partly at the instance of our "Board of Council," on business appertaining to the college, and partly to enjoy the privilege of seeing our General Conference in session. This is perhaps second to no deliberative body in the world for sanctified learning. The impression it made in Boston was very favourable to the Methodist Episcopal Church. The municipal authorities of that city showed a respect to this body that was unprecedented. They invited the members and visiters to take an afternoon excursion in a fine steamer, to visit, in and about the harbour, places of greatest interest, particularly one of the forts. The repast which was here served up was truly sumptuous. The Mayor of the city, and other prominent speakers of Boston, welcomed them to the hospitalities of the city. To the speeches of these gentlemen, Rev. John A. Collins and Rev. John Kennaday, D. D., replied, on behalf of the Conference, in an able though impromptu manner. Everything passed off pleasantly. This body was also invited to visit Faneuil Hall, the cradle of liberty, to hear a speech by the great statesman, Daniel Webster. Seats were specially reserved for the members of the Conference. And, when it was proper, the orator of the day made some appropriate remarks bearing upon the Church which this body represented. Said he: "It has been remarked truly, 'Methodism is Christianity in earnest.' I have not been an idle spectator of the movements of this Christian organization." He spoke of it in high terms of commendation, as a pure system of Christianity, and as doing much for the amelioration of the condition of the human family. He seemed to be well posted in Methodistical language. He quoted the words of Charles Wesley, referring to the perpetuity of Methodism: "Though the workmen die, the work goes on."

It speaks well for the Christian religion to have such a bright intellect as the great Webster was blessed with, enlisted, even in theory, "on the Lord's side." To the religion of the Lord Jesus Christ, he clung in the hour of his dissolution. If such men as Newton, Locke, Chalmers, Webster, and myriads of others who might be named, endorse the Bible, and the religion of the meek and lowly Jesus, how impudent it is, for pigmies in science and reasoning powers, to raise the hue and cry that the Bible is full of contradictions, and will not bear investigation; to place a low estimate on the Saviour of mankind, and to say of the "Mighty God, the everlasting Father, the Prince of peace," in the language of Infidelity, "Crush the wretch!" "The fool hath said in his heart, There is no God."

There are, however, a great many who profess Infidelity, and abhor the word of God, who are consummate hypocrites. To demonstrate this, I will mention a case or two. They may not be new, however, to some of my readers. "There were two persons travelling in the west on a collecting tour. To some extent they had been successful. One of them was a professed Infidel, the other a Christian. It was requisite when nightfall came on, to stop at a house that looked suspicious; and, before they took up their abode there, they entered into an arrangement, which they deemed prudent; viz. while one should sleep the other should watch. The lot fell upon the Infidel to be wakeful during the first half of the night. But before they retired to their humble and rather unsightly room, the head of the family took down from a shelf an old copy of the Bible, that looked as though it had been studied from Genesis to Revelation, and said to his guests, 'It is my practice to read a chapter in the Bible and pray every night before retiring.' He accordingly read in a solemn manner. There was feeling in his prayer. The travellers immediately after were shown to their place of rest. The Christian said his prayers and retired; and only a few moments elapsed before the Infidel followed him to bed. The Christian man said, 'You are to watch the fore part of the night, according to arrrangement.' The Infidel replied, 'What is the use of watching here? There is no danger to be apprehended in such a place as this, where the Bible is read, and where there is such praying as we have heard here to-night.'"

"A prominent Infidel gentleman had a wife who was a deeply devoted Christian lady. They had a lovely daughter, to whom they were strongly attached. The father's example and theory had been of such a character, as to impress the mind of the young lady unfavourably towards religion, as practised and taught by her pious mother. The young and only daughter was called to a sick-bed, and it was but too evident that she must die. She was not prepared for this critical hour; her mind was naturally much distressed in view of going before the bar of God in her sins. Her father watched the progress of the disease with the deepest solicitude. However, Infidelity had not a word of comfort for the dying girl! She asked her father in great agitation, 'Which must I believe, father; what you or what my mother has taught me?' He loved his daughter fondly; ay, better than his theory. And he said, 'My child, believe what your mother has told you.' 'For their rock is not as our rock, even our enemies themselves being judges.'"

From what has already been said, it will be readily concluded that our branch of the Christian Church in this city, Boston, occupies a prominent place in the affections of the people. Our churches are numerous, and some of them truly magnificent. I saw the one, among others, which our people purchased of the Unitarians. I was informed it originally cost about *one hundred thousand dollars.* Our people bought it very low, for, I was told, *forty thousand dollars.* I doubt not but the change will redound to the glory of God.

We are all ready to say, while considering the prominence of Methodism now in Boston, "What hath God wrought?" Especially when we recollect that in 1791, when Bishop Asbury first visited that place, the few friends that our cause had were so destitute of energy, and so timorous, that the venerable Bishop met with a very cold reception; so much so, that even this unflinching man, in view of the discouragements thrown in his way in this place, says, "I have done with Boston until we can obtain a lodging, a house to preach in, and some to join us." In Lynn he was cordially received, and this faithful man seemed to be inspired with the prophetic spirit, when he remarked, "Here we shall make a firm stand, and from this central point, from Lynn, shall the light of Methodism radiate through the state."

No place in New England seemed so difficult of access as Boston. It was hard here to plant the tree of Methodism. Rev. Jesse Lee did, perhaps, more than any other man in establishing our cause in this place. He could not, at first, procure even a private house to preach in. A school-house was procured, but the despised sect were not long permitted to retain possession of it. But this Apostle of Methodism in New England repaired to the Common, stood upon a table, and began to sing and pray. Only *four persons* were present when he commenced; before he concluded he supposed he had *three thousand hearers!* The next Sabbath, at the same place, the number of hearers was greatly increased. And notwithstanding the strong opposition to Methodism, a small society was established, which has grown to be very formidable, and so fulfilling the prediction of Bishop Asbury, "I am led to think the Eastern Church will find this saying hold true in regard to the Methodists: '*I will provoke you to jealousy by a people that were no people, and by a foolish nation will anger you.*' Says the Bishop, "They have trodden upon the Quakers, the Episcopalians, the Baptists—see, now, if the Methodists do not work their way."

The first Methodist church was built in Boston in 1795, a wooden house, forty-six feet long, thirty-six feet wide; and I am pleased to state, on the best authority, that a good portion of the money for this church was sent from the Eastern Shore of Maryland, from Delaware, and Philadelphia, in the bounds of my own beloved Conference. And it may be pleasing to my readers to know that the last sermon that the pioneer of Methodism in New England preached was within our bounds, on the Eastern Shore of Maryland, at a camp meeting, and that the remains of this "thunderbolt of war" in Israel's army, rest in my own native (Caroline) county, close by the quiet waters of the romantic Tuckahoe. Sleep on, and take your rest; but as Christ hath risen, so shall ye arise.

Rev. Jesse Lee and the fathers "lie by, in the bosom of the earth, as a weary pilot in some well-sheltered creek, till all the storms which infest this lower world are blown over; here they enjoy safe anchorage, are in no danger of foundering amidst the waves of prevailing iniquity, or of being shipwrecked on the rocks of any powerful temptation. But ere long we shall behold them hoisting their flag of hope, riding before a sweet gale of atoning merit and redeeming love, till they make, with all the sails of an assured faith, the blessed port of eternal life."

Mr. Lee and his co-labourers were frequently objects of ridicule; but it often happened that Mr. Lee, who was a shrewd man, and seldom at a loss for an answer suitable to the occasion, would fairly outstrip those who were disposed to make light of his learning and talents. On a certain occasion a young lawyer, with a view to puzzle Mr. Lee, addressed him in Latin; to whom he replied in German—a language not understood either by the speaker or his friends, who were anxiously listening to the conversation. "There," said a gentleman, who was in the secret of the lawyer's intentions, "the preacher has answered you in Hebrew, and therefore he must be a learned man."

At another time, some lawyers were disposed to have some amusement at the expense of Mr. Lee. Said they, "You generally preach extemporaneously, do you not?" To which Mr. Lee replied in the affirmative. "Do you not often make mistakes?" The answer was, "Sometimes it is likely I do." "Do you stop to correct them?" Mr. Lee said, "That depends on the character of the mistake. If I were quoting 'all liars shall have their part in the lake which burneth with fire and brimstone,' and should happen to mistake and say, instead of 'all liars,' *all lawyers!* I should suppose it so near the truth that I should not feel it my duty to stop and correct the mistake." They found that Methodist preachers were not *all Know-Nothings.*

As I was homeward bound, I passed through the Boston Common. I visited the old Elm Tree, prominent in the history of the Revolution, and on that account there was an interest in it; but it was more particularly interesting to me on account of its associations with the introduction of Methodism into the city of Boston. Under its foliage Mr. Lee is said to have preached to the listening multitudes, as I have before stated, owing to the fact that there was no house to be had. This no doubt was Providential: many more heard the Methodist preacher than could have been seated in any house that could have been obtained. John Wesley did more good preaching on his father's tombstone, after he was refused the Church, than he could have done in the church itself. Persecution generally results in the good of the cause opposed.

I felt a desire to be in possession of a piece of that

old Elm Tree, and I hardly knew how to contrive to get it. The branches were too high for me to reach, being somewhat like Zaccheus, low of stature. I set my valise erect, and then, from the top of it, made a successful spring, obtained a piece of that venerable tree, but fell at full length upon the ground, greatly to the amusement of the thousands who were there enjoying the refreshing breezes of a sweet May evening. The Boston Common is a place of great resort. I was apprehensive some one, who did not appreciate my feeling relative to the twig from this notable tree, would reprove me. I thought of the verses,

"Woodman, spare that tree,
Touch not a single bough,
In youth it sheltered me,
And I'll protect it now.
'Twas my forefather's hand
That placed it near his cot;
There, woodman, let it stand,
Thine axe shall harm it not.

"My heart strings round thee cling,
Close as thy bark, old friend;
Here shall the wild birds sing,
And still thy branches bend.
Old tree, the storm still brave,
And, woodman, leave the spot,
While I've a hand to save,
Thine axe shall harm it not."

I was permitted to be present in the Senate Chamber of Massachusetts, when the original Prohibitory Liquor Law in that state passed. There were many frowning faces, as well as cheerful countenances, at the result. This seemed to me to be a dignified body, and I judge, from this very vote, that they are lovers of good order and sound morals. The fact is, they could have given me no better evidence that they are patriots and philanthropists, in the truest sense of the word.

I visited Bunker's Hill, located in this city. I was in the high monument, and had a fine view of the city. I thought of the horrible battle that was here fought in the Revolution. I saw some of the ordnance that were used on that bloody occasion.

While musing upon surrounding circumstances, I was led to think of a thrilling incident which was connected with that memorable battle. I take this incident from one of Bishop Morris' sermons. "A man by the name of John Randon fell in this battle. He belonged to the British line, and after receiving his death-wounds, wrote a letter to his wife in England, which he commenced thus: "Before these lines reach you, grim death will have swept me off the stage of life, and filthy reptiles will be feeding on that form once so dear to thee. Yesterday we had a bloody and obstinate fight. I received two balls, and am now so weak from the loss of blood, that I can hardly write these few lines, as the last tribute of my unchanging love to thee. The surgeons inform me that three hours will be the utmost I can survive." And after narrating his voyage, his conversion by the instrumentality of a Methodist soldier, expressing his wishes respecting his business, and giving his dying advice at length to his wife and children, he closed with these memorable words: "More would I say, but life ebbs out apace. My senses cease to perform their office. Bright angels stand around the gory turf on which I lie, ready to escort me to the arms of Jesus. Bending saints reveal my shining crown, and beckon me away. Yea, methinks my Jesus bids me come. Adieu! adieu! adieu!" and soon expired.

For the first time in my life, being the agent of the college, I visited some of the more Northern Circuits. My visit to Dauphin county was, to me, deeply interesting. Reaching, however, the camp meeting near Millersburg, in that county, was attended with some difficulty. I had the company of two young ministers. Opposite to Millersburg we were under the necessity of crossing the Susquehanna river in a little boat. We were, on arriving in the canal boat at this point, invited to take passage with a man that had not signed the pledge, or if he had, we were inclined to think he had broken it, yet we resolved, if we could not do better, to go with him. The kind-hearted preachers of the Circuit, however, knowing that we were coming, had sent a young man, with instructions to convey us over. We left the former ferryman, and went according to instructions. This greatly offended our anti-temperance friend, and he threatened to turn our boat over, pursued us closely, and our helmsman was a little timorous. He worked manfully, however, and kept considerably ahead of our pursuer, and landed us on the Dauphin shore safely, and with all despatch made for his moorings. Up to this time we had said nothing to him ; but now, fearing that he would carry his threats into execution, and perhaps maltreat the young man who had so generously served us, I felt it my duty to say to his pursuer, "You should not molest that young man, he has only done his duty in bringing us over; there is no occasion for you to wish to injure him." Then using a horrible oath, he exclaimed, "If you take it up, I will flog you!" His boat was brought nearly to the shore where I was standing. Coat off, sleeves rolled up, he leaped into the water, and made towards me. I was perplexed; my companions had passed on ahead; he evidently had fight in him; he was an athletic man. I was not able, had I been pugilistic in my feelings, to meet such a stout man. In an instant it occurred to me, to "fight him with spiritual weapons!" I said sternly and with emphasis, "Come on, I am ready for you in the name of the God of battles. I have put on the whole armour of God, I am able to stand against the wiles of the devil. Come on! come on!!" Said he, "Who are you, and where did you come from?" I replied, "I am a soldier of the cross; I fight not with carnal but spiritual weapons; I have the shield of faith, wherewith I am able to quench the fiery darts of the wicked; I use the sword of the Spirit, praying always with all prayer. I will conquer you; come on; get down here on this river shore; I will pray God to have mercy on your soul; and, in this whole conflict, I will not hurt a hair on your head." He retreated to his little boat "speechless," and I went on my way rejoicing, without being the least injured in my person by this Susquehanna bully. "They shall not hurt nor destroy in all my holy mountain."

The camp meeting was upon an "exceeding high mountain." It was well managed by the preacher in charge, Rev. John Cummings—the Presiding Elder being under the necessity of leaving to meet other engagements. There were not many converted; yet it was not altogether in vain. God's people were revived, and I can truly say, I had my own spiritual strength renewed. From that meeting I went into the town of Halifax, the principal appointment on that Circuit. I rode with a good local preacher, by the name of Singer. He was not only a *Singer*, but he was a great shouter. He is one of the pillars of the church in that place. That day, as we rode along the road, we came to a large house by the way-side. He remarked, "A rich man lives there; he is a very wicked man; he had recently a very loud call, which, I did hope, would lead him to repent and be converted. Under that tree," pointing to an apple-tree near the road, "he had two sons, who had, in the time of a thunderstorm, taken shelter, and they were struck by lightning, instantly killed, and carried lifeless corpses to their father's house." It was impressed on my mind, It is my duty to stop, and warn this family to prepare for death; and I thought I would take for my text the crcumstance in God's Providence just related to me. My friend doubted whether this would be acceptable; he did not know but that we should be ordered out of the house. I told him positively, "In the strength of the Lord" I was going. He kindly consented to accompany me. We entered. I said to the rich man, "I am a preacher of the Gospel, have just heard of the calamity you have experienced, and have come to warn you and your family to prepare for death. I shall never see you again till I meet you at the bar of God." I then gave out the hymn,

"God moves in a mysterious way."

While this solemn hymn was being sung, the old gentleman and his wife also were very much wrought upon; they trembled, tears flowed freely. By this time, many returning from the camp meeting, and otherwise travelling the road, halted, so that we had a house full; many vehicles and horses were seen all round the premises. We went to prayer; the old people cried aloud for mercy; God's people shouted for joy. After praying, exhorting, and singing there, some hour or two, we bade them adieu; they, however, promising by God's help that they would meet us in a better world. It can be said, I think, with much truthfulness, "This day is salvation come to this house." It was a great cross for me to pursue the course I did, yet I am glad I did it; I was blessed in the deed. The man of that house has since been called out of the world. I hope he was saved, "yet so as by fire." Should not the minister of the Gospel be as "bold as a lion?"

In the town of Halifax I found a magnificent brick Methodist Episcopal Church, the finest building in the place, an honour to Methodism. Rev. John Cummings felt it his duty there to use his efforts to get the great evil of ardent spirits removed from the town. He considered some of the hotels nuisances, and being sustained by some leading temperance men, energetically prosecuted this matter, until they succeeded in getting, during his administration there, every bar closed in that place, and each man's license taken from him. There was an effort, however, made to have them restored. The tavern-keepers came before the court, with their lawyer, to plead for the cause of alcohol. The preacher,

Paul-like, "reasoned of temperance," and outreasoned the lawyer, and the court decided against the tavern-keepers of Halifax. This investigation lasted three days. It seems they were "tormented before the time" that prohibition came to pass; and when I was there, actually as far back as 1853, they had the Maine law in practical operation. This Methodist preacher was a target for this class to hurl their darts at. They wrote him anonymous letters, and threatened to cowhide him. He bravely told them, "I don't care for a whole regiment of you." They burnt him in effigy before his door. But this, bad as it was, was better than literally to burn up the people with their liquid fire! The point was gained. One of them undertook to sell without license; the preacher gave him no rest; he was fined *fifty-five* dollars. He found this an unprofitable business. Thus this brother prevented a multitude of sins, and the town was completely changed; and ere that brother's time expired among them, they could but see, he is our friend, he is a benefactor. The pulpit should generally be arrayed against this evil. All good people should heartily enlist in this great cause, and

> "Make the temperance army strong:
> And on to victory."

We should preach sermons on this evil that has slain

its thousands—destroying both soul and body in hell. We should pray in our pulpits, families, and closets,

> "Hasten, Lord, the happy day,
> When beneath the gentle ray,
> Temperance all the world shall sway,
> And reign triumphantly."

This summer, I was not only in the northern, but, at least to some extent, also in the southern portion of the Conference. In company with Rev. John C. Thomas, agent of "Dickinson College," I attended a camp meeting on Deal's Island. The agents, both of the Female and Male College, had cause to think that this people appreciate education. I know not how many scholarships my worthy colleague disposed of, but I can positively say, this people did nobly for the "Wesleyan Female College."

There was to me a very interesting personage in attendance at that camp meeting, of whom I must speak at some length. I allude to Rev. Joshua Thomas. Upon being introduced to him, I was ready to say, "I have heard of thee by the hearing of the ear, but now mine eye seeth thee." I found him very old, rather helpless, travelling from his tent to the preacher's stand in a small four-wheeled carriage, drawn by his friends, after he was assisted in taking his seat. But he "was strong in faith, giving glory to God." I had much conversation with him, and found him an uncommonly interesting man.

He was brought up in the Protestant Episcopal Church, and did not get among the Methodists till 1807. In the summer of this year, he attended two camp meetings, one in Virginia, and one in Maryland; at the last of which he fully gave his heart to God. He at once began to labour on Tangier Island, in the Chesapeake Bay, where he resided. His meetings would hold frequently all day on the Sabbath. Two local preachers, hearing of the work, went over with their tent, and laboured with the islanders. Many were converted. This was the beginning of the great camp meetings on that island; to which thousands, if not tens of thousands, from various parts, resorted. The British took possession of this island in 1813, and Rev. Joshua Thomas and all his people were prisoners. He was much respected by the Admiral and the whole army, and preached to them just before they made their attack on Baltimore. He had probably *twelve thousand hearers!*

For an account of this service, I am indebted to the manuscript of the late Rev. Levin M. Prettyman, which was kindly furnished me by his daughter, Mrs. Mary Ridgeway. "They were all drawn up in a solid column under the pines of the old camp ground, which was the centre of the British camp. I stood on a stage at one end of the column, all the men facing me, and an officer on my right and left. I never had such feelings in my life. I was determined to give them a faithful warning, and did not know but that the officers would cut me in pieces for it. After singing and prayer, I began to feel better; and soon all fear was taken away from me, and I warned them of the wickedness of killing men, and told them that, if they were going to Baltimore to take it, they could not do it, and they might prepare to die. When the battle was over, I saw them coming back. I went down to meet them. The first officers I met, I asked if they had taken Baltimore? They said, No, but hundreds of our men have been slain; it turned out just as you told us the Sunday before we left. We have had a bloody battle; and, all the time we were fighting in the field, we thought of what you told us. You seemed to be right before us, still warning us against the attempt to take Baltimore." This good man was much respected by the British, and had great influence with the officers. The soldiers were cutting down the trees where the camp meetings were held. Brother Thomas told the Admiral they were the Lord's trees, and under them hundreds had been converted, and he hoped hundreds more would be, after peace was declared; and he wanted him to have them protected. This was promptly attended to. In 1815, in the month of January, there was great rejoicing in the camp; the islanders could not tell what it meant. Soon, however, some of the officers rode up to Mr. Thomas's house, crying out, with joy, "O! Parson Thomas, there's peace! there's peace!" The ship was seen down the bay, the flag of peace flying at her mast. "We shall have no more war."

I found Brother Thomas a great man to shout. A few years before my interview with him, at a camp meeting he was lodging with his brethren in the ministry. One of the number was powerfully blessed in the night season; he sung and shouted, and every one felt that sainted man, Rev. W. S., had a good right to do so. Rev. Joshua Thomas awoke and said, "Brother S., you understand" (this was a great expression with him) "you are not going to beat me;" and he deliberately went at it with all his might and main. I tried to preach and exhort several times at the camp meeting on Deal's Island, in the summer of 1853, where I first met with this brother. I suppose I was animated and inclined to enjoy myself, as the Lord seemed to direct. He would sit and praise God, and say, "I have seen the day when I could *outshout you*—I only wish I was young once more." There was a peculiarity about his shouting, and an unction that attended it. Cases could be given of powerful conviction, brought about in this way, when other means had proved unavailing. He was an eccentric man, but accomplished a vast amount of good. On a certain occasion, he had business with a court-house officer in one of the counties of the Eastern Shore of Maryland. It was a small matter, not sufficient in the estimation of the kind-hearted officer to make a charge for. Mr. Thomas asked, "What is the charge?" The officer said, "Mr. Thomas, we charge you nothing but an interest in your prayers." Mr. Thomas said, "I don't like to be in debt; let us pray;" and knelt down on the office floor, and devoutly invoked God's blessing on the gentleman, who was not a religious man. He became from that time concerned for religion, and afterwards, like his father in Israel, who so earnestly prayed for him, became a most ardent, faithful member of the Methodist Episcopal Church. Brother Thomas was greatly attached to the ministers. His house was always a home for them; it afforded him great pleasure to take them from island to island in his canoe, called "*Old Methodist.*" To enable them to itinerate and meet their appointments every two weeks, "*Old Methodist,*" with Captain Thomas at her helm, would sail some thirty miles. This rough craft, made of a solid tree, and very large, has borne many a valuable cargo. Not a few who have sailed thus with their Saviour beneath, have reached the harbour of glory, and Brother Thomas now in their number; they

"Have crossed o'er the stream, and have reached the bright coast."

He died, as he lived for nearly fifty years, a witness that the blood of Jesus can save to the uttermost. In his declining years, he always manifested his love to the ministers on parting, by getting them to kneel down at his feet, and by praying over them, and, in a most solemn manner, laying his hands on their heads. When

Brother John C. Thomas and myself left that camp meeting, we received before leaving, his blessing. We did not perhaps feel more solemn when we were together ordained to the order of Deacon or Elder in the Church of God. Rev. Joshua Thomas was eminently useful on the islands and elsewhere in the region where he lived. When I saw him he was "old and grayheaded," but God had not forsaken him. His children were devoted to him, and, like Demetrius, he had "good report of all men, and of the truth itself."

In the autumn of the year, one of the flowers of the "Wesleyan College" was found to be fading; and it was soon evident to us all, that "Matilda" must die. This was a severe trial to us all; for we all loved her: she was buoyant, amiable, and intellectual. She was away from her paternal home; but, I can testify, that everything was done, and done cheerfully and tenderly, that could have been done, even in her own sweet home. I frequently visited her in her death-sickness. I felt it my duty to pay special attention to her; I knew her parents well; spent many happy hours at her father's house, in the first year of my itinerancy; I was the means of her going to the college; she accompanied me from her home to Wilmington in order to enter the college. Only a few months rolled round ere it was my painful duty to accompany her back. It was, however, only the body that was taken back; the intellectual part that promised so much, the soul, had "returned to God who gave it." The little company, some of her relatives and myself, travelled all night with the corpse; and just as the sun, on a beautiful Sabbath morning, was beginning to gild the heavens, we reached what once had been Matilda's home. The wailings of the mother I cannot forget; the tears of the feeling father I saw copiously flowing. I told them all the circumstances connected with the case. They were satisfied, and cheered themselves with the thought, "Although the child cannot come to us, we can go to her." Arrangements were made for the funeral to take place on Monday morning. The attendance was very large. I was called upon to preach the sermon. The text was, "The Lord gave, and the Lord hath taken away; blessed be the name of the Lord." Many reasons were assigned why we should, under such circumstances, bless "the name of the Lord;" and, among the rest, I took the ground, that God in his wisdom takes some to Heaven; those, too, that we think we can least part with; and by their death, surviving friends are won to Jesus. I stated to the congregation, that the death of this young girl who clung to the cross of Christ and died in peace, would produce results in the Wesleyan College, where she was so generally esteemed, that the most eloquent preaching would not accomplish. Before we left Wilmington, the corpse was brought into the largest room connected with the property, and an appropriate address delivered, by Rev. Francis Hodson, D. D., to the numerous students. Doubtless, great good was done; impressious made, deep and abiding; many vows made; and one after another, they took their leave of Matilda Bailey, dropping affection's tear, and imprinting a kiss upon the pallid cheek, with the determination, "We will meet our classmate in bright glory." While I was dwelling on this topic in the way of illustration, I related an incident that I had recently read in some religious journal, in substance as follows: "A father and his two children were rambling by the side of a river for pleasure and recreation. The father ventured on the river in a little boat, leaving his children on the beach. After he had gone some distance from the shore, a storm suddenly arose, the fog and gloom were intense, the river began rapidly to swell and overflow its banks. This truly was a distressing hour. The father felt great apprehension not only for himself, but also for his children. It was dark, he did not know which way to row his boat, he feared he would be lost, and his children also find a watery grave. In this critical hour he heard a voice—'Steer this way, father!' It was the excited voices of his children. The shore was reached, all were safe. Only a few weeks thereafter, both the children were taken ill and departed this life; they were buried side by side in the cold grave. The father was a stranger to religion; but this affecting circumstance led him to serious reflection. He could imagine, after he lost his children, that he could hear them saying, 'Steer this way, father!' He knew they had gone to Heaven, and he determined he would meet them there."

I told these weeping parents there was, in their case, a little resemblance at least to the one just referred to. Some years before this solemn event, they had a lovely daughter, that suddenly died, just at the age of Matilda at her death. I said, "They will sleep side by side, in the family graveyard, but their souls, redeemed by the precious blood of Jesus, are safely moored in the heavenly port. As you are navigating the sea of life, 'By winds and waves tossed and driven,' may you hear them say, 'Steer this way, father! steer this way, mother!!' Will you do it?" It was a funeral occasion, but it was a season of refreshing from the presence of the Lord. And we all felt "it is better to go to the house of mourning than to go to the house of feasting

A model Methodist Episcopal Church was consecrated in October of this year, to the worship of Almighty God, in Cantwell's Bridge, now Odessa, New Castle county, Delaware. Bishop Scott preached in the morning to a delighted audience. This is the native place of Bishop Scott, and yet no minister could be more universally esteemed than he, in that region of country. At night it was my privilege to preach in the new temple. I do not wish to speak to the disparagement of other churches in Delaware, but I am compelled to say, this, in my opinion, is unsurpassed for neatness, substantiality, suitability, and beauty. One of the most interesting things about it is, its freedom from debt. I will mention a fact with which I was that day made acquainted. The builder complained that he had lost money by the transaction. Be it spoken, however, to his credit, he did not slight the job, and his work will praise him. The trustees and congregation were most generously disposed, and, as there was a sufficiency of funds subscribed and given in the morning to cover the claims, at night there were a few hundred dollars subscribed as a donation to the builder. This looked to me highly honourable and Christian-like, and the impression made on my mind by my visit that day, both in regard to the minister, Rev. Joseph Aspril, and his flock, was, that they delighted "to do justly, and to love mercy, and to walk humbly with their God." Bishop Scott was at that time on the eve of sailing to Africa. He nobly that day made a subscription, remarking—and it went to our hearts—"*If I live to return from Africa I will pay it.*" Unexpectedly, however, to him, before we left that town, by the kindness of some of his numerous friends, this matter was adjusted, and duly paid. I came to the conclusion that this people are not classed with those who act as though they believed *that the ministers are all rich, and especially the Bishops of the Methodist Episcopal Church, who, according to the theory of some, hold all the Church property,* and are "lords over God's heritage." I need not say that this is vile slander, and that when one writes it, or preaches it, he is guilty of "bearing false witness against his neighbour."

The last Sunday in the year 1852, I tried to preach among my old friends, at the Union Methodist Episcopal Church, in Wilmington, Delaware, from "They all with one consent began to make excuse." In the crowd, that night, I saw a dear friend, not religious, much moved. He went home, deeply impressed with the importance of at once giving his heart to God. He said to his pious mother, "I never felt half as much under any sermon I ever heard Brother Manship preach. Mother, I will be religious." It was a late hour that night before he retired, and when he did go to rest, he went in the spirit of prayer. It was well for him he had a praying mother, and wife, the latter of whom I saw converted to God, and took into the church when she was a young girl, in Milford, September, 1845. This friend also had pious sisters. His family was greatly attached to him, and well they might be, for his generosity to his aged parents, and other members of the family, knew no bounds. They had shared his kindness in temporal things, and how eager these pious ones were to be of service to him in spiritual things! Many prayers were offered, and many tears were shed in his behalf. It was my privilege, about this time, to converse freely with him on the interests of his immortal soul. Said he, "I firmly believe in the reality of religion; I want it, and I will have it." A week only elapsed, and this noble son of the ocean, at the helm of his vessel, started with a valuable freight to a prominent port. He had not been at sea very long, before the winds escaped from their prison-house, roaring indignantly at having been confined so long. All was commotion. Behold the frail vessel, exposed to all the fury of the ocean. The weather was excessively cold; the freezing waves and billows go over the captain and his crew. Loud roars Neptune; loud roar the winds; loud, too, snap and crack the cordage and the sails. One or more were swept overboard, to feed the hungry monsters of the deep. When it was evident the vessel must be lost, orders were given to lash themselves in the sails and rigging. The captain was thus well fixed; but seeing one of the crew in a perilous condition, the compassion of his noble heart led him to give the sailor his place, and look out for himself. He made another arrangement for himself, far less likely, however, to secure his safety. One of the crew, looking to that God who is "the confidence of all the ends of the earth, and of them that are afar off, upon the sea," made an effort to reach the shore. Strange to tell, he was successful; but when he gained the beach, though so cold and exhausted, he contrived to bury himself in the sand, and after awhile revived, and proceeded to ask for assistance. The perishing condition of Captain A., and those on board his vessel, led to the launching of a boat into the terrific ocean, as soon as it was deemed possible for it to live, and as soon as the distress could be made known. She leaps from billow to billow—on she dashes. But, alas! when she reaches the unfortunate vessel, the noble Captain A. had just breathed his last. How awful it is to freeze to death! He was there more than twenty-four hours, exposed to the storm that raged furiously. No kind wife, mother, or sisters to administer unto him, but their prayers were going up to Heaven in his behalf. What would have been their distress had they known his lamentable condition! There was, however, an Invisible, Omnipresent Being ready to hear the prayers of those "who go down to the sea in ships, that do business in great waters." The crew heard him praying hour after hour; and he sung (and how appropriate!)—

"Jesus, lover of my soul,
Let me to thy bosom fly;
While the nearer waters roll,
While the tempest still is high.
Hide me, O! my Saviour, hide,
Till the storm of life is past!
Safe unto the haven guide;
O! receive my soul at last!

"Other refuge have I none;
Hangs my helpless soul on thee:
Leave, O leave me not alone;
Still support and comfort me:

The grounds of hope in Captain A.'s death.

All my trust on thee is stayed;
All my help from thee I bring;
Cover my defenceless head
With the shadow of thy wing."

He was brought home a few days thereafter a lifeless corpse. This mournful, unexpected circumstance was too much almost for his parents, wife, and sisters to support themselves under. I went to weep with those who wept; and they would have refused to be comforted, but for the hope they cherished: "Our prayers in his behalf have been heard, and the Lord did receive his soul at last." I owned a burial lot in the "Wilmington and Brandywine Cemetery;" this family were away from their place of burial; an arrangement was made, and my friend, Captain A., occupies the place where I expected myself to repose. My respect for him was great; and my confidence is strong in that scripture: "For he will finish the work, and cut it short in righteousness." The prayers of his pious friends, his own fervent petitions under those solemn circumstances, and the powerful exercise of mind he was under, and his determination to be a Christian just before he went on this fatal voyage, lead me to believe that this friend, who lost his vessel and his life, *saved his soul*, by stepping on the gospel life-boat, which, through God's amazing love, has been launched; Jesus being in the midst of her, guiding her movements. This boat is taking sinners from off the waves that are bearing them on to death, and placing their feet upon the Rock of salvation. What a merciful arrangement! Man is "tossed upon life's stormy billows;" wave after wave rolls him on to destruction; the whirlpool opens wide its mouth to "swallow him whole, as those that go down into the pit." Poor, perishing sinner! I will lay aside figurative language, and call your attention to the passage—and this is our only hope:—"God so loved the world, that he gave his only begotten Son, that whosoever believeth in him should not perish, but have everlasting life."

The little but enterprising society in St. George's, New Castle county, Delaware, had finished a neat brick church, in the winter of 1853. I was associated on the occasion of the dedication with the venerable Bishop Waugh. This house was commenced under the labours of Rev. Elon J. Way, and Rev. John B. Dennison. I was with them when the corner-stone was laid, the preceding summer. There was but a handful in the society, but preachers and people were united. No man worked, literally, on that house with more energy than Rev. John B. Dennison. He is a practical mechanic. My readers will not be surprised at success in this place, when I inform them that the ministers and brethren had the hearty co-operation of the women. One instance of zeal which occurred on the day of dedication I will mention. After we had accomplished apparently all that we could, an aged sister, who was much interested, took the matter in hand. Her object was to get twenty persons to give five dollars each, which would make one hundred dollars. It was strange to see a lady going up and down the aisle; but she accomplished the work. The brick edifice, here completed, and dedicated to the worship of God, was blessed with a gracious outpouring of the Holy Spirit, and the little society was immediately strengthened. The brethren realized the fulfilment of God's word: "They shall not labour in vain." St. George's was exceedingly feeble, Methodistically, when this work was commenced. But they went at it in a right spirit, feeling "except the Lord build the house, they labour in vain that build it."

If such a work could be accomplished there, shall not our societies in other villages and towns feel, we can "do likewise?" And will they allow the cause of the Redeemer to languish by saying, "the old church was good enough for our fathers, and it is good enough for us." Our fathers did nobly in this respect, considering they were few and feeble. But now we are numerous, second to no people in the nation, and have pecuniary ability, and, in many regions, have the influence to accomplish whatever praiseworthy end we may desire. If we do not provide for the people, shall we not be held responsible?—For Methodism is in many places the only religion among them, and through no other instrumentality "have they so much as heard whether there be any Holy Ghost." The little house that answered our purposes forty or fifty years ago, is not now sufficiently capacious. And while there are improvements going forward in everything else, should not our churches be neat and inviting and suitable edifices, and erected in proper places? May we all, preachers and people, feel like David on this subject! Then God's House would have the first claim upon us, and not be a secondary matter. Hear David's expression: "Surely I will not come unto the tabernacle of my house, nor go up into my bed; I will not give sleep to mine eyes, or slumber to my eyelids; until I find out a place for the Lord, an habitation for the mighty God of Jacob."

CHAPTER XI.

I will go in the Strength of the Lord—Nazareth Methodist Episcopal Church, Philadelphia—A young Man flying from the presence of the Lord—The happy End of a Youth—Church Locations a very important matter—Organization of Hedding Church—A little Missionary Station near a Catholic Church—"Have Faith in God"—Enlarge the Borders by pitching Tents—Interesting Incidents in the Tents—Philanthropists and Benefactors advised to build Churches—Rev. David H. Kollock—Future Place of Worship described—A Brother shouts prospectively.

AT the Conference in 1853, which was held in Harrisburg, the capital of Pennsylvania, Bishop Morris presided. I was desired at the "North City Home Mission, Philadelphia." One object that was contemplated, was the building of a church of respectable quality and dimensions. As I had had so much of that kind of work to do, be it spoken to the credit of that kind-hearted superintendent, he refused to appoint me to this field without mentioning the matter to me. He requested me to think of it, and let him know the next day. I did so: I dropped him a short note, in which I said, "In that field I must necessarily look for much labour and perplexity. But this is not our rest; and I am too young a man, and, I trust, too true a Methodist preacher, to refuse to go anywhere: therefore, if you and the council think I am the man for the place, 'in the strength of the Lord I will go.'"

I was appointed to be the successor of Rev. Thomas C. Murphey. This brother had acquitted himself on this field of labour well, and had been successful at several points, especially at the place where the new church was to be erected. Through his instrumentality, at least fifty had been added to the Church. His predecessor, Rev. George Quigley, had laboured at this point successfully, and had loudly called attention to the importance of rising up and building a house for the Lord.

The house in which we preached was comfortable, but it was "a little one." I suppose it would accommodate about one hundred and fifty persons. It was originally built by the Nazareth Methodist Episcopal Church, or more particularly, by the Sunday School of that Church, about the year 1842, and in honour of the parent Church, called "Nazareth No. 2." The original cost was about one thousand dollars. Much credit is due to Nazareth Methodist Episcopal Church for sustaining the gospel here for a series of years. Her pastors and local preachers delighted to face the storms of winter, and encounter the heat of summer, to publish glad tidings of great joy to this then neglected neighbourhood. In order to offer greater facilities to the people of the neighbourhood, the Nazareth brethren several years asked for the appointment of a junior preacher more exclusively for the little Nazareth. Among those who toiled here to cultivate Immanuel's land, was Rev. Robert R. Richardson. He fell in the work, after labouring in this and other fields a few brief years. His end was peaceful. In the winter of 1846–7, I aided Rev. Henry R. Calloway in a protracted meeting at this place. Services here were owned of the Lord. One evening I endeavoured to preach in this little temple. But little as it was, I found God did not despise it; for he was there to convict and convert souls. There was a young man deeply affected. He left the house, and tried hard to shake off his "guilty fears." He returned, if possible, more swiftly than he left, feeling that he could say, "For thine arrows stick fast in me, and thy hand presseth me sore." He pressed into the City of Refuge, feeling the avenger of blood was at his heels.

One of the first things that the people of God attended to here, was the formation of a Sunday School. This grain of mustard-seed has gradually grown; this little leaven is still at work. Through its influence many received their first religious impressions. I know not how many have, by this very agency, escaped the pollutions of the world.

About 1835 or 1836, the Lord put it into the heart of a Christian female to bestir herself, and do what she could to reform the wicked children, by starting a school in Coates Street. She reconnoitered the neighbourhood. While she looked on, she felt compelled to say of the people in the neighbourhood, "The heart of the sons of men is fully set in them to do evil." As she was passing around among the people, she met, greatly to her delight, with a female that knew the Lord. She spent several hours with her. These two Christian women started also a prayer meeting, and many attended; and there were none but the two females referred to, that could pray in public, or take any part in the exercises. Their cry was, "Come over into Macedonia and help us." The Nazareth brethren heeded that cry. Good came out of Nazareth. This beginning, made by the two pious females, who are still living, and ready to say, "Behold," our "eyes have seen thy salvation," led to the erection of "Nazareth No. 2." The good accomplished by this feeble and humble effort, will not be known this side eternity. Some converted here are now in Heaven.

I will give one instance; and if there was not another case, those who laboured in this work, and contributed their means to establish this little place, might truthfully say, "We are repaid, we have not lost our reward." The case I allude to was that of Thomas Willday. He for years attended Sabbath School at this point, and through this instrumentality was brought to God and to Heaven. Young readers, especially Sabbath School scholars, look at Thomas on his death-bed particularly, though only in his fifteenth year. He had been a delicate child from his tenth year; he used to say to the physician, "I shall never get well till I go to the Great Physician;" speaking of the Saviour, he said, "He will cure me." While on his dying-bed he would sing frequently the little hymn, the chorus of which was,

"Then our troubles will be over."

Rev. John Kennaday, D.D., the pastor of Nazareth Methodist Episcopal Church, visited him the day of his death, and asked the dying youth relative to his prospects. He replied, "I am fully prepared; I thank

God, that my parents, and especially my Sunday School teachers, have directed me to the Saviour. I am at the edge of the river, and the waters do not affright me." The minister inquired, "Do you think, Thomas, your faith will carry you through?" "Yes; Jesus is there to receive me." He called all around him, and said, "I see, I see the city of light; the host is come, and the chariot is waiting." He then sung,

"Hark! hark! my Lord, my Lord and Master calls me;
All is well, all is well;
I soon shall see, shall see his face in glory;
All is well, all is well.

"Farewell, my friends, adieu, adieu,
I can no longer stay with you,
My glittering crown appears in view;
All is well, all is well."

Thus this Sunday School scholar passed away. Young reader, may you and I likewise be honoured in our closing scene, and be promoted from the Sabbath School on earth, to the *higher* school in Heaven, where we shall increase in heavenly knowledge; "Now I know in part; but then shall I know even as I am known."

The first day I spent on the mission, I officiated at "Hedding" Church; for this was now the name of "Nazareth No. 2." This change was made after it became an appointment on the "North City Mission," and in honour of Bishop Hedding, who is now dead, but his "works do follow him." The last time he presided in our (Philadelphia) Conference, I heard him say in substance: "I have been an Itinerant Methodist preacher for about fifty years; I have endured hardness; often been persecuted and slandered; but, if I had my life to live over again, I would sooner be a poor Itinerant minister in the Methodist Episcopal Church, than anything else—yes, I would be, if I thought I should die in a ditch." These words fell from his lips with great weight, and sunk deeply into our hearts. When I found the church that was to be built was to bear his name, I was much pleased; for such a man as Rev. Elijah Hedding is rarely met with, and "shall be in everlasting remembrance." I told my little flock that the borders must be enlarged, and there was no time to be lost; the sooner we commenced the better. I asked that *one thousand dollars should* that day be raised, as a begining towards effecting this important work. This was pledged; and, what was truly interesting in the evening service, there were several seeking religion, and one precious soul happily set at liberty. This we all felt was a good Sabbath, and "a day's march nearer home." An important step was now to be taken, viz. procuring a lot on which to erect the structure which had been for some time contemplated. Several lots had been spoken of; barriers were thrown in the way; but finally, it was deemed judicious to purchase a lot of "St. George's

Methodist Episcopal Church." The lot fronts on a main street, viz. Sixteenth, south of Coates. This street is wide, and fine improvements have succeeded the church arrangement. This always is the case, and it speaks in language that we cannot misunderstand, in favour of Christianity. This, were I a property-holder in a neighbourhood where a church of the right grade was to be built, would induce me, if there was no other consideration, to aid in its erection. Who wants to live in a Christian land where there are no facilities for spiritual improvement? And where they are at command, who does not know that the value of property is very considerably enhanced?

We were led to settle on the "St. George's" lot, because we would then be at a considerable distance from any other church, of our own or any other denomination; because it was to be had on much more reasonable terms than any other in the neighbourhood; and because the people most generally wanted it there, and we firmly believed that their reverence for their dead all around it, would lead them to aid us in paying for it. And I do positively assert, that not only hundreds of our own denomination have expressed their approval and great pleasure at the location, but not a few of other denominations, ministers and members, have borne their testimony in favour of the location;

and all unite in saying, it is "beautiful for situation." The last argument, though not the least, that I shall present, to prove that it is rightly located, is, that the people from every quarter delight to flock to the standard of the cross, planted on this consecrated spot, and that already it has been said in hundreds of instances, "This and that man was born in her; and the Highest himself shall establish her."

When we consummated the lot business, and saw the light dawning, we were all inspired with strong hope that we should be able to accomplish the work, which was certainly likely to be arduous, provided we could have the entire time of a pastor, to co-operate energetically with the society. Hedding Church had already its separate Board of Trustees, the mission only providing for the support of the ministry while they officiated here and at other points. The field was too wide to do justice to all points; and, as there was to be a large church erected, the Hedding Board of Trustees and the society unanimously asked the "Missionary Board" to allow them to be disconnected from them, and to have the *entire services* of a pastor, whom they thought they could by a strong effort support. This important change was calmly, and in a Christian-like manner, discussed in the Missionary Board, and though the members of the board saw, as plainly as the brethren of Hedding society, the necessity of having the entire services of a minister devoted to that point, yet they were fearful of a *failure*, not only in carrying the Church enterprise to a successful issue, but also in regard to the ability of this infant church to support a pastor. Still, having a desire to adopt the best means for the accomplishment of the greatest amount of good, they resolved in the right spirit, to acquiesce in the proposal made by "Hedding Society," provided the proper church authorities would sanction the course. The regular steps were taken to lead the appointing power to make the proposed alteration; and, after due consideration, Bishop Morris, who was the proper superintendent to act in this case—for he made the original appointment at the preceding Conference—approved the measure, which however was carried out by Rev. Joseph Castle, Presiding Elder of the District, who was on the ground, and understood fully the merits of the case. Accordingly, by proper ecclesiastical authority, "Hedding Church" was made a distinct charge, on the 9th day of August, 1853, and I was appointed pastor of the "little flock;" and at the same time, another brother, Rev. Mr. Nixon, was appointed to the supervision of the "North City Home Mission." I should not do my duty, if I were not to say, that, in this transaction, the most fraternal spirit pervaded the different meetings which were held on this business, and that the "Missionary Board" unanimously agreed that "Hedding Church" should have the use of their parsonage furniture until the following spring, as the missionary, who succeeded me, did not need it.

As this arrangement was made, my stay on the mission was a brief one. I found the field difficult, but vastly important—the work consisting in holding little meetings in upper rooms, and out-of-the-way places, preaching and exhorting to a little company of saints and sinners, and, as opportunity offers, scattering tracts from house to house. How precious! these are leaves shaken off the Tree of Life. They speak where the living minister cannot. Let them be disseminated everywhere. Here is not only a fine field for the brethren, but also for our Marys and Lydias, who have "chosen the good part," and whose hearts "the Lord" hath "opened." This class of the Church were helpers to the great Apostle Paul: "*Those women, which laboured with me in the gospel.*" I am glad that the Methodist Episcopal Church is waking up to the importance of the tract cause, in saving souls. I saw some good accomplished on the mission in this way. This cause will save its thousands and tens of thousands. I was much interested with the Mission Schools. One of them, formed by one of my predecessors, from the force of circumstances had been disbanded, but the Lord raised up a man in that location, though not a member of any Church, who took an unfinished house on his own responsibility, and used his best endeavours to perpetuate the existence of this cause in the neighbourhood. I tried my utmost to encourage him in his work, reported the effort to the Board, and they encouraged me to do what I could for that populous, but mostly Roman Catholic district. Their Church was most extensive, and the minister thereof appeared to think he was "Lord of all he surveyed, his right there was none to dispute." And like Goliah of old, he was disposed to "defy the armies of the living God." This little Methodist missionary station was aroused, and ready to ask, David-like, "Who is this uncircumcised Philistine, that he should defy the armies of the living God?" We began to sing; we could not make such exquisite music with our uncultivated voices, as a well-trained orchestra, which they had at a heavy expense. They must have *something* to attract. And while they chanted, and we heard peal after peal from the deep-toned organ, we tried to lift up our voices like a trumpet, and fulfil the command, "the great trumpet shall be blown;" and we also sung with earnestness—

"O! for a trumpet voice,
On all the world to call!
To bid their hearts rejoice
In him who died for all.
For all, my Lord was crucified;
For all, for all, my Saviour died."

This little band was ready to say, "Let no man's heart fail because of him; thy servants will go and fight with this Philistine." But the Methodists were "disdained;" and the enemy was ready to say, "Am I a dog, that thou comest to me with staves?" The means that we use in triumphing in every place are very simple; we will not fight the enemy with Saul's armour, but the sword of the Spirit, and the shield of faith, and other weapons that are despised. David's faith and God's providence carried him in this conflict triumphantly through, and fulfilled his fearless declaration: "This day will the Lord deliver thee into mine hand; and I will smite thee, and take thine head from thee; and I will give the carcasses of the host of the Philistines this day unto the fowls of the air, and to the wild beasts of the earth; that all the earth may know that there is a God in Israel." Victory after victory has perched upon the banners of the Church of the Lord Jesus Christ. We verily believed, then, that in that hard field the tree of Methodism would be planted; "and this is the victory that overcometh the world, even our faith." Christ will "reign and triumph." There is many a battle yet to be fought, but the Lion of the tribe of Judah shall conquer. "These shall make war with the Lamb, and the Lamb shall overcome them; for he is Lord of lords, and King of kings; and they that are with him are called, and chosen, and faithful."

The worthy man who held on to the Sunday School cause in this neighbourhood with an unflinching hand, was one of the first to join our little society, which was reorganized while I was on the mission. This little band has considerably increased in numerical strength and influence; and they are building a house for the Lord, on the same street where the spacious cathedral stands, which, in size and quality, will be second to but few in our city, of our denomination. This little missionary station also has become a regular self-sustaining charge, with its own pastor, labouring to complete the stately edifice. The foreign missionary work is glorious, but the home department must not be neglected. And, in view of all the circumstances, the Protestant community in our city ought to feel a holy ambition in accomplishing this great work, and in opening an effectual door for the preaching of the pure gospel. The ministers of the word, and God's people here, should not only say to sinners, but to Roman Catholics, kindly: "Come thou with us, and we will do thee good; for the Lord hath spoken good concerning Israel." Many of them would accept the invitation. This would be a great salvation.

On the day we were organized into a distinct charge, we entered into a contract to have a church built at a cost of about *thirteen thousand dollars.* This amount was independent of the ground. We could scarcely tell where the money was to come from. I thought of an incident in the Life of Rev. John Wesley, which is as follows:—

"In one of his tours through England, Mr. Wesley stopped for a day and night in a small town where the members of the church were comparatively few and feeble, and worshipped God in a private house. As was his custom in all his journeyings, he gathered them together, and preached to them. Early in the morning he arose and walked through the town, for the purpose of selecting a suitable site for a chapel. He fixed upon a lot occupied by an old frame building. After ascertaining it could be purchased, he sought out a master mechanic, who had been recommended to him as a worthy and responsible man. He requested him to examine the premises, and to let him know the cost of clearing them, and erecting a chapel of the dimensions and character he gave him. The workman made the calculation, and assured him it would cost, including the land, one thousand pounds. Mr. Wesley directed him at once to proceed with the work, and have it done in a specified time. The gentleman accepted the offer of the work, and requested to be informed to whom he should look weekly for any amount of funds he might need to pay his hands, remarking, that he supposed Mr. Wesley had means sufficient to leave with some authorized agent. Mr. Wesley assured him he had no money himself, but that he must proceed at once with the work, and 'have faith in God.' The funds necessary would doubtless be provided as they were needed.

"The workman told Mr. Wesley it would not do for him to undertake the work without knowing on whom he could rely for the money, as he might need it. Mr. Wesley told him that all that was necessary was to 'have faith in God.' 'Faith in God,' said the builder, 'may answer you in your course, but in this case it will not answer my purpose, inasmuch as it will not pay off my hands at the end of each week, when they call upon me for what may be due them.' While thus engaged in conversation, on the site where the chapel was to be built, a venerable Quaker gentleman, who knew Mr. Wesley, stopped and accosted him by saying, 'Good morning, Friend Wesley, I hope thou art well.' 'Quite well,' replied Mr. Wesley. 'Friend John,' said the old gentleman, 'I had a singular dream about thee, last night.' 'Ah?' said Mr. Wesley, 'what was it?' 'I dreamed there was under thy charge, in this town, a small flock of sheep, and that they had no fold for their protection, and were suffering greatly from wolves, and dangers arising from other sources. I think, Friend John, thy people should be provided with a meeting-house, in which they may worship, and be secure.' Mr. Wesley assured him he was of the same opinion, and was at that moment in treaty with the workman then present, for the erection of such a chapel as he thought the necessities of the case required. 'I am pleased to hear it, Friend John,' replied the old gentleman. 'How much will it cost thee?' 'One thousand pounds,' said Mr. Wesley. Extending his hand, he said, 'Friend John, take this, it will aid thee in the accomplishment of thy purpose. Farewell.' When Mr. Wesley examined the paper, he found it to be a draft, upon the old gentleman himself, for eight hundred pounds. Mr. Wesley showed it to the astonished workman, and said, 'Did I not tell you to have faith in God, and the funds would be provided?' On Mr. Wesley's arrival in London, he found a letter from the same gentleman, containing a draft for two hundred pounds additional, the whole amount necessary to complete the chapel."

This circumstance encouraged me to hope we should be able to raise the means as they were required. We felt, *what ought to be done can be done*, and we had "faith in God." While we had faith in God, we all thought of the teaching of the Scripture, "What doth it profit, my brethren, though a man say he hath faith, and have not works?" Preacher and people well knew that, to accomplish this most desirable end, and to fulfil our contract, which was heavy for a handful of feeble members, we must have "a mind to work."

On the 11th of September, 1853, the work was so far advanced as to enable us to lay the corner-stone. The weather being warm, we arranged to have tents pitched on the adjacent lot, to protect the people from the heat of the sun; and we provided seats for the accommodation of a very large audience, and published through the papers of the city, and otherwise, our plan of operation, heading our advertisement with "To your tents, O Israel!" The meeting was largely attended. The principal address was delivered by Bishop Waugh, and the corner-stone laid by that good man. His address and labours told on the hearts of the people, and as their hearts were warm, great liberality was manifested. In this important respect, our most sanguine hopes were more than realized. There were suitable articles, such as the Bible, Hymn Book, Discipline, and "Christian Advocate and Journal," placed in the corner-stone, and last, though not least, the names of all the children connected with the Sabbath School of the church. We felt this will attach them to this sacred spot, and it was our hope that this course would create, in their tender hearts, a respect and love for the "habitation of" God's "house" that would grow with their growth, and strengthen with their strength. The Church should use every proper means in saying, "Come, ye children, hearken unto me, I will teach you the fear of the Lord."

At night (being Thursday night), we held meeting under the tents, for a twofold purpose. First, to increase our subscription list, which we did, to something over *two thousand dollars.* Secondly, to labour for the salvation of souls. Our meeting was so well attended, that we gave out for the next day—afternoon and night. On Saturday we had an addition of tents, working till just twelve o'clock at night to get ready, and on Sunday, 14th of September, 1853, we had accommodations for at least *two thousand persons.* Our places were all occupied, and hundreds, if not thousands in attendance, that could not procure seats. Excellent order prevailed throughout the day, except in the morning service some son of Belial threw at us, in the pulpit, with considerable violence, about a pound of soap; it struck one of the posts of our large camp-meeting-like stand, and fell harmless at our feet. I presume the intention was to do us injury. I remarked, "This is likely to turn out to advantage. If I am spared, I shall take this home with me, and as to-morrow is wash-day, I shall place it in the hands of the washerwoman, with instructions to wash out linens that I shall soil this day in trying to get just such hardened wretches converted to God." We remained in the tents for nearly three weeks. In the mean time the equinoctial storm came upon us, and just after a large and very happy meeting was dismissed, and all the people had made their exit, the tents were blown down, with a considerable crash. Had this taken place an hour sooner, limbs might have been broken, and possibly some one killed. Another circumstance, which took place during the tent meeting, and which leads me to believe in a special Providence, I will mention. One evening, while the prayer meeting was in progress, the large stand was occupied by the singers. I presume there were in it, at the time, at least thirty or forty persons. A little boy was asleep, under the stand, and the pressure on the floor causing it to give way, the bottom of the stand, with thirty or forty persons on it, came down upon the little sleeper. I was much alarmed; for I feared the result. I inquired, "Is anybody hurt?" There was a vociferous reply, "No, blessed be God, not a bone is broken, not a hair of any one's head hurt." "Ye are of more value than many sparrows."

In the presence of perhaps three thousand persons, in and about our tents, one of the Sabbath afternoons while our tent arrangement was the order of the day, an interesting young lady came forward to our humble altar, and meekly knelt down upon the straw, and earnestly sought for "peace." It was not long before she realized the evidence that God hath power on earth to forgive sin, and felt from the heart she could sing—

> "The smilings of thy face,
> How amiable they are!
> 'Tis Heaven to rest in thine embrace,
> And nowhere else but there.

"Thou art the sea of love,
Where all my pleasures roll;
The circle where my passions move,
And centre of my soul."

This young lady's parents were not favourable to Methodism, and her profession of religion in this place was so offensive to them that she either had to renounce the meeting and Methodism, or leave home. Of the two evils she chose the latter, (if it was an evil!) and took leave of her father's house. And, strange to tell, her mother was more antagonistic than the father; but the girl had faith to believe that the Lord would provide, and in her Bible she read, for her comfort in this hour that tried her soul, "When father and mother forsake me, then the Lord will take me up." She had not been in exile long before her mother was taken sick, and that sickness ended in death. How great the change, and how soon did she require that E—— should come home! She was not only ready to ask pardon for the course she had pursued, but desired her daughter to pray for her. The affection of that child was never so strong before for her mother. She wept over her parent; she spent days and nights in prayer that her mother might be prepared to meet her God. She was a prevailing Israel. Under the circumstances, she had more influence with her mother than any other person could have had. This child was used as God's instrument in the salvation of her mother. And awhile before the mother closed her eyes on all terrestrial things she said to her, "I commit the younger children to your care; raise them right, and to love and serve the Lord." Dear reader, under all circumstances "be kind to thy mother." "Honour thy father and thy mother, that thy days may be long in the land which the Lord thy God giveth thee."

I hope, young reader, if you should, upon embracing religion among the Methodists, or elsewhere, be opposed, you will be firm, as was the young lady referred to. And if it is necessary, *sooner leave your own father's house*, "forsake all," rather than "cast away your confidence." You will be brought back again, and be the bright star to guide your parents, and the entire family, to the haven of repose. The young lady of whom I have been writing is still happy in religion, and, as my readers might suppose, useful in the church, of which she is a burning and a shining light.

It is said in God's Word, "Woe to him that striveth with his Maker." There was, one night, a strife in our tents, when this scripture forcibly presented itself to my mind. The circumstances were as follows:—A young lady was at our altar, seeking the Lord very ardently; her mother, who was very indignant towards "the people called Methodists," heard what was going on; she came into our meeting much excited, and said to me, "You have my daughter down there," pointing to the mourners' bench, "and I want her out as soon as possible." I did my utmost to induce her to let her alone. I told her, she was very sincere, and it would be very wrong to remove her. An influential gentleman, not a member of any church, saw the state of the case, and he united with me in persuading the furious mother to be calm, and not to think of removing the young woman. Said I to her, "If you will not hear me on this matter, hear Mr. T——." She was more than ever excited, and said, "I don't care for any man, I will have her; and if you don't give her to me at once, I will go home, and get the *old man*, and we will take her by force." She went, sure enough, like an arrow flying through the air. I went into the centre of the meeting, took my stand upon a bench, and elevated my voice as much as possible. The case was fairly stated; and I said to the brethren, who were all deeply interested, "If ever you prayed in faith, do it now; if possible, before the old people get here to bear off the young woman, we will have her converted, and then she will work her way." I never in all my life saw a greater disposition to conquer—such praying I never heard before. It was effectual; just as the opposing parents made their appearance, the blessing came, the shout of the new-born soul was heard; the daughter sustained a new relation; she was adopted that moment, and could say,

"With confidence I now draw nigh,
And *Father*, Abba *Father* cry."

Her Heavenly Father gave her "good things." Such things she never realized before. The old folks looked on with amazement, but did not lay hands on her. In this we see the fulfilment of the word of the Lord, "Every one that asketh receiveth; and he that seeketh findeth; and to him that knocketh, it shall be opened."

The meetings were earnestly conducted, and I felt it my duty then, as at other times, to adhere to the direction, "Remove not the ancient landmark, which thy fathers have set." In order to carry forward our enterprise, and in order to make this world a Paradise, I believe that extensive, thorough, and numerous revivals of religion are requisite. We felt willing to have a revival here in God's way. It is too frequent that we want revivals in our own style. "There must be no deep sighs, heavy groans, loud songs, fervent prayers, awful sermons, rousing exhortations; and, above all, there must be no shouting; for this is confusion." My doctrine is, if he "come in the sweet still voice," Amen! if "in the fire," Amen! if "in the whirlwind," Amen! if "in the earthquake," my soul says, Amen! In my heart, I wish all the people would say, Amen! especially all our Methodist people. Then I think, "they that wait upon the Lord shall renew their strength; they shall mount up with wings as eagles;

they shall run and not be weary; and they shall walk and not faint." And soon the happy day would roll on, when "the wilderness and the solitary place shall be glad for them; and the desert shall rejoice, and blossom as the rose."

The pitching of the tents at the corner of Sixteenth and Coates Streets, and the revival of religion that followed, were events not soon to be forgotten. Near this spot are the *State's Prison* and *House of Refuge*, and, formerly, near this place *criminals used to be hung;* and here the *military* used to encamp, and be disciplined and reviewed. These things have called out the co-operation of the talent, wealth, and influence of the great of our state and country. And what have they done? How many have our expensive "Houses of Refuge," and our "Penitentiary," near us, reformed? I would not be considered as arraying myself against them. They are necessary, in the present state of society. But this spiritual work is above all. It is true, in our enterprise, we could not boast of "many wise men after the flesh, not many mighty, not many noble;" and, emphatically, many considered this arrangement for purposes of salvation "foolish" and "weak." Nevertheless, about *one hundred* souls, during our tent meetings, were saved by the "foolishness of preaching." And who can tell where it will stop? "As the pebble, dropped into the lake, puts its waters into motion, and circle rises after circle, till all is stirred, and the whole borders around are bathed by the waters"—so, we think, this gospel beginning, though small at first, and despised by many in the neighbourhood, has proved the means of an *excitement*, which shall grow and increase, from person to person, and from place to place, and from age to age, until the influence shall reach eternity itself, and encircle the throne of God with a halo of glory. If the gospel of Jesus Christ could be preached everywhere, and if the people could everywhere in our land be brought to "bow to the sceptre of his word," the founding of Penitentiaries and Houses of Refuge would not be requisite; for there would be none to occupy them. And the death-warrant of a fellow-citizen would never again be signed, or a gallows ever erected for the purpose of dealing out death to the murderer. If the gospel can have a general sway, then the "trump of the warrior and the clangour of arms will never be heard to echo on our mountains, or in our valleys; garments dyed in blood will for ever pass away." May the day come, speedily, when the "everlasting gospel" shall be preached "unto them that dwell on the earth, and to every nation, and kindred, and tongue, and people!" Then our armies might be disbanded, and a general rally take place under the banner of Him who said, "My kingdom is not of this world. If my kingdom were of this world, then would my servants fight."

It would be well for philanthropists and benefactors

to inquire, How can we most efficiently, with our means, ameliorate the condition of our fellow-men, and bring about a state of pure morals? How can we raise the fallen and cheer the faint? I would answer, One of the most effectual ways is, to aid the cause of "*church extension.*" Let these "bulwarks of our land" be reared in every proper place, and let the pure gospel be faithfully proclaimed. And let measures be adopted to convince the "poor" and the "outcasts" that they are welcome, and that it is desired that they should, with their wives and children, "assemble themselves together" at the house of prayer. What changes in the moral aspect of affairs take place speedily in every location where this course is pursued! The gospel can effect what other things *fail to accomplish.* This may be represented in a striking light by a verse of one of our hymns:—

"But something yet can do the deed,
And that blest something much I need;
Thy spirit can from dross refine,
And melt and change this heart of mine."

The ministers, both local and travelling, aided me in this camp meeting, as it was called by some of the city papers, who took occasion to speak of our affairs, not, however, in a disrespectful manner. I do not think any preacher did me more efficient service than Rev. David H. Kollock, of this city, who has since crossed the stream of Jordan. For more than a quarter of a century this beloved brother did "the work of an evangelist." I had the pleasure of forming his acquaintance in the summer of 1840, at a watering place, before I was a minister of the gospel. I observed him closely; he was not there "ashamed of the gospel." He preached in the church of our denomination with uncommon power. I thought to myself that that brother could with propriety say, "The zeal of thine house hath eaten me up." I found him ever after the same faithful labourer in "the vineyard of the Lord." The sermons he preached in our tent meetings surpassed any for effect I ever heard him preach—not a few were convicted. And not only in this place, but elsewhere, his labours were profitable. He "turned many to righteousness." The Church sustained a great loss when he fell a victim to death, but our loss is his gain. He could say with Paul, "For to me to live is Christ, and to die is gain." This event took place May 12, 1855. Awhile before the time of his departure arrived, a friend said, "Brother Kollock, this is a severe ordeal you are passing through." His reply was, "Yes, but the grace of God is all sufficient." He frequently said, as the cancer was doing its work, "All is well, all is well." His pastor, Rev. M. D. Kurtz, informed me he was frequently with him. Among his last visits, he asked him, "Do you find the Saviour precious?" He answered, "I do." The passage was quoted, "Yea, though I pass through the valley of the shadow of death, I will fear no evil, for thou art with me; thy rod and thy staff they comfort me." He could scarcely then articulate, but looked at his pastor, and assented. He tried, in the hour of death, after calling his children to him, to exhort them to meet him in Heaven. And now he is gone. The struggles of reluctant nature are over. The body sleeps in death; the soul has launched into the invisible state, surrounded by guardian angels instead of weeping friends. The vale of tears is left behind. Farewell, for ever, the realms of woe. No doubt he has safely arrived on the frontiers of inexpressible felicity. The funeral was largely attended; he was generally esteemed. Business in the part of Philadelphia where he resided, to a considerable extent was suspended. Rev. Francis Hodson, D.D., and Rev. Thomas T. Tasker, officiated. The latter had been intimately associated with him for many years, and knew him well. Among other things, he said, "I do not believe Rev. David H. Kollock ever preached a sermon, or offered a public prayer, but that the convicting power of the Holy Spirit accompanied those efforts to some poor sinner's heart."

The weather becoming cool, we found it necessary to strike our tents, and make other arrangements for future toils and triumphs, until we could get the new church completed, the corner-stone of which had recently been laid. The plan that we adopted will be seen in the following chapter. The last night we held meeting in the tents, the plan of our future place of worship was pointed out. Some thought it was impossible; but one faithful brother shouted prospectively, and came to me, and said, "Brother Manship, I see it by faith, now. Glory! Glory!!"

> "Faith lends its realizing light,
> The clouds disperse, the shadows fly;
> The Invisible appears in sight,
> And God is seen by mortal eye."

CHAPTER XII.

"Plank Temporary Hedding Church"—Difficulties to be surmounted —The Work completed in *ten days*—Dedicated by Rev. John Hersey—Wanted one to cover an Acre of Ground—A noble Bequest by a coloured Man—Rich Members should remember the Church in their Wills—Names given to our temporary Church—Mrs. Palmer—Gas-lights suddenly go out—Husbands, love your Wives —German Infidel wants to drag his Wife from the Altar—Not much Difficulty in Revival Work, with Men of Reason—Revival carried on through Christmas Holidays—Nine Sermons at the Dedication—Missionary Meeting—James Stewart "Crossing Jordan"—"Out of the Eater came forth Meat, out of the Strong came forth Sweetness"—My first Donation to a Church—Saint Peter's Church in Reading—Bishop Ames.

AS my readers will naturally conclude, there was at this place much religious interest. A large congregation had been meeting here from time to time, and as the revival work had been going on, the people eagerly desired to worship with us. The new church would not be ready for use, as it related to the main part, under twelve months; and the little church only held about one hundred and fifty. What must be done? was the natural inquiry. It was in my heart "To build an house for the name of the Lord God of Israel." My proposal to the brethren was to let the house be plank; in dimensions to be about forty by one hundred feet. A number of difficulties were presented; it was thought it would be burnt down. I told them we would have it insured, and, Phœnix-like, another would arise from its ashes. It was thought, as it was against the law to rear frame houses, we could not get a permit. We were soon relieved of this difficulty, as there were good men in the Board of Commissioners who took an interest in our welfare, and through their agency we had the privilege to proceed. It was thought those who owned the land would not allow us the privilege to locate this temporary house. Be it spoken to the credit of the "St. George's Board of Trustees," the request for the use of the ground was unanimously granted. Some members of the "Hedding Board of Trustees" thought they could not conscientiously go into this arrangement; supposing that the community would charge them with a foolish outlay of money. I told the brethren I did not wonder that they hesitated; for many, even of the members of the Methodist Episcopal Church, would regard this as a piece of folly; but I told them, it was the only thing, in our weak state, with such heavy liabilities upon us, that would save us; and, as I was deeply concerned in the success of the enterprise, I should, if necessary, buy the lumber on my own responsibility. Three gentlemen of our Board united, however, with me, viz. John Miller, Morris Morris, and Abner F. Old; and we purchased the lumber, and called for volunteers to aid in the erection of the "Temporary Hedding Methodist Episcopal Church." There were, some days, as many as forty employed, some with their mallets and chisels, some with their saws and planes. Much of the work was done gratuitously. Mr. Rifford R. Hollowell was the supervisor of the work. This matter was so energetically prosecuted, that in *ten days*, it was accomplished in a workmanlike manner. Gas and fixtures being introduced, all things being ready, the arrangement was made to have it solemnly dedicated to the worship of Almighty God, on the 16th of October, 1853.

The dedication services were performed by Rev. John Hersey. We had a plain house, and a very plain minister, who preached so plainly, that the "wayfaring men, though fools," could readily understand. Brother Hersey was very happy in his labours that day. His sermons proved him to be no novice in the Holy

Scriptures. I never saw a more attentive audience. The meetings were very large, and, at the evening service, several were at the altar, and, at least, two professed to obtain religion. My poor heart was greatly cheered to see so many attend. No more attended, however, than I expected, as my readers will perceive from the following interview and conversation, that took place between myself and a brother in the ministry, while we were building the temporary house. Said he, "Brother Manship, what is the use of building the house so large? Do you suppose the people in Philadelphia will attend preaching in such a place as this?" I replied, "Most assuredly I expect them to fill the house. I deeply regret we have not more ground; we are, as you see, occupying every inch we can; and if we had an acre, and were to build a Methodist Church of this description to cover it entirely, it would be filled." He replied, "You have more faith and enthusiasm than I have." But what has the sequel proved? The reader will see by perusing this narrative.

Many interesting circumstances may be mentioned in connexion with this plain house, which stood exactly twelve months, and in which meetings were continued, with but little intermission, during the entire year; and during that year, memorable in the history of "Hedding Methodist Episcopal Church," at least *five or six hundred souls* were happily converted.

We were glad to get help in our beginning from any quarter; and I wish to mention the services of an aged, but active and industrious coloured man, by the name of Saulsbury. He hauled the lumber for the "Plank Church," as he kept a horse and cart, and took a deep interest in our welfare. About the time the house was finished, he was taken ill, and he soon died, and I delivered a funeral discourse to a large audience. This faithful coloured man, on his dying bed, bequeathed to the Plank Church committee the sum of five dollars! Soon after his burial, his widow paid it in gold, baptizing it with her tears. We did not wish to take it, but she insisted upon it, and said, "It was his last wish, and she desired to carry it out." Has not this simple-hearted coloured man set an example worthy of imitation? How comparatively few, of the many able members of the Methodist Episcopal Church, in making their wills, think of that church, that has been, in many cases, the means of making their estates; but give a direction to their property, which leads to its being "wasted with riotous living."

Among the thousands that attended this remarkable church, as we might reasonably suppose, many attended that were disposed to apply hard names to our place of worship. Some for sport called it the "*Crystal Palace*;" and others called it, while they saw persons getting converted, "*The Plank Road to heaven.*" The people of God also would piously give it names. I have heard it called, "Noah's Ark." There was force, I thought, in this name. When Noah was constructing his huge building, many thought, he is beside himself, what is the use of building such a mammoth vessel to sail on dry land? The "Plank Church" was called the "*Life Boat.*" Many a perishing soul was rescued and saved by it. No name that I heard applied to it, however, pleased me better, than the one given by Rev. Thomas J. Quigley; when he preached in it, and saw the many there, that wished to learn of Jesus, he said, "Brother Manship, I think the '*Central Salvation Seminary*' is a most appropriate name for your church."

We were favoured with the presence and labours of Mrs. Palmer, of New York. She attracted much attention, as it was uncommon to hear a lady speak in public. She spoke with great modesty; so much so, if I had been previously a little prejudiced, that feeling would all have passed away. Her views on *sanctification* were simple, and easily comprehended. Many were ready to say, through her labours among us,

> "O! for a closer walk with God!
> A calm and heavenly frame;
> A light to shine upon the road
> That leads me to the Lamb."

I found this Christian lady not only ready to work in this way, but she was efficient in pointing the penitent to the Lamb of God. In company with her, my wife, and others, I spent an afternoon at the house of a hotel-keeper. His wife was pious, and I was intimate with the family. I always had felt much timidity in pressing religious matters upon the gentleman of the house, who was a very kind man, and did not throw any obstructions in the way of his family on matters of conscience and religion. At the tea-table, Mrs. Palmer felt it her duty to urge him to give his heart to God, and that very night to go to the church and put in his plea for mercy. I shuddered; I was apprehensive of an eruption; I feared, as she was a stranger to him, her feelings might be wounded. I was agreeably disappointed. When the time came to depart, I sung a hymn, and called on Mrs. Palmer to pray. I think it likely that *that prayer* made an impression that will never, as long as memory lasts, be effaced. When she gave him the parting hand, he said, "I have been much pleased with your visit; I believe in your piety; and, if ever you come this way again, believe me, I shall be very glad to see you. I will think of what you have said to me." "Blessed are ye that sow beside all waters."

The second Sunday night that we spent in the *Plank Church*, was a memorable time, in more ways than one. Many were in attendance; a house was never more densely crowded. The altar was filled with penitents; and, in the midst of the prayer meeting, a lady sitting in her seat, about midway the house, was suddenly and most powerfully converted. She arose in the greatest ecstasy, and praised the Lord for the great things which he had done for her. She was the daughter of one of our oldest and best members; much interest was felt in her case, and "all partook the glorious bliss." And in the midst of our triumph, as quick as thought, the gas-lights were extinguished, and we were left in total darkness. There were, perhaps, from twelve to fourteen hundred persons pressed into our chapel. Some were shouting, some were crying for mercy. Persons, in some instances, were much terrified; they concluded an enemy had done it. But it was purely accidental; the fluid had leaked out of the meter, or exhausted itself in some way; and, as soon as it was filled up, our lights resumed their brilliancy. The darkness remained for about five or ten minutes; the singing went steadily on at the altar, and, in the mean time, two souls were brought out of *darkness* into *light*. They could joyfully say, God "hath shined in our hearts, to give the light of the knowledge of the glory of God in the face of Jesus Christ." There were several Roman Catholics there, that night, from the Emerald Isle; one or two, I was informed, affrighted, leaped out of one of the windows. A friend of mine took a seat in the midst of them; they were females; there was a great panic among them, and mistaking my friend for one of their company, she was laid hold of with much eagerness, and addressed as follows: "And, Biddy, is this you? this must be the devil's works." I suppose they concluded they were very near purgatory. In a little while the agitation was over, and God's people could sing,

"In darkest shades, if thou appear,
My dawning is begun;
Thou art my soul's bright morning star,
And thou my rising sun.

"The opening heavens around me shine
With beams of sacred bliss,
If Jesus shows his mercy mine,
And whispers I am his."

In our Plank Church meetings, there were persons that attended that would not have thought of attending a Methodist meeting in a regular city church; and occasionally we had, among others, a Roman Catholic converted to God. A very valuable man of this persuasion experienced with us the "peace of God, which passeth all understanding." He found his wife a great barrier. She would, if she had an opportunity, destroy his hymn book and Bible; and did everything in her power to keep him away from the class meeting, and other Methodist meetings. The last time I conversed with him, he informed me he experienced much difficulty, owing to her disposition to hide his clothes, and thus keep him away from church. He also stated to me, however, that she said:

"Henry, your Methodist religion makes you a better husband." May this brother, or any other brother in similar circumstances, *never* say, "I have married a wife, and cannot come!" I say you can come, in a free country; and you can, by being faithful and persevering, bring your wife with you. The apostle says, "Husbands, love your wives." And shall we not give an evidence of our love by exerting all our power, in the name of the Lord, in converting them from the superstitions of the Church of Rome?

I saw a lady converted in the Plank Church one night, greatly to the annoyance of her wicked husband, who came there to drag her from the altar, if she went to it. Notwithstanding his threat, she did go. And, be it spoken to his shame, he undertook to carry his purpose into execution. He was a German infidel. I saw him coming towards her; he was very angry. I spoke to him as one having authority. Said I to him, "I am the captain of this ship, and you can't have this penitent yet awhile." I took him down to the door, and reasoned with him. He said, "It is hard a man can't control his own wife." I told him, in matters of religion and conscience, he had no right to interfere. He threatened to use harsh means. I said, "If you do, you are a demon in human shape. Still, she should not fear you; 'fear not them which kill the body, but are not able to kill the soul; but rather fear him which is able to destroy both soul and body in hell.' " While our conversation was going on, she was happily converted, and leaped and shouted all over the house. He was in a great rage; I felt for her, and in my heart desired, almost, that she could take wings "like a dove," and "fly away and be at rest." After awhile, I exhorted her to go along with him. As she passed out, she said, "Pray for me! pray for me!!" They went down Coates Street, the furious husband cursing and swearing, and using abusive language towards her and the Methodists; but she went rejoicing, filled with glory and with God. "Can two walk together, except they be agreed?" She joined our Church, but had to do it in a clandestine manner, this unfeeling husband watching her like one who "doth hunt a partridge in the mountains." "Some men use their wives as farmers' girls do split brooms; when new, they only sweep the parlour with them; then the kitchen; then scrub with them; then take them for oven-brooms; and, when the splits are burnt off, they use them for cow knockers. O! shame, where is thy blush!" While I looked at him, and heard his threatening remarks, I was reminded of the lines:—

> "The man who lays his hand upon a woman,
> Save in the way of kindness, is a wretch,
> Whom 'twere gross flattery to call a coward."

I, after awhile, missed her from the church; I do not know but that she "cast away her confidence," under the circumstances. How awful will the case be, if she should say to him in death, or at the judgment seat of Christ, "Thou art the cause of my damnation!" It is very difficult to manage an ignorant, wicked man. Though it is said "Ignorance is the mother of devotion," it is only so to Popery, not to pure Christianity. In our revivals, we seldom, if ever, have much difficulty with sensible, well-informed persons.

I will give an instance in my experience—it did not however occur in this charge. The leading facts are as follows: At a Methodist protracted meeting, the lady of an eminent lawyer was powerfully wrought upon. She, with deep humility, presented herself at the altar of prayer, her cheeks bathed with tears. Much interest was manifested in her case. And, after struggling hard for peace, in answer to prayer, while the hymn was being sung, entitled,

"Mercy's free! mercy's free!"

she felt she could, in the language of that hymn, "Plant herself beneath the throne" and realize in her soul that mercy is *free*. She was very happy; she began to feel and pray for her husband. He was not present, but, at the time, away from home. No sooner was he at home, than he was informed, "Your wife has been converted in the Methodist meeting." He was greatly displeased, and said to her, "I am not willing for you to join the Methodist Church, but I wish you to unite with the Protestant Episcopal Church." She replied, in substance, "I have been converted among the Methodists; my heart is with them; you must allow me, my dear husband, in this important matter, to take my own course." He was much excited, and no doubt powerfully tempted by the devil, and exclaimed, "You will have every ragamuffin in this town calling you sister." And in his frenzy he laid hands upon a loaded pistol, and said, "I had as well die at once." At this crisis, his angel-like companion, who loved him fondly, flew into his arms, and exclaimed most tenderly, "My dear husband, do thyself no harm." The weapon of death fell from his hand; he fell upon his knees; his proud heart yielded. He was anxious for the hour to come for the exercises at the church to begin, and he was ready to say to his wife, "Whither thou goest I will go; thy people shall be my people, and thy God my God." He came promptly to the altar, was gloriously converted, and was not ashamed to confess it to the world. He arose in the presence of the vast congregation, and sung with great spirit, and with amazing effect,

"I have sought round the verdant earth."

One object among others, which has led me to introduce this incident, with which I am familiar, is to show that when we meet with persons opposed to the work of revival and Methodism, it is well for us that we can say, "Come now, and let us *reason* together;" for religion and Methodism are reasonable things, and we, as a people, will try to "Be ready always to give an answer to every man that asketh *us* a reason of the hope that is in *us*, with meekness and fear."

Are we not too apt to think protracted meetings cannot be successfully held through Christmas holidays? It is true there is generally much drinking and sporting. Theatres, circuses, and other places of amusement, calculated to decoy, are at this season of the year at their acme. Should not the Church spread out her wings, and cover the defenceless heads, especially of the young, and her ministers affectionately say, "God forbid that I should sin against the Lord in ceasing to pray for you; but I will teach you the good and right way." Our meetings on this occasion were deeply imbued with the Holy Spirit. The Sabbath was Christmas day. Long before the break of day, our forces were assembled in the Plank Church. The day was spent in devotional exercises. There was not any adjournment till about eight o'clock at night. The Rev. John D. Onins was to preach at the usual hour that night; but, when he came in and saw the salvation of God, the altar being crowded with mourners, several about that hour being converted, he said like a wise man, "Brother Manship, it is no use to preach here to-night, God is doing his work in his own way." He heartily united with us in the altar work. There was a stirring love feast in the afternoon; at least one thousand attended it. Young converts would arise, and, ready to face a frowning world, many of them said, "I have spent many a Christmas in sin and folly, but never knew what pleasure is before." New Year's day, 1854, also came on the Sabbath. The Saturday night preceding, the watch-night, was a time never to be forgotten. We watched the old year out, and the new year in, and not a few watched all night. Among the many, converted on this day, was a lady advanced in life, and who, for a quarter of a century, had been a member of another Church, but had never known her sins forgiven. She had been *hoping*, but all her lifetime she had been "subject to bondage" "through fear," until this happy day in her history, when she, at our humble altar in the Plank Church, received powerfully the witness of the Spirit. She exclaimed joyfully, "Glory be to God, he hath given me a *New Year's gift* that I shall never forget! Glory! glory!!" She is a faithful and substantial member of our Church. She has not only come herself, but all her house.

While the work of revival gloriously went forward, the builders were doing their part faithfully in completing the substantial building. And, in the month of March, 1854, the lecture room and class rooms were in order to be occupied. And the Sabbath preceding our Conference, March 19th, 1854, was fixed upon for the dedication. There was much interest at the time, and we well knew the lecture room would not hold the people who would attend on this interesting occasion. It was requisite, that day, that we should raise *fifteen hundred dollars;* therefore we endeavoured to make arrangements for the accommodation of all who might favour us with their presence. The "Little Brick" was close at hand, the Plank Church still closer to the new edifice; therefore we resolved to have services three times in each place, during the day. By this means we had *nine sermons* preached.

In the new church the following ministers officiated: Rev. Bishop Scott, Rev. Francis Hodson, D. D., and Rev. John Street. In the Plank Church, Rev. Joseph Castle, Presiding Elder of the North Philadelphia District, Rev. David W. Bartine, and Rev. Thomas Jefferson Quigley. In the little church, Rev. William E. England, Rev. William B. Wood, and, at night Rev. William E. England again. It devolved upon me to do the best I could in supervising the whole. Each place was filled to overflowing, but, of the three places, the Plank Church was evidently the most popular. It was the banner church, in the way of finance. The day was pleasant, heaven smiled upon us, the ministers were all in the Spirit. How truly we could sing,

"See where the servants of the Lord,
A busy multitude, appear;
For Jesus day and night employed,
His heritage they toil to clear."

We realized all we asked for. But could it have been done by simply confining ourselves to the lecture room that day? I answer unhesitatingly, it could not. Is it not well for the Church to be "wise as serpents, and harmless as doves?"

On Monday night following the dedication, we had a love feast in our new place of worship. All was love and harmony; we felt it was God's house. The meeting, from the experience of a young man, whose heart glowed with the missionary fire, assumed the character of a "missionary meeting." We felt for the heathen, and in order to save him from his blindness, we raised the sum of *twenty dollars.* This amount, *under the circumstances,* was a noble offering; it was voluntarily brought forward to the stand, while we were heartily singing the composition of Bishop Heber:

"From Greenland's icy mountains,
From India's coral strand,
Where Afric's sunny fountains
Roll down their golden sand;
From many an ancient river,
From many a palmy plain,
They call us to deliver
Their land from error's chain."

I wish to notice the experience, for a moment, of a faithful brother that night. He was one of our trustees; he had done much in accomplishing this important work. He was a noble-hearted Scotchman; I allude to James Stewart; he arose, and said, "I feel happy somewhat, but strange, just as I have done when I have first put on a new coat. They do not generally seem to set well. I always feel awkward." And while he talked, the fire began to burn in his noble soul. He shouted out, "I begin to feel the garment just fits me, I am just suited." Early in the year 1855, he left this city, to reside on a small farm he owned in Luzerne county, Pa., hoping that his declining health might be restored; but, in this desire, he and his friends were doomed to disappointment. When, however, the final struggle came, he was ready for his change. When asked relative to his prospects for the future, he said, "I am going down to the waters!" A few moments before he left the world, he said to his companion, "I am crossing over Jordan." And when he could no longer speak, one saying to him, "Is all well?—if so, give me a sign;" with eyes uplifted towards heaven, he waved his hand several times, in token of victory over the last enemy. Soon thereafter he fell asleep, beloved and esteemed by all who knew him. His funeral sermon was preached where he died, September 26, 1855, to a large audience, though he was comparatively a stranger. And, through respect for him, in the Hedding Methodist Episcopal Church, Philadelphia, of which he was a faithful member, trustee, leader, and steward, a discourse was delivered by me on Sunday, October 21, 1855, to a large and weeping audience. We were all ready to say, "Let me die the death of the righteous."

I went to the Conference in the city of Reading, Pennsylvania, with a cheerful heart. I was, by God's blessing, able to report a larger list of probationers than I ever reported before. And I might say, "Out of the eater came forth meat, and out of the strong came forth sweetness." By the goodness of God, it often happens, those things which appear unpleasant or injurious, become real blessings. It was said to me, when I was assigned to this weak appointment, "You will starve!" I remarked, "I will throw myself upon the promise; 'If ye be willing and obedient, ye shall eat the good of the land.'" I never was better supported. I did obtain honey from the carcass of the lion. Our support now, brethren in the ministry, is abundant, compared with what our fathers received. But sometimes we are tempted to think we should be better sustained in some other Church. When we come to this conclusion, we only see the bright side of the picture. As a general thing, no set of ministers in our country are better provided for, than the Itinerant ministers of the Methodist

Episcopal Church. Our people love us. A holy, working ministry among us, shall "have lack of nothing." The people see their ministers are constrained by the love of Christ; and they see them "Spending their sweat and blood, and pains, to cultivate Immanuel's lands;" and they delight to honour them "with many honours," and to lade them "with such things as are necessary." We will labour on, taking "No thought for our life, what we shall eat, or what we shall drink; nor yet for our bodies, what we shall put on." We know that "birds, without barn or storehouse, are fed;" and, with great propriety, the minister may be asked, "Are ye not much better than they?" Wherever, then, the powers that be send us, we will go, notwithstanding the work be arduous, and the prospect for support meager; and, as we occupy our humble station, or go round the Circuit, we will sing,

"No strength of our own, nor goodness we claim,
Our trust is all thrown on Jesus's name;
In this our strong tower for safety we hide;
The Lord is our power—the Lord will provide."

Brethren, let our motto be, "God and the people." God first of all, then the people. The people have been, and I believe ever will be, true to us, as long as we are true to God and ourselves. We have our difficulties, but we know our refuge and resource. Our high-toned enemies have cried, "Who are these ignorant, incompetent, unauthorized teachers, travelling out of *the regular line of succession?*" We answer in a voice of thunder, "Ask the people." We wish to hold no controversy; we merely say, Let us alone: and if perchance we should encounter, in our itinerant course, one of these lofty successors of the apostles, we would meekly act toward him as Mr. Wesley did to the country magistrate. It is related of Mr. Wesley, that, riding one day to preach, he met a pompous country magistrate, mounted on his stately charger; who, looking with ineffable scorn upon the little apostle of Methodism, exclaimed in a rough tone of voice, "I shall not give the way to a fool." Wesley very cordially reined his horse to the left, and quietly replied "*But I will.*'

The session of our Conference in the city of Reading was highly beneficial to us as a denomination. Methodism there is of recent origin, and there has been much prejudice against, and much ignorance of us. But this tree of God's planting is taking deep root in that soil. There are two excellent churches of our denomination. When the first one was built, the society being weak, the pastor, Rev. John A. Roche, in the year 1839, volunteered to visit many of the churches and Circuits to solicit pecuniary help. He came into my native place; I heard him preach a most solemn sermon, and then plead in eloquent strains for his infant church. I felt, a person to resist such an appeal as that, must have a heart of adamant. I remember that day, that, to aid his cause, *I emptied my scanty pocket, and gave him every cent I had*, and did it cheerfully. That was the first donation I ever gave to a church. I was a poor boy, but over that act I was happy. My means then and since have always been humble; but, as it was said of the woman in the gospel, who had an alabaster-box of ointment of spikenard, "she hath done what she could," I think I can say, I have done what I could; and my experience is that it is "blessed to give." The church, where the Conference was held, "St. Peter's," was more recently built. It was deemed proper to rear a more modern, and larger house. It was well to heed the direction of the prophet: "Enlarge the place of thy tent, and let them stretch forth the curtains of thine habitations: spare not, lengthen thy cords, and strengthen thy stakes." But in this "great work" the brethren found themselves much involved in pecuniary embarrassment. And as a parent will protect a child, the Conference was disposed to relieve, in every possible way, this beautiful temple from difficulty. But it cannot be denied, that that church, and the entire Conference, owe Rev. Newton Heston a debt of gratitude that can never, in this world, be paid. He traversed through the length and breadth of our territory, *feeble* as he frequently was, leaving sometimes a *sick family* behind, stemming torrents of opposition, through wet and dry, heat and cold, labouring in the pulpit and at the altar. His mission, unwelcome as it sometimes was, had to be made known. No one, who has not had the experience, knows the difficulties connected with such matters. Yet his success, by God's blessing, was complete. This was a great salvation; but what, at the Conference, was still more encouraging, was, we found that sinners, by scores, were being emancipated from the thraldom of sin. And over all these excellent things, who can wonder that "there was great joy in that city."

In connexion with "St. Peter's" Church in the city of Reading, I will mention an anecdote in which I was a party. There was a certificate presented to me of church membership from the pastor of this church. My location then was contiguous to a Roman Catholic church by the name of "*St. Peter's.*" I began to read, "This is to certify that —— is an acceptable member of *St. Peter's.*" It did not occur to me at the time that we had a church of this name; and I was so close to the one bearing the same name, and not a few of that church having attended our meetings, my readers will not be surprised when I tell them, that when I read as far in the certificate as "St. Peter's," I suddenly stopped, and was getting ready for a shout; for I was sure, this is a conquest from my Roman Catholic neighbour; but, just as I was about to say in the way of exultation, "we come not to call the righteous, but sinners to repentance," I saw on the paper "Methodist Episcopal Church," and the name of my friend and fellow labourer. I would not be understood to intimate, that I object to the name being given to a Methodist Church. We claim to be an apostolic church, and we revere the name of Peter, and have as good a right to affix his name to our churches as they. But while we revere the name of Peter, we are *more* absorbed in the name of Jesus. And we mean Christ when we say, "Upon this rock I will build my church; and the gates of hell shall not prevail against it."

Bishop Ames presided at this Conference for the first time, greatly to the satisfaction of the entire body. The General Conference did well, when they chose him to fill that responsible office. He is an excellent presiding officer, commanding in appearance, and "kindly affectioned" towards the brethren. He is a thorough Methodist. He said, in an address to the Conference, "I have frequently been honoured with a seat in the General Conference; and such has been my esteem for the Book of Discipline that I have never felt free to propose an alteration." Exhorting the brethren to go to their work in the right spirit, and assuring them that all would be well, he added; "I have been coasting round these capes for twenty-five years, and have never wanted for a harbour." How well it is, for our superintendents to have had experience in the hardships as well as the pleasures of the Itinerancy! then they may duly sympathize with us, and understand practically the "shades" as well as the "lights" of a travelling preacher. We all felt Bishop Ames is one of us, and this feeling, so far as I know, is general towards our superintendents. When we heard him preach during the session of the Conference, we could say the gospel which he proclaimed "Came not unto *us* in word only, but also in power and in the Holy Ghost and in much assurance." All felt he is to the flock of Christ a shepherd, not a wolf; he will feed them, and not devour them. He will heed the direction in the ordination service, "Hold up the weak, heal the sick, bind up the broken, bring again the outcast, seek the lost." The Bishop closed the Conference by reading our appointments, and, I presume, all thought they never were more judiciously made. The people of Reading, who had endeared themselves to us by their great kindness and hospitality, crowded St. Peter's to hear the conclusion of the whole matter. It was good to be there, but it was requisite that we should sever. Our motto is, on such occasions,

"O let us still proceed,
In Jesus' work below,
And, following our triumphant head,
To further conquests go."

CHAPTER XIII.

Revivals increase our Congregations—Are we immortal till our Work is done?—Sometimes we go a Warfare at our own charges—The old Rye-field—Reported to be Dead!—Life Insurance—Rev. John Lednum—Recovery of Health—Camp Meeting Arrangements in Philadelphia—Ministers deceived—Rev. A. L. P. Green, D. D., of Tennessee—A Methodist Preacher at Home, preaching anywhere—Feast of Dedication—Special Love Feast—Farewell or Anniversary Meeting in Plank Church—Driving a Stake, and shouting "Glory"—"Prepare ye the Way."

I WAS returned to Hedding Church in the spring of 1854. The Plank Church remained until the following autumn, when the upper part of the brick church was completed. We found it opportune; for the congregations were frequently so large that we had it as well as the lecture room occupied, and two distinct meetings in progress at the same time, notwithstanding some had entertained fears, and loudly expressed them, that the location was not a suitable one, and that the congregation would be small. But where the work of revival progresses, and the Church is in earnest for the salvation of souls, the people will flock together, filled with wonder and amazement; and when they thus come, we are to be successors of Peter, and proclaim, "Repent ye, therefore, and be converted." People generally like a ministry in earnest. If there is any subject about which the children of men should be in earnest, it is the salvation of the soul. Our founder, Mr. Wesley, was an earnest minister; his sons, for the last century, have in this respect followed in his footsteps, and the Methodist Church is a revival Church. Those who preceded us preached good doctrine, and it may be said of Methodist preaching and religion as it was once said of Mr. Whitefield, "The religion which he teaches is but the old, revived with energy, and heated as if the minister really meant what he said." Wherever the Church is in a languishing state, congregations small and feeble, I would modestly suggest that the best method to be adopted is for the ministry to ask—the Church heartily uniting—and persevere in asking God, "Wilt thou not revive us again, that thy people may rejoice in thee?" This being the case, every evil is corrected, and we may say, "The flowers appear on the earth, the time of the singing of birds is come, and the voice of the turtle is heard in our land." Our fields of labour blossom as the rose. How fragrant is the odour which is imparted to all around! We are compassed about with a great cloud of witnesses, so great, indeed, that we have to say, in regard to our places of worship, "The place is too strait for me; give place to me that I may dwell."

My readers would conclude naturally that I had work enough at home to do, but I did about this time what I could in assisting my brethren abroad at dedications and corner-stone layings of new churches. I think we should "bear one another's burdens;" and if we would have friends in the time of need, we must show ourselves friendly. I presume we are "immortal till our work is done." I have gone, however, frequently, when physically I did not feel able, to assist weak points. About this time I dedicated two Methodist Episcopal Churches for our coloured people. One in St. Michael's, Talbot county, Md., the other in Dover, Delaware. For the first enterprise, much credit is due Rev. John D. Long, supernumerary in the Philadelphia Conference, and our brethren in that place. I preached in the forenoon to the white people only, who raised a respectable amount to aid in freeing the new church for the coloured people from debt. In the afternoon the service of dedication took place. The new house was not large enough, and the case was somewhat relieved by pitching a large tent in front of the church. I stood in the front door of the new house, and preached to a mixed multitude; for very many of the white people cheered the sons of Africa with their presence, and aided them financially. I looked on with admiration, and thought of the passage, "He that hath pity upon the poor lendeth unto the Lord, and that which he hath given will he pay him again."

After the services at Dover were all over, and the Church was dedicated to the worship of Almighty God, the committee came to me and said with tears, "We are under great obligations to you, Mr. Manship, for your pains in coming to help us at our dedication; you will never be forgotten by us; what shall we give you? if you say twenty dollars, here it is." It was not in my heart to take it; they were allowed only to pay the travelling expenses. But they acted like Christians, and manifested a nobleness of soul that does not always characterize such occasions. And I presume I am not the only minister who has been sent for to go a distance to labour, and been permitted to go "a warfare, at his own charges."

In the month of April I was invited to visit the neighbourhood where I preached the second sermon I ever preached after I was licensed. The Church was a temporary affair there, of the tabernacle character, situated in the "Old Rye Field," near Bloomery Mills, Caroline county, Maryland. It was a very cold day, in the month of January, 1842. The clap-boards trembled, while the western wind roared, and through the crevices we felt its chilling blasts. There was also a heavenly breeze; I may say, "there came a sound from heaven as the rushing of a mighty wind." The few (for it was a little flock) that loved and served the Lord, could say,

"O, joyful sound of gospel grace!
Christ shall in me appear;
I, even I shall see his face,
I shall be holy here.

"The promised land from Pisgah's top
I now exult to see:
My hope is full—O glorious hope
Of immortality."

A little more than twelve years rolled round, ere I again preached the gospel at the "Old Rye Field." The little leaven that began to work twelve years before, had, in a great degree, leavened the whole lump. There was not a more wilderness place to be found in the county. The land was poor, much of it turned out as worthless; the people many of them made and drank brandy, and said, "Let us eat and drink, for to-morrow we shall die." When Rev. Joseph Carlise was preacher in charge, he did much for this neighbourhood, and, being aided by Samuel G. Smith, who was almost entirely alone, a house was built to take the place of the original tent in the Rye Field, in which I preached my second sermon. In this second tabernacle, which was temporary also, many were converted. This answered very well for several years. The labourers were few, but their faith was strong, and they could sing in faith,

"Rejoice, rejoice, the promised time is coming,
Rejoice, rejoice, the wilderness shall bloom."

Near the same spot where the work was first begun, it was my privilege to dedicate to the worship of Almighty God, the best church edifice on the entire Circuit, on the 9th of April, 1854. The congregation was immense for a country place. In and out of doors, that bright day, there were about a thousand people. Rev. Lewis C. Petit was an earnest fellow-labourer in this important work with Samuel G. Smith, the leader of the society in that place from the beginning. Brother S. wept, prayed, exhorted, and freely gave his money, to better the state of society. I thought on the Sunday of the dedication, when I saw such an immense number collected together, and remembered the state of the church twelve years before, This is a fulfilment of the Scripture, "One thousand shall flee at the rebuke of one!" Brother Smith, while labouring to build this house, had many discouragements. Some said, "The neighbourhood does not require such a church." Some, "We are not able to build;" some, "The old one is good enough;" while others said, "It is pride that makes people desire new churches." Is it not the love of the world, too great a fondness for the filthy lucre, that leads people to start so many objections to new churches? But, nevertheless, the work was vigorously prosecuted: "Let us not be weary in well-doing, for in due season we shall reap if we faint not."

My disposition to go forward, and labour more than my strength would sustain me in, superinduced an attack of indisposition that threatened to put me in the grave. In the month of June, my health so far failed, that I was not able to preach during the entire summer. A report was put in circulation that I was dead; perhaps hundreds read it, as it was in several newspapers. My situation for some days was, by medical men, considered critical. I did not know but that my work was done. I thought of the cold grave. Trusting solely upon the Lamb for sinners slain, it was not to me altogether gloomy. I felt desirous (if it was God's will) to live, that I might labour in his vineyard. I was much concerned also, in this dark hour, for my wife and children. This is a great trial to a man on the verge of the grave. I had seen the widow and orphan children, even of the faithful minister of the Gospel, greatly neglected. I asked myself the question, Will mine, when they are thrown upon the cold charities of an unfeeling world, fare any better? "There dies a father; and behold, the widow descends from the sofa of ease to the oar of labour; and the children lose the caresses of the neighbourhood; are scattered, oppressed, injured." For few in our world act according to the laws of genuine friendship; or inquire, like David, "Is there any left of the house of Saul, that I may show him kindness for Jonathan's sake?"

In the hour of affliction, how much can be done by sympathy! "Weep with those that weep." The kindness of my brethren and friends who visited and prayed with me, made a deep impression upon my mind, and a letter from Bishop Waugh about this time drew from my eyes tears profusely. I introduce it, to show the kindness of his noble heart towards an humble fellow-labourer in the kingdom and patience of our Lord Jesus Christ. It is dated Baltimore, July 4, 1854; and is as follows:—

"Dear Brother,—I learned, on my way home, of your severe affliction. It afflicted me. I was afraid that the tendency of my Brother Manship to gigantic labours had carried him too far for his physical resources. And now, just at this point, let me tell you, with the concern of a father, that I am fearful that the abundance and ceaselessness of your labours are leading to premature death or superannuation. My motto, in theory, at least, is, "It is better to *wear* out, than to *rust* out." I would not that you should be less zealously affected in the great work of the Christian ministry; but I would have you remember that the house in which the immortal spirit lives and labours, is of clay. It cannot with impunity bear the unremitted toils of day and night. There must be time for rest and repair, else the frail habitation will tremble, totter, and fall. Cannot you be less laborious without being less zealous? I am happy to learn your health is somewhat recovering; but let me urge you, Brother Manship, not to recommence your public labours too soon; and when you do begin them, do not forget that you have had a severe shock, whatever may have been the immediate cause of it. I hope you will visit Cape Island or some other sanative place again, before you resume your work."

In my critical state, in view of my domestic affairs, next to the grace of God and the sympathy of my friends, I found my mind relieved, by having, when well, taken out a life insurance policy. This arrangement was entered into with a well-regulated, old, and honourable company, in Philadelphia. From the standing of that company, I have not the shadow of a doubt, in case I had died, that the policy, which I held, would have been promptly paid to those dear to me. I desire to call the attention, particularly, of my brethren in the ministry to this subject. It is a rare case for a minister, from the salary which he receives, to lay up anything, for the education of his children, and support of his family, that he is quite likely, in the providence of God, to leave behind. I do not mean to assert that ministers are not supported. There are, however, so many demands made upon them, and they are so generous in contributing to every good cause, that they are able only, generally, to meet expenses. What provision, then, can they make for those whom they may leave behind? The prospect is gloomy. One way, however, is open to them. For a small *yearly payment*, for a *life insurance*, they can insure to those loved ones who may survive them, a respectable sum, which, with industry and economy, will place them in circumstances of comparative comfort.

There are, however, objections, says my reader:—

1. The idea of insuring life is impossible. I do not mean to intimate that it is to add to life, but it is a prudential regulation in case of death.

2. Some may say it implies distrust of Providence. If this be a valid objection, it will apply to lightning rods, insurance in general, and a thousand other regulations, entered into heartily by the best of men in the land.

3. Some may think this has somewhat the aspect of a lottery, or gambling affair. If it had, no man would be more denunciatory than myself. This class of objectors will say, "Suppose I pay one year's premium of fifteen or twenty dollars, and then die; and the company is compelled to pay to my estate one thousand dollars; is this not sinful and unjust?" I answer, not at all. The company, by mathematical calculation, know the general average of human life; and, in a given number of years, they can tell how many of those insured will die. They know not upon whom the lot will fall; but they do know, that while some of the insured may die prematurely, others may live to a good old age. And the latter are better off than the former, even though they should pay in annual instalments more than the amount of their policies. "For all that a man hath

will he give for his life." What is the amount of our policy, compared with sweet life? What, therefore, the company may lose in some cases, they make up on others.

4. My readers may say, I cannot pay the yearly premiums. The amount will be small; and, for the sake of our little ones, let us practise a little self-denial, and be economical.

5. One will say, I prefer taking the little I can save, and investing it otherwise. But here is the difficulty. It is perhaps so small, you will think it is useless to undertake to invest so insignificant an amount. Who knows that he is to live even a year to make an investment? But even in case of death, if that small amount had been invested as pointed out, the widow and orphan children might have had a respectable sum.

6. Others will say, "I am afraid of these insurance companies; they will break, and all will be lost." Banks break, stocks which we may deem the most safe, sometimes become worthless, and every earthly investment is liable to fail us. Hence we should not fail to "lay up for ourselves treasures in heaven, where neither moth nor rust doth corrupt, and where thieves do not break through nor steal." But so far as earth is concerned, I know nothing so well suited to a man of limited means, who has a desire to provide for his household, and leave them something to lean upon when he is gone, as a

responsible, well-regulated life insurance company; in which he agrees to pay an annual amount within his reach; the company, on their part, agreeing to pay to his wife and children a certain sum when he can no longer go in and out before them. I have myself seen the widow and orphan children gladdened in the hour of adversity by this means. When we see its good effects, who will gainsay it?

Reader, if we pursue this course, it will, I think, be loving our neighbour as ourself. It will be a triumph over selfishness. When we insure a house, a leading idea is, if it is burnt down, we will have money in hand to build another; but when we insure our life we are ourselves not to be benefited, but our families, when we are no more. In *every respect*, let me say to my reader, "Set thy house in order, for thou shalt die and not live." *Be, however, careful in regard to the character of the insurance company.*

Rev. John Lednum, an elderly member of the Philadelphia Annual Conference, who sustains a superannuated relation, filled my appointments during the summer. He filled my place in every respect; and he could not have been more faithful had he been the regular pastor. He, like God's ancient prophet, resolved that he would receive nothing from the hands of the brethren. There is much originality and power in the preaching of Rev. John Lednum. His labours were owned in this charge, in the awakening and conversion of many souls. From this minister, all through my career at Hedding Church, I realized much assistance. He was one of my most efficient "helpers in Christ Jesus."

In the month of September, 1854, my health was so far recovered, by God's blessing, that I was enabled to resume my labours in the Hedding Church. The dedication of the new edifice was approaching; we desired to have another extra meeting in the Plank Church before we abandoned it to occupy the permanent building. Many of our members were not, for various reasons, able to go to the great Red Lion camp meeting, which they most earnestly desired. I told them I would arrange for them to have a camp meeting at home. This was good news to them. At first we held what we called a camp meeting prayer meeting in the Plank Church, on a Sabbath afternoon. The night meetings that followed were so large, that we resolved to make more room, by taking out about forty feet of the south side of the church, where there was a vacant lot, situated immediately between the new brick and the plank house, and we proceeded to rear tents, which we obtained from our sister churches. The pulpit in the plank house was removed to the centre of the building, and the several tents faced the same. The minister had the people on his right and left; one of the large tents immediately faced the speaker, another was in a south-western, and the third in a south-eastern position. The minister, by this arrangement, could see the audience readily, and every person, from any point, had a full view of the speaker. We often had every place filled to its very utmost capacity. The best ministerial talent in our church was called into requisition.

While I had the co-operation of our brethren in this city, I was also highly favoured with the labours of several prominent ministers from the South—Rev. Dr., now Bishop Early, Rev. Dr. Summers, and Rev. A. L. P. Green, D. D. All these brethren preached for us, and seemed to be very happy in their efforts. Dr. Early said, "This is not unlike a camp meeting; I have preached at many a one, where the audience was not so large, or so attentive." I admired that aged minister's course; he concluded his sermon, and then went through the congregation, urging persons to seek religion. To my knowledge, he was the means of one soul's professing to obtain the pearl of great price the night he preached for us. He made an effort to get a man forward who is an adept in deceiving ministers and others. He practised deception on me once, as follows: In Chestnut Street, Philadelphia, "Brother Manship," said he, "allow me to introduce you to Mr. S., a friend of mine; he will, I think, give you a donation for your church." I said, We have no claims on Mr. S.; but, if he chooses to do so, we shall be thankful. Mr. S. took my book, and wrote his name, street, and number, affixing the amount of twenty dollars thereto, and directed me to call on such a day. I did so, but he was not to be found. I plainly saw this whole matter was a hoax. When I saw good Dr. Early urging him to come to the altar, I thought of the saying of the old coloured man, when the lightning struck the gum-tree: "*You have got your match dis time!*" After awhile I had an interview with Dr. Early, and found, sure enough, he was deceived. He said to me, "Brother Manship, —— is under powerful conviction; his heart is very soft; follow him up." I did not tell my venerable friend, at the time, this man's predisposition, but I knew that he, as well as myself, had been trifled with. How wicked is such a course! The wise man says, "As a madman who casteth fire brands, arrows, and death, so is the man that deceiveth his neighbour, and saith, Am not I in sport?"

The Rev. Dr. Green took great delight in aiding us at this point. He preached several times in our temporary place of worship, while in this city on business relating to the Methodist Episcopal Church, South. He is as a minister a great favourite in this city in all our churches. There is much simplicity in his manner. A child can understand him, and a sage may sit at his feet and learn of him. For effect, I know none to surpass him in my range of acquaintance. One shining grace in this distinguished man that won my heart's affections, was humility. I was in his company much. I saw in him what is admirable in a minister of the gospel, viz. a great love for the children, and a disposition to impart instruction to the juvenile mind. Another mark of his humility that struck my mind forcibly was, his great willingness to preach in our Plank Church. After having officiated in our place several times, being in our city again, I was emboldened to ask him to give the people another sermon. Said he, promptly, "Brother Manship, I am glad to see you. I was afraid I should not get there this time; I am already engaged for two sermons for to-morrow (Sunday), but if you will accept me in the afternoon, I will cheerfully preach, for, to tell the honest truth, I had rather preach in your Plank Church than in any house in this city."

That is right; a Methodist preacher should feel inclined to glory in preaching the cross in the most humble place. *If it be requisite,* stand on a butcher's block in the market, or a stump in the commons, in the woods at the camp meeting, in the spacious hall or theatre, or, last though not least, in the estimation of some, in a populous city in a Plank Church, with its appendages, such as we had during the last protracted meeting we held in it. Such places answer for an extemporaneous preacher whose heart is in the work; and I am happy to say such a preacher was Rev. Dr. Green, of Tennessee.

I would also strenuously maintain that our doctrines are so excellent that they should be proclaimed everywhere, and our ministry, moved by the Holy Spirit to the work, is fully competent for the task. It is true, "we utterly disclaim all pretensions to what Papists and High Churchmen call the divine succession, and with it we disclaim all Popish infallibility, and all that high-toned priestly authority which lords it over God's heritage, or interferes with the rights of conscience; but we do humbly claim to be men whom God has called, commissioned, and sent to preach the everlasting gospel; and if any doubt this, we refer them to the thousands of sinners who have been reformed and saved through our instrumentality." These are our epistles of commendation, known and read of all men. Such a ministry is good enough for the most costly edifice, not passing by the "Metropolitan Church," now being built in the city of Washington. Under *peculiar circumstances*, it may be necessary for us as a people to have a place of worship bordering on the magnificent; and should we object, if immortal souls may be saved, even if there should be a spire pointing to Heaven, or a bell, reminding the people that the hour for worship had arrived; or a deep-toned organ, skilfully managed, with a thousand hearts and voices uniting in sacred song, making one think of the music of the skies, where, "with our harps in our hands, we'll praise him evermore."

Perhaps my plain reader will think, if this should be the case in the Methodist Church, "Ichabod, the glory is departed from Israel," might be written upon our walls. No, never! While, however, in some *remarkable emergency*, I would advocate such an arrangement as a prudential regulation, in no case would I admit that our old-fashioned preaching of Christ and him crucified, "in demonstration of the spirit, and of power," can be dispensed with.

Let us, indeed, have the people, by some means, but when we get them assembled together, even in our fine churches, let us try to make them feel, as a prominent gentleman once said, he liked preachers to make him feel;—"I like," said he, "the preacher to drive me up into the corner of my pew, and make me feel as though the devil was after me!" If the pulpit is kept pure, and flames with the glory of God, and our ministry walk by the same rule, and mind the same things which characterized our fathers, the ship built at the Foundry, city of London, under the direction of Messrs. John and Charles Wesley, will be ever well balanced, in sailing trim, and continue to move forward (though winds blow a dreadful hurricane, and the waters roll mountains high); she will float her triumphant course over the main, and wave her joyous banner to the nations, till she circumnavigates the world, for she was never designed for a mere coaster. Mr. Wesley said, "The world is my parish;" so must his sons feel. One even higher than Wesley says, "Go ye into all the world, and preach the gospel to every creature."

Our builders, the Messrs. Ginnodo of this city, gave us to understand that, on the 15th of October, 1854, the new brick Hedding Methodist Episcopal Church would be ready for use, and that we might make our arrangements accordingly. We are much indebted to this firm, for undertaking to build for us when they plainly saw our weakness in funds; there are but few builders, in all probability, that would have done it.

The venerable Bishop Waugh again came to our help, and preached the opening sermon, and performed the dedicatory services, in the presence of a large and delighted audience. Many of the original little band had feared that they would never see this day: they had waited so long. Some months before the dedication, one of them, a zealous labourer in this work, was, as every one thought, near the close of life. I visited him often while in this critical state. He expressed a great desire to get well; he frequently said, "I would like to live to see Hedding Church finished." His desire was gratified; but, shortly after, he had a relapse, and died on the 9th of November, 1854. He could say, "Lord, now lettest thou thy servant depart in peace: for mine eyes have seen thy salvation." The enemy of souls followed him almost down to the waters of Jordan. He died on Wednesday. The Sunday night before his death, he received the sacrament of the Lord's Supper about midnight; and that night every cloud vanished. There never was a happier man, certainly, than George M'Caulley on his death-bed. He said, frequently, "Glory to Jesus! Hallelujah to the Lamb!" A little while before the redeemed spirit left the clay tenement, he was in a transport of ecstatic joy, and so extended his voice that all about the premises heard him triumphing over the last enemy. He assisted in every possible way in building this house for God; and the Lord built an house for him, "eternal in the Heavens." His funeral sermon was preached in the new church, from "I have fought a good fight, I have finished my course, I have kept the faith."

Rev. John Kennaday, D.D., and Rev. Professor Wentworth, were associated with Bishop Waugh in the labours of the dedication occasion. It was just before Professor Wentworth sailed as missionary to China. Before he commenced preaching at night, the congregation sung the hymn, with much pathos, beginning,

"Away from his home and the friends of his youth,
He hasted, the herald of mercy and truth,
For the love of his Lord, and to seek for the lost;
Soon, alas! was his fall, but he died at his post."

We felt the presence of that God, in the house and in our hearts, of whom it was said, "Behold, the heaven, and heaven of heavens, cannot contain thee!"

Rev. John Kennaday delivered, in the afternoon, a very appropriate discourse. His numerous friends in this city flocked to hear him. He has laboured much within the bounds of the Philadelphia Conference, and is deservedly a popular minister; and his popularity among us has never waned. Several of our best church edifices have been reared through his instrumentality. He has assisted in relieving many from pecuniary embarrassment, within our bounds. It may be truly said, he is abundant in labour, perfectly at home in the work of revival, and he has, a thousand times, perhaps, led on the armies of our Israel. Who ever witnessed his management of a protracted or camp meeting, and could not well say he is a good tactician? He has the happy art to interest the children. The morning of our dedication, in order to have the room for adults, we held a meeting expressly for the children, in the lecture-room, where Bishop Waugh presided, and Dr. Kennaday was the chief speaker. This great privilege reconciled them to give their places, that morning, to their parents entirely.

In the afternoon the congregation was too great for all to hear, and hence, Rev. Irvin Torrence, of the Baltimore Conference, kindly consented to officiate, though he had not previously been called upon. I presume he believes that "a Methodist preacher should always be ready for two things: First, always ready to preach; Secondly, always ready to die." He was in the spirit of the glorious work. This worthy brother had frequently laboured for us in the Plank Church, acceptably to all; as he did on this day of the feast of dedication. We may truly say, we "kept the dedication of this house of God with joy."

On Monday night following the day of dedication, we had arranged to have a love feast in connexion with our dedication, on a somewhat peculiar plan. The tickets were printed on various colours of card paper, worded, "Special Love Feast Ticket, Hedding Methodist Episcopal Church, Philadelphia." Bishop Waugh, in order to have an interview with many ministerial brethren, and many of the members of the other Methodist Churches, and to aid us all he could in our efforts to pay for our church, consented to remain and preside over the Love Feast. At my request the good bishop endorsed all the tickets. He wrote his name *a thousand times!* That name is embalmed in many a heart in our wide-spread connexion, and those tickets he had the kindness to endorse, are sacredly kept through respect for the senior Bishop of the Methodist Episcopal Church, who is now feeble, and soon expects to lay his armour by, and be with Christ at home. When he is gone, great pleasure will be realized by my brethren and sisters here, who were fortunate enough to get his autograph in this way.

Another feature of this love feast that startled some of the Methodists, was, the tickets were sold, to aid in liquidating the debt. They were bought cheerfully. To those who desired to make a mountain of this molehill, and "strain at a gnat and swallow a camel," and who said, "Who ever heard the like before—*selling love feast tickets?*"—we replied that we were old-fashioned Methodists, and in this respect we copied after our Wesleyan brethren. The members of that body, universally, so far as I know, buy their love feast tickets. The love feast was blessed of God, and it was a memorable season. It was a feast "of fat things full of marrow." It was also a source of pecuniary advantage to our church, and we thought the end justified the means.

On the next night, we held a farewell meeting in the Plank Church. This temporary structure stood precisely one year, and hence we called the meeting the anniversary of the temporary Hedding Methodist Episcopal Church. Accordingly, at an early hour on Tuesday evening, October 7th, 1854, a vast crowd assembled, anxious once more, before this tabernacle was taken down, to have the privilege of worshipping in the place dear to many of them, made so by the fact that it was the place where they experienced that change of heart without which we cannot enter the kingdom of God. The meeting was organized by calling Rev. Joseph Castle, Presiding Elder of North Philadelphia District, to the chair. He offered a fervent prayer, after *the whole* congregation had sung the hymn, beginning,

"Jerusalem! my happy home!
Name ever dear to me!
When shall my labours have an end,
In joy, and peace in thee?"

I have heard, occasionally, the best choirs in different churches; but the singing that night in our Plank Church was not a whit behind any I ever heard. "Not one in ten only" was engaged in this delightful work, but all sung with a spirit, I think, worthy of imitation. Some will say that such singing answered at an earlier day, but it will not do now. Would that our singing now was more generally congregational and spiritual! It does not appear to me to be Heaven-like, for a very small number to do the singing for a vast assemblage in a formal manner. On this subject, I will introduce an incident. Rev. A. A. Willets informed me, that a highly intelligent and devoted lady, the wife of a Congregational minister of New England (who was present with her husband the Sabbath afternoon that he, Mr. Willets, preached in the Plank Church for us), came up to him at the close of the service, and, while the tears streamed

29

down her beaming countenance, said, "O how thankful I am I came here this afternoon! I never before have been so near Heaven, as I have been this hour under this humble roof. *O that singing! that singing!* how it lifted up my soul! I shall never forget this hour;" her emotion fairly choking her utterance as she turned away.

It is not my purpose to oppose the study of music; for "that which is worth doing at all, is worth doing well." We cannot sing correctly without a knowledge of the notes of music, any more than we can speak correctly without a knowledge of the rules of grammar; yet I have sometimes feared that our scientific singers, and those who are well skilled in music, lack, in many instances, a devotional spirit, and "are proud, self-willed, contentious, and arrogant." I am tempted, in this connexion, to give an incident in my own experience. When a youth, I visited a large city for the first time in my life. The vessel, on which I was a passenger, arrived on a Sabbath morning, in the month of May. I no sooner landed than I started in search of a meeting. In the part of the country where I lived, the Methodists were the principal religious sect. A few Quaker meeting-houses, and, now and then, a dilapidated old Episcopal Church, could be seen in my county. The first church I came to I entered, asking no questions. Everything inside was truly magnificent; and, of course, the singing was of a high order. I seated myself, after kneeling down and praying, in a pew that was finely cushioned. I saw a hymn book not in use. I felt desirous to participate in the devotions; and although things were on a much grander scale than I had been used to, still I did not realize but that I was in a Methodist Church, until I saw the minister clad in vestments of various colours, and heard the deep-toned organ. I suddenly asked myself the question, "Where am I?" Still I did the best I could in singing. And I do not believe that there was a more sincere worshipper there that day than I was. I was in a happy mood, and sung, I think, with the spirit and with the understanding. But, alas! I could not stay to see the conclusion of the whole matter. A tall man looked steadily on me, and said, "Your singing makes discord." I replied to him, "I am in the habit of singing at home, and the spirit moves me to sing here." I suppose he thought I would continue to sing if I remained; therefore he said, "Your absence will be good company; you are in another man's pew anyhow, and the sooner you go, the better!" That was too plain to be misunderstood; so I quietly retired. I obtained afterwards some direction from a captain that enjoyed religion; and before that day passed, I was permitted to join a pilgrim band, composed, in part, of converted sailors and their families, in an humble room; and, like the Congregational minister's wife just referred to in the Plank Church, I was ready to say, "O that singing! that singing! how it lifted up my soul!" This company of humble worshippers were singing,

"The old ship of Zion."

In my Itinerant life, I have been pastor where the choirs have been a great blessing; and, *properly* managed, will generally be. On this subject, finally, however, let me say to choirs and congregations, so conduct this most interesting part of Divine worship, as to compel all to say who hear us, "O! that singing! that singing! how it" lifts "up my soul!"

In our anniversary or farewell meeting, after prayer, a report of the year was read, which proved, apparently, deeply interesting to all. How could it be otherwise than interesting, when it was stated in the report, that, in that humble house of prayer, there had been won to the Saviour about *five hundred* persons of different ages during the year!

Rev. John P. Durbin was the first speaker introduced to the meeting. He is more particularly absorbed in the foreign missionary work, being the secretary of the Missionary Society of the Methodist Episcopal Church; but his noble soul, that night, was deeply in this home enterprise. He has preached before the Congress of the United States, and in various parts of the world, to the most intelligent assemblies of our own, and other denominations; but never, perhaps, was he more inspired than on this occasion. Among other things, he urged the employment of temporary arrangements like this, for purposes of church extension, and as preparatory to permanent church edifices and congregations. No sooner was the Doctor through with his stirring address, than Samuel H. Aldridge, Esq., a prominent member of the church in this city, arose and asked, "Is this church for sale?" Previous to that meeting, an enterprising Baptist brother, John N. Henderson, Esq., had privately made us an offer for our Plank Church, and until we had an interview with Mr. H., who was present on the night of the anniversary, we were unable to give an answer to the question. This honourable fellow-citizen, seeing a zeal manifested on the part of the Methodist brethren to purchase the house, said to me, "Let it be offered for sale, and let the highest bidder have it." This was done, and Rev. John Kennaday managed this business with much ingenuity, and it was soon declared by him, "That Mr. Aldridge and other Methodist brethren were the purchasers." The arrangement was for the church, according to Dr. Durbin's suggestion, still to be a pioneer Methodist Church. This business being adjusted, the Rev. John Kennaday and Rev. A. A. Willetts delivered appropriate addresses. The last-named minister is connected with the Dutch

Reformed Church. He was formerly an Itinerant in the Methodist Episcopal Church. In the labours of the Itinerancy, his physical strength gave way. So much was he broken down, that he was compelled to abandon the idea of ever being able to do the work of a Methodist preacher. While taking steps to go into a lucrative business, he was urged to take charge of the church of the denomination above named, in Crown Street, Philadelphia. But Mr. W. said to the gentlemen, "I am a broken-down man; I cannot do the labour of a charge." They replied, "Preach as you are able, and we will supply your lack." But Mr. W. said to them, "I am a Methodist preacher; the doctrines of that Church I firmly believe." The gentlemen said, "We have heard you preach; we want no better doctrine, and we want you to preach as formerly." Mr. W. consulted with judicious friends, prayed over this important matter, and, in the fear of God, resolved that he would try. God has smiled upon the course; the happiest results have followed. His health has very greatly improved. The church, over which he was placed as pastor, has prospered. It was then small and in a weak state in every respect, but it has greatly enlarged its borders. His prayer no doubt was, "Oh that thou wouldst bless me indeed, and enlarge my coast, and that thine hand might be with me." "And God granted him that which he requested." The new church, in

Spring Garden Street, which his flock have been enabled to erect, at a cost of about one hundred thousand dollars, and which will accommodate fifteen hundred persons, is filled with attentive hearers, to whom he preaches faithfully the "unsearchable riches of Christ."

He is deservedly popular among all classes, as an orator and preacher; but he is ever ready to say of Methodism, It shall not be forgotten by me. He does not imitate the example of the chief butler towards Joseph: "Yet did not the chief butler remember Joseph, but forgat him." The address he delivered in our Plank Church, at our anniversary, led me to say, "His tongue is the pen of a ready writer." His address told favourably on the collection, which was taken for the purpose of assisting in paying off the debt of the newly consecrated church.

The doxology was sung, and the large audience was dismissed. How reluctantly did we tear ourselves away from this place, where for one year we had witnessed the conversion of souls, the sanctification of believers, and had realized the Lord to be "unto us a place of broad rivers and streams!" This house was not only engraved upon many hearts, but our attachment to it was so great that in coming years we wanted to gaze upon it, and tell to our children the fame of its wonders; hence we had it engraved by an artist on a large scale, presenting both an exterior and interior view.

This picture is now suspended in many parlours, and those persons especially who were converted in the Plank Church, place a high estimate upon it. Can we blame them? After the Syrian general was cured of the leprosy, he loved not only the prophet and the water of Israel, but also the earth; and expressed a desire to carry some of it home with him. "And Naaman said, Shall there not then, I pray thee, be given to thy servant two mules' burden of earth?" Many a pious soul desired and obtained small portions of the very humble altar of the Plank Church, at which they had been converted, and which was now about being removed, saying in their hearts, "If I forget thee, O Jerusalem, let my right hand forget her cunning. If I do not remember thee, let my tongue cleave to the roof of my mouth; if I prefer not Jerusalem above my chief joy."

The spot where from above "I first received the pledge of love," I shall ever revere. I have often visited it since with emotion, and as I have passed the place, it being near the county road, I have always, in my thoughts, recurred with hallowed feelings to the memorable camp meeting held there in the summer of 1835, and I have a veneration for the place somewhat similar to that of a person in Virginia, many years ago, who was brought to God through camp meeting influences. The incident is as follows:—

"A gentleman visited a place where preparations

T. SINCLAIR'S.　　T. B. WELCH.

THE ORIGINAL PLANK CHURCH, PHILADELPHIA.

were in progress for a camp meeting. As he walked around the ground, viewing the laborious operations which, all who are acquainted with such meetings know are necessary in preparing the ground and erecting tents, and occasionally pausing to chat with a friend, his attention was especially arrested by the energy with which one man drove a stake into the ground. Each stroke was accompanied by some exclamation. Getting near enough to understand what was said, he found the man shedding tears profusely, and with every stroke of his axe, shouting 'Glory!' 'You seem to be excited, and happy,' said the gentleman.' 'Happy!' replied the man, 'I have enough to make me happy;' and down came his axe on the stake with increased energy, and up went the shout—'Glory!' He proceeded to explain: 'Twelve months ago, at a camp meeting held on this ground, and just here, God converted my soul!' The tears rolled down his brawny cheeks, his lips trembled, and with more than previous force down again came the ponderous axe, and, in harmony with the echo, up went the shout—'Glory! Glory!!'"

My readers will conclude I have participated with my friends in the feeling of attachment for the Plank Church, when they see in this work the engraving referred to, so far as the exterior is concerned, reduced, and given to them from a steel plate. I hope I shall not, in this respect, be charged with superstition; my motive is to do good, and only good, and that continually. Several similar structures in this city have sprung up, and the results have been felicitous. To the friends of church extension "all over these lands," let an humble fellow-labourer in the "vineyard of the Lord," commend this temporary arrangement PLAN to their consideration. Is it not better, for awhile, to worship God in an humble place, free from debt, than to have a more magnificent church edifice, heavily encumbered? Such an arrangement, properly entered into, and carried forward with due energy, will be like "The voice of him that crieth in the wilderness, Prepare ye the way of the Lord, make straight in the desert a highway for our God."

CHAPTER XIV.

A Family in Distress—Death of the Mother and the Son—Mrs. Ann B. Castle—Her Death—A Course of Lectures—Compass the Church seven times—Some offer objections to Revivals—" A more excellent Way"—Supernumerary Relation—Sent back to Hedding Church in charge—Encourage worthy Men to enter the Ministry—Insure a Horse's Life—His name is "Itinerant"—Friendship—Start to Europe—Kindness of Friends—Greatly disappointed—All for the best—A Storm—Ship still sails—Day for Camp Meetings not over—Ex-Governor Hazzard—Eastern Shore of Virginia—" Fall a-crying"—Interesting Anniversary—Concert Hall—Home and Foreign Missions—The Itinerancy divinely instituted—Anecdote of Mr. Wesley—His happy Death—Methodists die well—Powerful Argument—Let these Men alone.

THE remarkable meetings, an account of which has been given in the preceding chapters, drew persons from all parts of Philadelphia; this extended my range of acquaintance very greatly. I sometimes was called upon to visit the sick and bury the dead at remote points.

It may not be unprofitable for me to describe a case. I entered the little court, and, after inquiring at several places, I was directed to the house, where I found a female dying. There were several children; the husband and father was far away in the South, endeavouring to do something for his family, as he had been thrown out of employment at home. I feared, however, from all I could hear, that he was a poor provider, and that the main part of what he did make was worse than thrown away; for he looked upon "wine when it is red." How many innocent children have to say (O, how pathetic!),

"My father is a drunkard, but I am not to blame!" I found the son, who was about twenty-one years of age, to be a consumptive. He had been, as I was informed, the main support of the family. I found him, weak as a "bruised reed," sitting at a table, trying to write to his father. He was not able to do it, but it was the best he could do, for there appeared to be none to do for him! It was cold; there was scarcely any fire in the house, and but little to subsist upon. Everything looked cheerless. The young man, addressing me with a tremulous voice, said, "Sir, I knew you in Wilmington, Delaware. I have sent for you; I knew of no other person to send for; my poor mother is about to die, and father is away from home. I have done all I can. I, too, must die; I am growing weaker every day. Can you do anything by which I could have my poor dear mother buried in Wilmington?" The circumstances of that suffering family were made known, and their wants, to some extent, relieved. I returned the next day, and said to the young man, "It is not in my power to do anything now beyond this city—I am too much engaged; but, if you are willing for your mother to be buried in a Methodist burying-ground, I will see that a lot be procured, and she put away decently." With cheeks bathed with tears, he said, "God bless you! that will do." How I was affected, when he asked, as I was passing away, "*Will there be room enough there for me, too?*"

I answered, Yes; when he kissed my hand, bedewing it with his tears. Sure enough, they were both interred decently in a beautiful lot, and there was but a short interval between their death—the devoted son following his mother in the space of a few weeks. What a pleasing thought it is, that, though we may be poor and comparatively friendless in this world, Jesus is a friend "that sticketh closer than a brother!" I have good reason to believe that this mother and son made a happy exchange, and realized the truth of God's immutable word: "He will swallow up death in victory, and the Lord God will wipe away tears from off all faces." We should, dear reader, feel for the poor. We have never known, perhaps, what it is to want; God hath dealt bountifully with us. But there are those in our midst that suffer for the necessaries of life; especially in affliction. Fly to their succour. Give relief, and Heaven will bless your store. "Blessed is he that considereth the poor; the Lord will deliver him in time of trouble."

During the winter of 1854–5, there was much suffering in our city. The benevolent societies did much in relieving the wants of a very large class, and churches and individuals did what they could in this Christ-like work. We had no Dorcas Society in our church regularly organized, and yet, considering our circumstances, I do not know that we were a whit behind others. We were materially aided in this work by a neighbour—I may well say—a modern Tabitha. This Christian lady "was full of good works, and alms-deeds which she did." I allude to Mrs. Ann B. Castle, wife of Rev. Joseph Castle, Presiding Elder of the North Philadelphia District. From her the poor were the recipients of many favours. However, "it came to pass, in those days, that she was sick, and died." Only a few weeks before her death, which took place Sunday morning, March 11, 1855, knowing that there were many in our congregation, as well as most others that needed clothing, she sent to my residence a large quantity of wearing apparel, which was by judicious females distributed to the necessitous. She forwarded to one of the towns, where she formerly had resided, a large package of goods, for similar purposes, which did not arrive at their destination till after her death.—"She died in the work." As in the case of Tabitha, who had won numerous friends by making "coats and garments while she was with them," and they manifested their friendship by standing by her dead body "in an upper chamber, weeping," so had this excellent Christian lady a large circle of friends, not only in Philadelphia, but everywhere, wherever with her companion her lot had been cast. It is not strange that such a person should be appreciated. I have heard it remarked, in regard to her, "She had a kind word for every one." From early years her unselfish and affectionate disposition made her a general favourite among all who knew her. Innocence and love were stamped upon her features. She was blessed with a pious mother, who instructed her in the things that made for her peace, and from a child she feared the Lord. When about seventeen years old, at a camp meeting in Pittston, Wyoming, she consecrated fully her youthful heart to God, and on the following Sabbath united with the Methodist Episcopal Church. From that time she became decidedly pious, walking in all the commandments and ordinances of the Lord blameless. The Sunday School, the class and prayer meetings, and other means of grace, were not only religious duties, but religious privileges and pleasures.

In the autumn of 1829, in her twenty-third year, she was united in marriage to Rev. Joseph Castle, then a member of the Genesee Conference, and cheerfully left the beautiful valley of her infancy and girlhood, to make sacrifices and encounter difficulties incident to an Itinerant minister's wife, which are neither few nor small; but in every place her loving nature, humble piety, and active benevolence, attracted to her the hearts of rich and poor, and ever formed a bond of delightful union in all the congregations where her husband was stationed. She was a "help-mate," indeed, lent for a season, but taken away when husband, children, and friends least knew how to spare her. While she was greatly admired in her large circle of friends, she was specially beloved in her own family. She was the constant light and joy of their dwelling. A more exemplary Christian, or devoted or affectionate wife or honoured mother, perhaps never lived. Her death was so sudden it took every one by surprise; but it was like her life, unselfish, uncomplaining, patient, and serene. She expressed her willingness to die, or readiness to live, for her family's sake. Christ was her hope in life, her stay in death—and her mind was kept in perfect peace while passing the dark valley. Her equanimity was undisturbed throughout the whole distressing scene, and her consciousness remained perfect to the last. A few minutes before eleven o'clock, on the day of her death, she opened her bright black eyes, and cast, for a moment, an intelligent look of love on husband and children weeping around her, and then closed them for ever.

> "As sets the morning star, which goes
> Not down behind the darkened west, nor hides
> Obscured among the tempests of the sky,
> But melts away, into the light of Heaven.

The funeral concourse which assembled at Green Street Methodist Episcopal Church, of which she was a faithful member, was very large, and with weeping eyes witnessed the solemn services.

> "Peaceful be thy silent slumber."

Our friends, who have "passed on before," have

thrown off every burden, and escaped from every snare. "The head aches no more; the eye forgets to weep; the flesh is no longer racked with acute, nor wasted with lingering distempers." Released from pain and sorrow, danger never threatens them, tranquillity softens their couch, and safety guards their repose. "Blessed are the dead which die in the Lord from henceforth: Yea, saith the Spirit, that they rest from their labours; and their works do follow them."

In our newly dedicated house, we found it good to wait upon the Lord. Many predicted that, when the Plank Church excitement was over, the congregation would diminish, but we found our large brick edifice, fifty-six by eighty feet, was filled to overflowing, and frequently hundreds had to go away for the want of room. Rev. Thomas C. Murphey, who only two years before had the little church in Seventeenth St. under his control, in connexion with other mission churches, was with me on a Sabbath evening in the new Hedding Church; and when he arose and saw such a vast crowd of persons, ready to hear the word, he said, "My feelings almost overpower me, and I am compelled to ask, What hath God wrought? the contrast is great." The circumstances apparently inspired him, and the sermon that followed "had free course and was glorified."

It was deemed expedient in the winter of 1855, to have a course of lectures in the church: which we supposed would be a source of improvement and also a financial gain to the trustees. Rev. A. A. Willetts, Rev. Alfred Cookman, Rev. George Loomis, Professor William Allen, and Rev. Col. Lehmanousky, all delivered very entertaining lectures. After the course of lectures was over, we resumed in our new church our *favourite work* of trying to get sinners converted. The minds of the people had been diverted, and there seemed to be a reaction in this absorbing business. Not a man came forward. It was a dark hour. The devil tried to tempt me that we had desecrated the house of God, and there never would be another soul converted in it during my connexion with it. I told the devil publicly, "You are a liar and the father of lies, and I will, by the help of God, prove you to be a liar this night." Quick as thought, without previous meditation, the directions given to Joshua, the leader of Israel, relating to Jericho, came into my mind. I gave direction to the brethren to march round the church, and if it were necessary, let the church be compassed seven times. The direction was strictly adhered to; at first when we began to walk about Zion, the number was comparatively small, but we had not passed round about the church more than twice, ere there was "an exceeding great army"—starting from the altar on the north aisle, going west to the back part of the church, then coming east in the southern aisle until they reached the altar. We had no "trumpets of rams' horns" to blow, yet we did the best we could in blowing the gospel trumpet by singing with much spirit,

> "Blow ye the trumpet, blow;
> The gladly solemn sound;
> Let all the nations know,
> To earth's remotest bound.
>
> The gospel trumpet hear,
> The news of heavenly grace;
> And saved from earth, appear
> Before your Saviour's face."

I can also testify that "all the people did shout with a great shout," and by the time we compassed the church seven times, the power of the enemy was curtailed, and "the mighty men of valour" were conquered, and sinner after sinner fell prostrate at our altar, and it was filled with earnest seekers of salvation. Several were powerfully converted. I felt free to say to the people, "Shout! for the Lord hath given you the city." This gave a fresh and powerful impetus to our spiritual operations. Does any one question the propriety of such a course? If so, I will inform him that on that night, a gentleman, the head of a family of the highest reepectabiliiy, and who never before was impressed, was led to fall prostrate at Jesus' feet. While the people of God passed on and compassed the church, singing and shouting, his heart melted, he trembled, he yielded and was happily converted. He only lived a few months. I visited him on his dying bed. I administered to him the ordinance of Christian baptism, a few days before he left the world. His end was not only peaceful, but triumphant. His wife, who survives him, and who is a valuable member of the Church now, was likewise arrested by this uncommon course. When the devil "Shall come in like a flood, the Spirit of the Lord shall lift up a standard against him." When this conflict commenced with the powers of darkness, many felt the "gates of hell" are likely to prevail against us; but soon all were ready to say, the troops of the enemy are receiving a "galling fire," and the field was left to Zion's sons.

Our meetings during the two years had been remarkably prosperous, unprecedented in my feeble Itinerant life. I had command of a Spartan band determined upon victory or death. We appointed the new converts to classes, and endeavoured to use proper means to confirm and establish them in the practice of true piety. We did what we could to place in their hands books and periodicals of the right character. The reaction, talked of by some, was to a great extent avoided. A few went back to the world, and this we shall generally realize in revivals; but some of the number have died happy in God, and have gone home to glory; while a large number are steadfast pillars in the Church of God. There are those in every church, ready to offer objections to revivals of religion, but the general spirit of the Bible is in favour of revivals. There are many signal instances in which God has poured out his Spirit, and effected a sudden and general reformation. The Church should continually pray for revivals. To them she must look for accessions both to her numbers and her strength. May the Methodist Episcopal Church ever remember she is a *revival Church!* Let this be her prominent characteristic, and we need not for one moment entertain fears that we shall decline, and lose our influence over the *people* and over our *children*. The praise of revivals is upon her lips, and upon the lips of her sons and daughters, who come crowding to her solemn feasts. He whose name is holy, will dwell "with him that is of a contrite and humble spirit, to revive the spirit of the humble, and to revive the heart of the contrite ones."

These were palmy days, and days never to be forgotten in the history of Hedding Methodist Episcopal Church, Philadelphia. There were over *ten thousand dollars paid* on the property, and enough money besides subscribed, to have swallowed up the debt entirely; but owing to the stagnation in business, and many of our subscribers being thrown out of business, it was impossible to collect it. This society, although it never had appropriated to it one dollar missionary money, provided for the pastor, and provided well. And last, though not least, the membership had been so increased, that I was enabled to report at Conference, in the spring of 1855, *four hundred and thirty-five in society!* and our usual congregation was about *one thousand.* We all felt, however, this work was "Not by might, nor by power, but by my Spirit, saith the Lord of hosts."

I may be considered an "*old fogy*," but when I hear persons calling for *alterations in Methodism, especially in the cities*, in order to make it more efficient, it is deeply impressed upon my mind to inquire modestly, is there not "a more excellent way?" I think so. If my readers ask what way I mean, I answer, "Stand ye in the ways, and see, and ask for the old paths, where is the good way, and walk therein, and ye shall find rest for your souls." As ministers, let us preach Christ and him crucified, attend prayer meetings and camp meetings, hold love feasts, visit the classes, go from house to house among the people, pray with them in their families, and labour constantly for revivals of religion, not recognising "the spirit of the age" as a controlling influence, but *control* "the spirit of the age." Invite *Young America* forward to the mourners' bench, and have him powerfully converted to God; and, while he prays, "God have mercy upon me a sinner," "Save, Lord, or I perish," sing over him,

> "The good old way is a righteous way,
> I hope to live and die in the good old way."

And exhort him to "Believe on the Lord Jesus Christ," and "walk by the same rule, mind the same thing." God's method of saving a soul never changes. Brethren in the ministry, should not our preaching be aimed directly at the conversion of sinners? Let us make this our first, highest, and only aim. Then the gospel would be "quick and powerful, and sharper than any two-edged sword, piercing even to the dividing asunder of the soul and spirit, and of the joints and marrow." If we can have wide-spread powerful revivals of religion, nothing will be left undone that ought to be done; we shall, as a church, accomplish that for which God raised us up, and it will be said of the Methodist Episcopal Church, "Who is she that looketh forth as the morning, fair as the moon, clear as the sun, and terrible as an *army* with banners?"

My attachment to Hedding Church was very strong; a large proportion of the membership I had seen converted, and had taken into society. They were brethren and sisters, "beloved, especially to me." I did suppose that it would be requisite at the close of this Conference year to say, "Finally, brethren, farewell." Had this been the case I would have urged, "Be perfect, be of good comfort, be of one mind, live in peace; and the God of love and peace shall be with you." However, in the spring of 1855, at the Conference held in Lancaster, Pa., I was induced, by the advice of my friends, to take a supernumerary relation. This I consented to do for two reasons: First, My health was much enfeebled by excessive labours in the Itinerancy, though only thirty-three years of age. Secondly, The *circumstances* called loudly for my return to the charge of Hedding Methodist Episcopal Church; and although I had not been in charge of that particular church two full years, yet I had been in charge one year and eight months, and it was a part of my field of labour also, from the Conference of 1853, till its organization into a separate station, August 9th, 1853; therefore it was decided that, according to our polity, I could not be sent back another year in the regular way; but that I could be placed in charge of the station, by taking the supernumerary relation. I did this conscientiously, as I was in comparatively ill health, and as a *prudential regulation* for the good of the infant church. To this arrangement I gave my assent, with the understanding that I should have an assistant sent with me, and that I should have the privilege to use means for the recovery of my health. Rev. William M. Warner, being deemed a suitable young man, was appointed with me, and has proved himself to be a "true yoke-fellow."

The Hedding Church was, this spring, the means of sending forth into the travelling connexion at least three ministers. Do we, as a general thing, do our duty in encouraging pious men to engage in the work of the

Itinerancy? The Church should, however, be careful not to lay hands suddenly on any man; and I doubt not but some have run before they were properly sent. Says one of high standing on this subject, "A call to the ministry may be defined a persuasion, wrought by the Holy Ghost in the mind of an individual, that it is his duty to become a preacher of the gospel. This impression varies greatly in clearness and intensity in different individuals, and in the same individual at different times. It is commonly developed and matured by prayer, by self-examination, by perusing the Scriptures, by hearing the gospel, by pious conference, by meditating upon the wants of the Church and of the world—in a word, by all those means which deepen piety, and make more fervent our love to Christ."

If a person is thus impressed, the Church should open, as far as possible, his way, and bid him God speed; for "the harvest truly is plenteous, but the labourers are few. Pray ye, therefore, the Lord of the harvest, that he will send forth labourers into his vineyard." While there are those over anxious to engage in this work, there is, frequently, in the different churches, those to be found—young men of sterling worth—deterred by modesty and self-distrust from making known to prudent and pious friends their exercises of mind with regard to engaging in the ministry.

One of the brethren who went forth from our church this spring, was a married man, and is now travelling, not in the Philadelphia, but another Conference, with great acceptability and usefulness. After he was assigned to his field of labour, and while he was arranging to move his family and enter upon the duties of his charge, he ascertained that his hopes, relative to obtaining a horse and carriage, were blasted in the direction he looked for help. His noble heart was about to fail him; his family were also in much distress. He visited me, cast down, ready to despair, and although, like Paul, he realized, "*Woe unto me* if I preach not the gospel," he said, "I thank you for what you have done in my case; I owe you a debt of gratitude I shall never be able to pay; but it is all over with me now; I cannot go without a horse at least, inasmuch as the Circuit is large. I have been disappointed in this respect." "The rich hath many friends." But can this be said of the poor? I saw tears in his eyes, and from the impulse of the moment I said to him, "In the strength of the Lord you *shall go*, and you shall have a decent outfit; go home, and tell your family to cheer up; all will be well." Their goods were accordingly shipped on that day (Thursday) for their destined place, and I took the cars for Wilmington, thinking I could make a better purchase there, and, in company with a friend, who was an excellent judge of horses, we went from place to place, and finally found a noble animal that we considered admirably suited to the purpose for which we wanted him; he was purchased. Not many words were used in buying either the horse or carriage. Together the cost was two hundred dollars. My notes were given and thrown into bank in that city. The intelligence was conveyed to the preacher and his family that night. It was like "good news from a far country." The horse and carriage were brought the next day to Philadelphia. I resolved, although the animal was fat, and bid fair to live many years, to have his *life insured!* He was taken to the "Live Stock Insurance Office," in Walnut Street, Philadelphia, of which Hon. Benjamin R. Miller is president, and his life was insured. The proper officer asked, "What is to be the name of the horse in the policy?" I told him to call him "Itinerant." On a Saturday morning in the month of April, this *Itinerant family* repaired in fine spirits to their field of toil, with a bright prospect of usefulness before them.

My object in insuring the horse was, that if he should die, another "Itinerant" might be purchased, so that the chariot wheels of my worthy brother might not be clogged in carrying the gospel into every nook and corner of his extensive field. Some of my very best friends upbraided me for making this outlay, and plainly told me, "You will ruin yourself, and bring your family to want." They asked, "How can you expect that dear man, with his family looking to him for support, to replace the money? It will require many years, if ever it is done." I felt in this case like saying we should "Be sure we are right, and go ahead." Have we anything to fear when we "trust in the name of the Lord, and stay upon our God?" The day for the payment of the notes rolled round; although I had received no tidings from my friend, I was enabled, in a way I knew not, to pay the notes promptly. In one or two days thereafter, I received a letter from the befriended one with the *entire amount enclosed!* The Lord was good to him, friends rallied around him, and enabled him to reimburse his fellow-itinerant. This overjoyed his magnanimous soul. There is much truth in the sentiment,

> "To generous minds
> The heaviest debt is that of gratitude
> When 'tis not in our power to repay it."

Pure, disinterested friendship ought to be appreciated. It is a rare commodity. There is much pretended friendship, but let adversity come, then we may know more of our friends. In too many cases we shall find they were sunshine friends, and will escape for their lives like rats from a barn in flames! "Ten to one, those who have enjoyed the most sunshine, will be the first to forsake, censure, and reproach. Friendship, based entirely on self, ends in desertion the moment the selfish ends are accomplished, or frustrated."

I have felt, myself, the force of the adage, "A friend in need is a friend indeed."

> "These I remember, these selectest men;
> And would their names record—but what avails
> My mention of their name: before the throne
> They stand illustrious 'mong the loudest harps,
> And will receive thee glad, my friend and theirs.
> For all are friends in Heaven; all faithful friends;
> And many friendships in the days of time
> Begun, are lasting here, and growing still:
> So grow ours ever more, both theirs and mine."

In the month of June, 1855, being thus advised by friends and physicians, I seriously thought of crossing the ocean, and looking upon scenes in the old world. Medical men expressed to me the opinion that such a sea voyage would be of great service to me; and gave it as their opinion that nothing that I could do would be so likely to restore my health, and add to my life many years. The expense of the visit to Europe was one of the barriers in my way; this, however, was a difficulty soon surmounted by the co-operation of friends. Be it spoken to the credit of my friend Alexander Cummings, Esq., who interested himself, and procured for me a passage in a splendid clipper ship, without any expense to me whatever. Through the influence of this gentleman, the firm of Bishop, Simons & Co. invited me urgently to sail on their noble ship "Monitou." As I had an assistant, who resided in my family, it occurred to me both the church and they could spare me now as well as at any future time. Therefore I resolved to make the experiment. This being the decision, I used all possible despatch in getting ready; for there was only a day or two ere the ship would sail, after I fully made up my mind to go. I supposed I had all things adjusted, and took my leave of family and friends on the 20th of June, and found myself slowly gliding down the Delaware river, fully expecting to be absent from my family, church, and native land at least three or four months. A fellow-passenger from Ohio was inclined to be very friendly and conversational. He asked me many questions, and among the rest, "Have you provided yourself with a passport?" This was a matter of great importance, which both myself and my friends, who kindly aided me in this undertaking, had lost sight of. The passenger alluded to, said, "I would not go on without it; I considered it of so much importance that I went all the way to Washington and procured my passport from head-quarters." I had anticipated going in another ship, which would sail five days later; and I came to the conclusion it would, under all the circumstances, be more judicious for me to return, (as we had not yet cleared the Capes,) adjust my neglected passport business, and re-start in the ship first thought of. The captain of our ship was a gentleman, and he and crew, as well as my fellow-passengers, appeared deeply to regret my leaving. This ship crossed from Philadelphia to London in fifteen days. When I reached home, I took my family and friends by surprise. I found difficulties to exist in the church that seemed to require that I should remain at home. My health required that I should go on; this voyage would have doubtless been to me a means of very great improvement. I felt as though I would take great pleasure in treading the soil of the Wesleys. I would have been much delighted to have "meditated amongst the tombs" in Epworth churchyard. I would there have seen the tomb of Wesley's father, and the birth-place of the founder of Methodism. I might have seen there that venerable pile, the parish church of Epworth, in which he was presented at the baptismal font by his illustrious mother, and consecrated to God, the Church, and the world. It would have afforded me much pleasure to see the graves of such men as John Wesley, Adam Clark, Richard Watson, and others of precious memory. I think I should have involuntarily exclaimed, May their spirit descend upon me! It would have afforded me unspeakable delight to worship the God of my fathers in the City Road Chapel and similar places; and to commingle and take sweet counsel with living Wesleyan ministers to whom I was to bear letters of introduction from many of our most prominent ministers, which would have guarantied to me a welcome; and from them I should have learned much, and doubtless had both my head and heart improved. I should have seen more clearly than ever, "The best of all is, God is with us." And, though I did not realize my hopes, I will say, and say it feelingly and understandingly,

> "Mountains rise and oceans roll,
> To sever us in vain."

Although this was the greatest disappointment of my life, yet, for *Zion's sake*, I felt willing to forego all the pleasure and benefit, every way, that would have accrued to me from the prosecution of this contemplated trip to the fatherland. I have reason to believe that my return was ordered by Providence; and I firmly believed all would "work together for good, to them that love God, to them who are called according to his purpose."

The Hedding Church had never seen a darker hour. The sun of prosperity, which had been shining forth so brilliantly, was suddenly obscured. The storm was upon us. Trusting in that God, who said in the storm, "Peace, be still, and there was a great calm," I said, "Brethren, I see the lowering cloud; a good captain will not desert his ship in time of a storm; I am, if it costs me my life, at the helm; if the ship goes down I go with her." We tried to undergird our ship, not literally with strong cables, but "with bands of love." Every one on board saw the necessity of the ship being lightened; not by throwing our guns overboard, but by throwing off some of our financial burden; and we fondly hoped she could live at sea. We did not wish to "let her drive." We were at our wits' end; but all hope that we should be saved *was not* taken away. I tried to exhort the brethren "to be of good cheer." Every man called on his God. Favourable winds that would waft us into the desired haven, soon began to blow softly. We could joyfully exclaim, "There is land ahead;" "we are rounding the cape." May she ever be in sailing trim, and heavily freighted with passengers, bound for the Celestial City, the Heavenly port; and as they glide over the sea of life, homeward bound, may they look to their Infallible Pilot, and say,

> "Be thy statutes so engraven
> On our hearts and minds, that we,
> Anchoring in death's quiet haven,
> All may make our home with thee."

There are dark seasons in every one's history; we must encounter storms in navigating life's sea. This will apply to nations, churches, families, and individuals. It is well it is so. "I went astray before I was afflicted." But we must not lose sight of those sweet lines,

"The gloomiest day hath gleams of light,
The darkest wave hath bright foam near it;
And twinkles through the cloudiest night
Some solitary star to cheer it.

"The gloomiest soul is not *all* gloom;
The saddest heart is not *all* sadness;
And sweetly o'er the darkest doom
There shines some lingering beam of gladness."

In order to "steady helm," however, an honourable and amicable arrangement was made with those to whom the Church was indebted. The agreement was, that three hundred dollars should be paid each month until a loan upon the property could be obtained; which was by all deemed plausible, and an entire settlement made. The trustees would have at once consummated this matter if they could, but in the effort they failed; this being the case, we fell upon the other alternative, *and all legal proceedings on the faith that this contract would be carried out were stopped.* In view of the weakness of the church, and of the much that had been done at home, I offered for a few months at least to go abroad and aid my struggling brethren. Persons that help themselves, as we had tried to do, will have sympathy and help in time of need from others. To aid the church, and for the improvement of my health, and to see the wonders of redeeming love, I spent several weeks in the tented grove. The camp meetings were specially successful on the Peninsula. Shall it be said that the days for camp meetings are passed? I attended one in Dorchester county, Maryland, which was held by Rev. Robert E. Kemp. A year previously, there was a similar meeting held in the same place by Rev. James Hargis, which was the means of building an excellent church not far from the encampment, in a neighbourhood which for many years had been much neglected. This church, on the last Sunday in the month of May, 1855, was dedicated to the worship of Almighty God. In the providence of God, it was my privilege to officiate on that occasion. And, after everything else was done, the ministers, trustees, and building committee held a meeting together to fix upon a name by which this church should be called. And my readers will be as much surprised as myself, when I state that it was resolved to designate it "Manship Chapel." I had received no intimation from the brethren to this effect, and I urged them to recede; but they said, preachers and people, *what is written is written.* I arose, and said, "Many among whom I have gone preaching have had the kindness to name their children after me, unworthy, unfaithful, and unprofitable as I am. I doubt the expediency of this course; this, however, is the first church edifice that has had my poor name applied to it. I think, brethren, you have erred; but, God being my helper, I pledge you 'my life, my fortune, and my sacred honour' that I will never bring a reproach upon it. I ask an interest in your prayers. 'Brethren, pray for us.' Neither you nor I should ever lose sight of the possibility of falling. 'Wherefore, let him that thinketh he standeth, take heed lest he fall.' My heart's desire and prayer to God is, that this neat church in the wilderness, built through camp meeting influence, may be the spiritual birth-place of scores and hundreds.

Here let the great Redeemer reign,
With all the graces of his train;
While power Divine his word attends,
To conquer foes, and cheer his friends.
And, in the great decisive day,
When God the nations shall survey,
May it before the world appear
That crowds were born to glory here!'"

The last though not least of the series of camp meetings I attended was in Sussex county, Delaware. In company with Bishop Scott, I went to this meeting comparatively a stranger. However, at a camp meeting, my spiritual birth-place, I never feel that I am out of my element, or that I am a stranger. There was much simplicity and power in the meetings; conversions at this camp meeting were very powerful. I will give a case. A stout young man, who attended the meeting for no special spiritual good, was deeply convicted. He started away from the aisle and went beyond the circle of the tents, trying to "shake off his guilty fears," but he fell under the power of God in the woods, and under the foliage of a stout tree he cried for mercy. The people of God instructed him, prayed with him, and sung sweetly over him. A little lamp was hung up over him in the tree to give light, for the night was dark. But the candle of the Lord, after a hard struggle, shone upon his head, and by heaven's light, he was enabled to walk through darkness. He realized the truth of the passage, "Weeping may endure for a night, but joy cometh in the morning." It was on Saturday night, and it was, I presume, near the break of day,

"When Jesus washed his sins away."

I never saw a happier man than he was on the Sabbath day that followed. He could scarcely tell "whether he was in the body, or whether out of the body." Many similar incidents might be given, for their name was legion, which came under my observation on this camp meeting tour.

I formed the acquaintance here more intimately of ex-Governor Hazzard, of Delaware. He is now, and has been for the last forty years, a devoted Christian, and a faithful class-leader, ardently attached to Methodism. Whether in the gubernatorial chair, on the judicial bench, in the halls of legislation, at home or abroad, he has maintained his Christian principles and character. Many public men, who seem to be pious at home, dispense with their religious duties and habits when they go abroad and enter upon public life. Not so with this venerable gentleman; he is the same man abroad as at home. His house has always been a home for the ministers of the gospel, where they are at once made welcome and comfortable. In company with Bishop Scott, Rev. John Hough, Rev. Adam Wallace, Rev. Jeremiah Pasterfield, and others, after the close of this camp meeting, it was my privilege to share in the hospitalities of his house. It is said, "The Lord hath blessed the house of Obededom, and all that pertaineth unto him;" and I felt this house will likewise be favoured of heaven.

This generous gentleman proposed at the camp meeting to give the church, of which I was pastor, a collection. His influence did much in opening the way. The circumstances were duly explained at the proper time, and no sooner was I through with my remarks than the Judge stepped forward to the stand and made a liberal contribution; and in all my experience I never saw such enthusiasm and ardour in giving as came under my observation on this occasion; and while the people gave their money, "not grudgingly, or of necessity," they realized the truth of that word, "God loveth a cheerful giver." The Lord paid them again by giving them such a blessing as there was scarcely in them room to contain, "pressed down and shaken together and running over." I was compelled to say, "Salvation belongeth unto the Lord; thy blessing is upon thy people."

I found the Presiding Elders of the lower Districts of our Conference, Rev. John T. Hazzard, and Rev. William McCombs, with the ministers of those Districts, were truly in the spirit of their work, "fervent in spirit, serving the Lord." At the different camp meetings I attended, I thought an ardour and zeal characterized them that was truly commendable. They were ready to strike blows for their conquering king and their beloved Methodism that should resound through the wilderness, and cause every tree to bud and blossom as the rose. Thank God there is vitality in the church, the days of camp meetings are not numbered; let me now make, to those who are inclined to bring them into disrepute, a statement. I saw in my camp meeting tour in the summer of 1855, at least *fifteen hundred persons converted to God!* When I am at a camp meeting my heart beats in unison with that of the poet—

"Hark! through the grove
I hear a sound divine! I'm all attention!
All ear, all ecstasy! Unknown delight."

Never mind the objections of infidels or formalists, or the falsehoods which have been fabricated and published to the world about them. We must admit, it is true, that many good people, and Methodists too, have objections, and think such meetings ought to be abandoned. We must differ with them; facts are stubborn things, and conscientiously I say to all my readers, "To your tents, O Israel." Go in the right spirit, and signs and wonders will follow. Fear not, timorous ones. "And I will make with them a covenant of peace, and will cause the evil beasts to cease out of the land; and they shall dwell safely in the wilderness, and sleep in the woods."

"Around the camp the power divine
Descends upon the saints below,
Immortal emanations shine,
And streams of life divinely flow;
The grateful tear which wets the eye,
Speaks to the soul that God is nigh."

In the month of September, for the first in my life I visited that portion of the Philadelphia Conference which lies on the Eastern Shore of Virginia, in company with Rev. John D. Onins, and took part in the labours of the dedication of Garrison's Chapel. The new church takes the place of one of the same name, which had been used for worship for sixty-six years. I trust the glory of the latter house may be greater than that of the former. A good beginning was certainly made. It was solemnly dedicated to God on Saturday, 22d day of September, by my associate brother Onins, who lives in the hearts of that people. The church cost between two and three thousand dollars, but the whole of the remaining debt was provided for in the forenoon of the day of consecration. God in a gracious manner poured out his spirit, and on Saturday night, a sweet little girl, the daughter of one of the trustees, who had given liberally of his means, was powerfully converted. Perhaps my readers will ask why lay any special stress upon the conversion of this little girl? It would seem she could do but little. But, reader, don't treat with inattention such a case. The heart of that father melted; tears bathed his cheeks; her influence was felt powerfully in that newly consecrated temple. Let me introduce an anecdote. "Four children, three brothers and a little sister, were enjoying a ramble along the banks of a river, when one of the boys accidentally fell into the water; just as he was sinking, another brother plunged in for his rescue, and when they were both struggling in the stream, the other brother reached out his hand and caught the second brother, who was about to sink also; and by the good providence of God, both found bottom and crawled ashore. When they arrived at home, the glad father, who had learned the jeopardy of his children, called them around him, and inquired of one, 'Well, what did you do to save your drowning brother?' I plunged into the water after him, sir,' was the reply. 'And what did you do?' he inquired of the next. 'I carried him home upon my back, sir.' Turning to his little daughter, he said, 'Well, my dear, what did you do to save your drowning brother?' 'I fell a crying, papa, as hard as I was able, all the time.'" There is eloquence and power in tears. Who can love and be loved like a sister? Is it not likely she did as much as any of them in saving the drowning one? Those tears prompted her little brothers to those desperate and successful efforts. I maintain converted children can accomplish much; though they may only *fall a crying as hard as they can, all the time.* My little Virginia friend did this work in a masterly manner, and she *cried* to the new altar several of much riper years. I was sojourning with the other ministers at her father's house. It was late on Saturday night, when we reached home; the influence of this child was felt there, both amongst white and coloured. A glorious revival followed in the new church. Let me say to my young readers, Seek until you find the Lord, and then *fall a crying as hard as you are able, all the time.* God will bless you and make you a blessing.

On the Sabbath the Lord poured out his Spirit and grace upon the assembled throng in a copious shower. The altar became crowded with weeping penitents, and the new song of souls pardoned mingled with the happy shouts of God's people, who rejoiced together in the manifestations of his holy presence and reviving power. We spent the whole day, the people having brought an abundant supply of refreshments. Many tables were spread in the wilderness. This meeting in many respects looked like a camp meeting. My colleague and myself remained till Tuesday with this loving people; between us we preached seven sermons. *They fed us well, and worked us hard.* "If any man will not work, neither shall he eat." But we felt so much of the presence and power of God that labour truly was rest. The kindness shown the coloured part of the community I found to be very great. The trustees set apart the entire gallery of the new church for the accommodation of this class. Hundreds upon hundreds were there of the sable sons of Africa; not only were they there on Sunday, but on week-days many were in attendance, and they obtained their portion of the spiritual manna, as it fell about the camp. They were so happy I was afraid some would do as I once knew one to do, viz., leap over the breastwork of the gallery. She came down with a considerable crash; not a bone, however, was broken, and no sooner was she on her feet than she resumed the work, "leaping and praising God." This was, all things considered, to me one of the most delightful dedication services I ever attended. Rev. Adam Wallace, the preacher on the Circuit, deserves much credit for his indomitable zeal in carrying this important enterprise to so successful an issue. He is deservedly a *beloved brother.* New churches are multiplying all through the Eastern Shore of Virginia, also in many other places on the Peninsula. But in this respect all over our Peninsula, the garden-spot of our Conference territory, we ought to pray "O Lord, revive thy work." The erection of a new church, and a good church, is the harbinger of spiritual prosperity. I was happy to see that on the Eastern Shore of Virginia peace prevails, and ministers and people of both divisions of the Methodist Episcopal Church are forgetting all sectional differences, in the promotion of the common cause of one who is our Master, and Head over all. I felt compelled to say, from what I saw, "For lo! the winter is past, the rain is over and gone; the flowers appear on the earth; the time of the singing of birds is come, and the voice of the turtle is heard in our land."

While away from home, at camp meetings, &c., I did not lose sight of our struggling church, and my pledge to aid our trustees to meet their monthly payments; which they were enabled to do promptly. The last instalment, however, was raised at home. The 14th of October, 1855, our new Hedding Church was just one year old. We held an anniversary, and endeavoured to improve "each shining hour," as my readers will see. We had on Saturday night an introductory service; Rev. G. C. M. Roberts, M. D., D. D., of Baltimore, preached a sermon on "Holiness," which was listened to with thrilling interest by the congregation, which was quite large. On Sunday morning, at nine o'clock, this good man held another meeting in the church, on the subject of *entire consecration* to the service of God. Many were inclined to "hunger and thirst after righteousness." At half-past ten o'clock in the morning, Rev. Henry G. King, of our Conference, preached, as he generally does, with great acceptability and profit, to a crowded audience. At three o'clock our friend, Dr. Roberts, delivered one of the most impressive discourses that it ever was my privilege to hear. I was greatly gratified to see representatives from the various churches; and all seemed to appreciate highly the lessons of instruction which fell from the lips of this deeply devoted minister of the Lord Jesus Christ.

Having had service morning and afternoon in the Hedding Church, at night we repaired, according to previous arrangement, to "Concert Hall," in Chestnut Street, and closed up our anniversary exercises in the most spacious room for public assemblies in the city of Philadelphia. Many regarded this part of our plan as being very much out of order, I have no doubt, and asked, "What does this mean?" "Is not the man beside himself?" It was said, "There will not be a hundred people there." And they supposed we should be objects of ridicule. "Nevertheless, we made our prayer unto our God;" and, while upon our knees, we felt that we heard "the sound of a going in the tops of the mulberry-trees." The victory will be ours, for we did bestir ourselves. Our motto was to "*trust in God, and keep our powder dry.*" But one asks the question, "Why did you abandon the church on Sunday night?" Our answer is: 1. We wanted a larger place; we were impressed that the church would be too strait to contain the people who would come "to the help of the Lord against the mighty." 2. We wanted to give an impetus to the home missionary and church extension work; and, believing that the people were with us, and that Methodism should be proclaimed everywhere, therefore we did not fear to urge our church, in the language of inspiration, "Lift ye up a banner upon the high mountain." We believed the effect would be glorious to let the Methodists, and warm-hearted Christians generally, sing, even in fashionable Chestnut Street, and "let them shout from the tops of the mountains." 3. Our Church had an obligation to meet the following Tuesday; we knew that we had done in the forenoon and afternoon about all that we could do in the church; hence we saw, on this account, the reasonableness of going to another place more central, where we could have a larger and somewhat different congregation. Certainly, it should be a part of every man's and every Church's religion to pay their honest debts. "Owe no man anything, but to love one another."

My reader will ask, "What was the result of the meeting in Concert Hall?" In the first place, I would answer, in regard to the attendance, it was the largest meeting in a house I ever beheld among the Methodists or any other denomination. As the ministers entered the spacious hall, they found it reverberating with the sweet songs of Zion. Nations have national airs, by which the love of country is deepened. The popular air of "Hail Columbia" will probably create an American feeling as long as our nation exists; and the airs "God save the King" and "Rule Britannia" will never cease to call the heart of the Briton to his own glorious isle. The soldier from Switzerland, and from the Highlands of Scotland, will weep at the national airs which call their hearts home to the place of their birth and childhood. In like manner is the Christian reminded, though here a "pilgrim and a stranger," of his *home in Heaven*, while he listens to sacred song, such as fell on our ears on this occasion:—

"'Mid scenes of confusion and creature complaints,
How sweet to my soul is communion with saints!
To find at the banquet of mercy there's room,
And feel in the presence of Jesus at home.
Home, home, sweet, sweet home!
Prepare me, dear Saviour, for glory, my home."

The American traveller, away from the land that gave him birth, though he be surrounded by crowned heads, and though he may be associated with those who have not the highest respect for America, and American institutions, or for the

"Truest hearts that ever bled,
Who sleep on glory's brightest bed,
A fearless host,"

yet, let him hear the "Star Spangled Banner" sung, or the name of the immortal Washington, the father of his country, mentioned; his heart leaps, his feelings overpower him, the love of country is deepened, and a national feeling is created and maintained. And wherever you find a true American, he will contend for *liberty*, and say, in substance, "I am in love; and my sweetheart is liberty. Be that heavenly nymph my companion." He exclaims, without regard to consequences,

"O land of good that gave me birth,
My lovely native land;
Enroll'd amidst the great of earth,
Thy name shall ever stand."

But if Americans be more loyal and devoted to their country and Washington than Christians are to "Canaan's happy shore" and to the name of Jesus, who has fought our battles and has triumphed over death, and ascended to God "as he captive captivity led?" Whenever, and *wherever*, the "fellow-citizens with the saints," hear the "Star of Bethlehem," "Round the cross," "Jerusalem, my happy home," and other *Heavenly airs*, almost Divine, they will shout Hosannah to the Lamb of God, "if there were as many devils in the way as there are tiles upon the houses."

James B. Longacre, Esq., a long-tried and faithful member of the Methodist Episcopal Church, was called upon to preside over this large assemblage. He did it with much dignity, and after singing and prayer by Rev. Henry G. King, he introduced the speakers; appropriate hymns being often interspersed. The addresses were of a *home missionary* character. Rev. Dr. Roberts and Rev. Newton Heston were deeply imbued with the home missionary spirit. No audience could have been more deeply interested. The collection was good, and the spirit of this Methodist meeting commended itself to all well-disposed persons. "Our hearts burned within us." A certain female said to the Saviour on one occasion, "Our fathers worshipped in this mountain; and ye say, that in Jerusalem is the place where men ought to worship." The Saviour, in reply, taught her the lesson that the *place* was an unimportant matter. And if any fastidious person should raise an objection to holding a religious meeting in "Concert Hall," or any other decent and convenient place, I would remind him that the worship of God is not now, under the gospel, appropriated to any place, as it was under the law; but it is God's will that men pray *everywhere*. "And in *every place* incense shall be offered unto my name," saith the Lord. The Saviour, though he made light of the place, he did not intend to lessen our concern about the thing itself, and says, "The true worshippers shall worship the Father in spirit and in truth." Readers, this is the main point. O for spirituality everywhere, in all our worship, and at all times!

The three brethren in the ministry, that assisted us throughout the day, were made, in an *impromptu* manner, "life members of the Methodist Episcopal Church in Philadelphia." Perhaps my reader will ask, What meaneth this? And what are the privileges of this life membership? First, These brethren were to feel themselves under obligation to assist, whenever called upon, if in their power, in planting churches in the suburbs of Philadelphia, and in every possible way, the home missionary work. Secondly, This life membership should entitle them to a lithographic copy of the "Original Plank Church, Philadelphia," neatly framed in gilt. This was to be their certificate. It required, according to our plan, *one hundred dollars* in each case; which amount, of course, went to the church; yet this was expressive of gratitude to the brethren who so efficiently served us; and the several propositions were nobly responded to and duly accomplished. The people, in this case, fulfilled the direction of the apostle Peter, "Love as brethren; be courteous." Why should we not have interest infused into home missions as well as foreign? The one must be done, and the other must not be left undone.

I strenuously maintain that "charity begins at home." Large mass meetings ought to be held in prominent places; powerful appeals ought to be made in behalf of the home missionary and church extension work. We are far from supposing that all the good done in the world is done through our instrumentality; but we do believe, that as a people, the Methodists are specially charged with responsible duties in reference to the poor; and thousands upon thousands are found in the suburbs of our large cities, and elsewhere in our bounds, without the gospel. We must not wait for them to come to us, but go in pursuit of them; plant churches and Sabbath Schools in their midst, and tell the story of the cross— "The poor have the gospel preached to them." But, reader, our charity should not remain at home. When the pressing wants of home are supplied, let us go forth like Noah's dove, on errands of mercy to the heathen in his blindness, and tell them of Jesus and his dying love. This is, we think, the spirit of the missionary commission, and such was the practice of Christ and his apostles. I hope and believe the Methodist Church will do her part. The means and men will be ready, I trust, for every emergency. There are those who do not count their lives dear unto themselves so that they might finish their course with joy. The lamented young

Stocker was on the eve of going to Africa; he was asked, "Do you not know that the climate of Africa is considered unfriendly to the constitution of the white man, and that he would be very liable to disease and death in that country?" He answered in the affirmative. He was then asked, under the circumstances, Are you willing to go? And his answer was, "None of these things move me." His bones rest in that dark land, near those of Wright, Barton, and Cox, the last of whom said, when dying, "*Don't give up Africa if a thousand fall!*"

A little more than thirteen years have rolled round since I joined the Itinerancy of the Methodist Episcopal Church in the Philadelphia Conference. I have done what I could in the vineyard of the Lord. I have not been idle or unemployed, and although I have, with the rest of my beloved brethren in the ministry, had some difficult fields of labour, yet, brethren, we have been enabled to say, "We are troubled on every side, yet not distressed; we are perplexed, but not in despair; persecuted, but not forsaken; cast down, but not destroyed." We have not, in the work of the ministry, laboured altogether in vain in the different Circuits and Stations we have filled, and amongst those where we have gone preaching—to God's name be all the glory!—we have had ocular demonstration that the word hath swiftly run. And to many, brethren in the Itinerancy, (and this is the best evidence that we are called of God to the work) we can say with humility, "Ye are our epistle written in our hearts, known and read of all men: for as much *as ye are* manifestly declared to be the epistle of Christ ministered by us, written not with ink, but with the Spirit of the living God; not in tables of stone, but in fleshly tables of the heart."

Methodist Itinerants are still with some an object of ridicule. Representing us, they will say, "They are well conditioned, jovial, idle, roving fellows, well mounted and living on the fat of the land, imposing upon the ignorance of the poor, and basking in the smiles of the rich; while there are others who seem to imagine the only proper idea of a Methodist preacher is that of a sallow-looking little man, of thin visage and thread-bare coat, mounted on a living skeleton across empty saddle-bags, and in constant jeopardy of perishing by hunger." Go on with your mischievous misrepresentations. You are trying to degrade as noble and as useful a band of ministers as the world ever saw. Amuse yourselves and the parties amongst whom you commingle, but recollect, you are to be brought into judgment for this slander. And don't lose sight of the fact that vituperation coming from such a source, cannot stop our chariot wheels, or quench the fire of love that burns in our souls for the salvation of our fellow men.

Thirteen years' experience in the Itinerancy leads me to say, "I love the glorious system of Ministerial Itinerancy, established by Jesus Christ, and owned and honoured of God. I particularly love the Methodist Itinerancy, uniting within itself an endless diversity of gifts and usefulness, combining the experience of age, the vigour of manhood, with the ardour and enterprise of youth: a system of missionary activity which directs its vigorous instrumentality over the Rocky Mountains, where the foot of neither prophet nor apostle has ever trod the soil, down through the swamps and canebrakes of the South, into every corner of this extensive and extending republic; planting its foot on the islands of the sea, and traversing the mighty continents of the earth." God being my helper, I will never clog its wheels, either by theory or practice. I will, so far as health and strength will allow, as a son in the gospel, *go forth*, "bearing precious seed," and try to preach Christ and him crucified, exclaiming—

> "His only righteousness I show,—
> His saving truth proclaim;
> 'Tis all my business here below
> To cry, 'Behold the Lamb!'"

And when I get sick for the last time, and friends and Itinerant brethren may around my bed their watchful vigils keep, and with affection wipe the cold sweat of death from my face, and hold the cordial to my quivering lips for the last time, I hope in death to be able, like the swan, to sing my sweetest song—

"Happy, if with my latest breath,
I may but gasp his name;
Preach Him to all, and cry in death,
Behold! Behold the Lamb!"

Rev. John Wesley, the founder of Methodism, was practically an *eminent Itinerant.* He travelled about four thousand five hundred miles every year. He often, in this Christ-like work, encountered pain and neglect; to which, however, he ever retained a cheerful insensibility. I will give one case. "As he was travelling with John Nelson, one of his preachers, from common to common in Cornwall, and preaching to a people who heard him willingly, but seldom, or never, offered him the slightest hospitality, he one day stopped his horse at some brambles, to pick the fruit. 'Brother Nelson,' said he, "we ought to be thankful that there are plenty of blackberries; for this is the best country I ever saw for getting a stomach, but the worst I ever knew for getting food. Do the people think we can live upon preaching?' 'At that time,' says his companion, 'Mr. Wesley and I slept on the floor; he had a great coat for his pillow, and I had Burkett's Notes on the New Testament for mine. One morning, about three o'clock, Mr. Wesley turned over, and, finding me awake, clapped me on the side, saying, 'Brother Nelson, let us be of good cheer; I have one whole side yet; for the skin is off but on one side.'" This great and good man, after suffering hardships and reproach in the work of the ministry for sixty-five years, finished his course with joy and great triumph. Having been laid on the bed from whence he arose no more, he called upon those who were with him to "pray and praise." Soon after, he again called upon them to "pray and praise." Taking each by the hand and affectionately saluting them, he bade them farewell. Attempting afterwards to say something which could not be understood, he paused a little, and then, with all the remaining strength he had, he said, "The best of all is, God is with us." And again lifting his hand, he repeated the same words in holy triumph, "The best of all is, God is with us."

This new religion, as Methodism was called, has always given its subjects wonderful victory over death. Speaking of a Sister Hooper, says Mr. Wesley, "I asked her whether she was not in great pain? 'Yes,' she answered; 'but in greater joy. I would not be without either.' 'But, do you not prefer either life or death?' She replied, 'All is alike to me; let Christ choose; I have no will of my own.' I spoke with her physician, who said he had little hope of her recovery; 'only,' he added, 'she has no dread upon her spirits, which is generally the worst symptom. Most people die for fear of dying; but *I never met with such people as yours.* They are none of them afraid of death; but calm, and patient, and resigned to the last.'" During my thirteen years' experience in the itinerancy, I have seen the proposition, *that the Methodists die well,* gloriously exemplified. I will give some examples. Stormy, indeed, had been their passage over the river of death; but was it not safe? was it not triumphant?

In my first year in the Itinerancy, the work of religion broke out in a prominent family. A little daughter was first converted; then the mother; the father soon followed, and they altogether told to sinners around "what a dear Saviour they had found." During the past summer, the head of that family came to P—— to die with his daughter, who contributed much in leading him first to the Saviour. I saw him on his death-bed, calm as a summer evening, not a cloud to obscure his spiritual sky. And, when about to bid adieu to earth and earthly things, he said, "*Now sing me home to Heaven.*" Yes the language of the Christian is,

"O! sing to me of Heaven,
When I am call'd to die;
Sing songs of holy ecstasy,
To waft my soul on high!

"Then, 'round my senseless clay,
Assemble those I love,
And sing of Heaven, delightful Heaven,
My glorious home above!"

A good brother in one of my fields of labour, long a Methodist, on his dying pillow, surrounded by his children and weeping companion, said to his wife, "*There is light in the valley, Mary! There is light in the valley, Mary!!*" Jesus does not send for us simply, but he will come for us, and return with us: "Though I walk through the valley of the shadow of death," like the one referred to, we shall be able to say, I trust, "*There is light in the valley,*" because the Sun of Righteousness is shining upon us and walking through the valley with us, and we must have comfort.

Not long since an esteemed young Christian friend, who had much to live for, fell asleep in Jesus. I allude to Mrs. Hannah Louisa Flinn, wife of Mr. Anthony B. Flinn, and daughter of Rev. Anthony Atwood. That religion which she obtained in early youth at a protracted meeting in Asbury Church, Wilmington, Delaware, and which shone with lustre in the Sunday School, the class room, the circles in which she moved, and in her own home, irradiated the chamber where she met her fate. A few weeks before her death the Lord favoured her with a fullness of joy. She thought she was stepping into the stream of Jordan. She called her husband, father, mother, sister, and brothers, gave them her last, as she supposed, affectionate kiss, and bade them farewell. Seeing her friends bathed in tears, she said, "Don't weep; my sufferings will soon be ended, and I shall be at rest." A few days after she was asked by her father, "Are you willing to depart and be with Christ?" She replied, "All ready, except a desire to see my dear husband once more." She requested her friends to sing,

"Jesus, lover of my soul,
Let me to thy bosom fly."

One of her friends remarked to her just before she closed her eyes on all terrestrial things, "You are *now* in the cold waters of Jordan." "Yes, but I am in perfect peace." So peaceful was her death, that it could scarcely be distinguished from the approach of a healthy slumber.

Early in my Itinerant life I formed the acquaintance of Mrs. M——, the wife of one of our Itinerant ministers. She was converted when but twelve years of age, and emphatically went "on to perfection." Liberally educated, and deeply devoted to God, she was an helpmate indeed. When informed that she must die, she said, "For my husband and children's sake I would prefer living, but I am fully resigned to the Divine will." She conversed freely about death and eternity, gave directions concerning her funeral and little ones, and about an hour before her death she repeated many sweet passages of Scripture and verses of hymns, and requested those about her to sing,

"On Jordan's stormy banks I stand,
And cast a wishful eye."

She then cried out in holy triumph, "O death, where is thy sting? O grave, where is thy victory?" Lifting her eyes and hands to heaven, she said, "Come, Lord Jesus, and receive my spirit." She exclaimed, with almost the eloquence of a seraph,

"Hark, they whisper! angels say,
Sister spirit, come away."

Then she said, "I come, I come, I come; glory, glory, glory." These were her last words. She waved a peaceful and final farewell to all sublunary things, and the happy spirit returned "to God who gave it." O, how rapid then is our homeward flight! "Scarcely shall we have lost sight of these mundane shores, till we shall behold the glory of the heavenly city. Scarcely shall we have ceased to hear the groans and conflicts of earth, till our souls will be fired with the shouts of angels, and the songs of the redeemed in heaven. Scarcely shall we have finished taking leave of our friends on earth, till we shall be greeted by our friends in heaven, and made welcome to the everlasting habitations which Jesus has prepared for us; that where he is there we may be also, to behold his glory."

In this work I have referred to several ministers and members of our church with whom I have been acquainted, who have "conquered death." "And what shall I more say?" For the time would fail me to tell of the scores which I have myself seen triumphing, finding "their latest foe under their feet at last." To this fact I desire to call the attention of those who would ridicule and make light of Methodism. Don't forget that the people called Methodists generally *die well!* And while for the last century the Methodists have done good "in every possible way," let me ask, especially, Is there another organization on the face of the earth that has been instrumental in enabling so many thousands, ay, tens of thousands, to sing, when mortality is about being "swallowed up of life,"

> "Jesus can make a dying bed
> Feel soft as downy pillows are,
> While on his breast I'll lean my head,
> And breathe my life out sweetly there."

This to me is an irresistible argument in favour of the divinity and excellence of our religion, an argument that neither the Infidel nor the devil himself can resist. "Let me die the death of the righteous, and let my last end be like his."

I owe my all to Methodism, but far be it from me to quarrel with any one else because of different views on the circumstantials of religion. But I must never lose sight of the passage, "Look unto the rock *whence* ye are hewn, and to the hole of the pit whence ye are digged." Looking at this form of Christianity in all its bearings, (with which I have been connected since my fourteenth year,) I am compelled to say, "*by the grace of God I am a Methodist.*" Have we not, as a people, had the most convincing evidence in the salvation of sinners, that it is of God? "Methodism has compassed both Indies, reached the four continents, visited the islands of the sea, and overrun the whole civilized surface of North America." It is destined to live and accomplish "many wonderful works." We won't give up the distinguishing features of Methodism. We endorse it heartily as a whole, especially its class meetings, and its Itinerancy, and in this work we will go forth at all seasons, and in all weathers, under all circumstances, for the love of Christ and a perishing world constraineth us; and we will "take joyfully the spoiling of our goods, knowing in ourselves that we have in heaven a better and an enduring substance." And we will proclaim in burning words a free salvation to a lost world. And to all the enemies of Methodism, and of her ministers, I would say, you had better "refrain from these men and let them alone; for if this counsel or this work be of men, it will come to nought: but if it be of God, ye cannot overthrow it, lest haply ye be found to fight against God."

THE END.

VALUABLE WORKS

RECENTLY ISSUED.

A Voice from the Pious Dead of the Medical Profeſſion;

Or, Memoirs of Eminent Physicians who have fallen asleep in Jesus; with a Preliminary Dissertation on the Cross as the Key to all Knowledge. By Henry J. Brown, A. M., M. D. Price, 90 cts.

NOTICES.

From Thomas E. Bond, M. D., Editor Christian Advocate & Journal. New York.—* * * * * We hail with joy the work before us. The author has done good service by showing examples of Christian belief and practice among the most eminent of the faculty, both in Europe and America. We especially recommend this work to our brethren of the Medical Profession. They will find, especially in the dissertations which precede the Memoirs, a fair exhibition of the peculiar difficulties which the study and practice of medicine and surgery present to the theory of Christianity; and are able and satisfactory solutions of these difficulties.

From G. C. M. Roberts, M.D., Baltimore.—After having carefully read the book, and *re-read portions of it*, with increased interest, I take great pleasure in returning you my sincere thanks for affording me the opportunity, through you, of commending it most earnestly to the community at large, and to the members of the Medical Profession in particular. At this particular juncture, when strenuous efforts are in progress for the purpose of elevating the standard of medical education throughout the land, this excellent Memoir of some among the most distinguished physicians, who have died in Christ, appears most opportunely. I trust you will be successful in placing a copy of it in the library of every medical man in our country; where it will not only prove the means of spiritual benefit to preceptors, but likewise to those who may be under their supervision.

From the Boston Medical & Surgical Journal.—This volume is written with a view "to refute a charge of incompatibility between the Christian religion and science, sometimes made by wicked and ignorant persons." It contains three short Dissertations on the subjects of The Cross in the Life-Union, The Cross in Nature, and The Cross in Medicine; which are followed by Memoirs of Wm. Hey, Dr. Hope, Dr. Good, Dr. Bateman, Dr. Godman, Dr. Gordon, Dr. Broughton, and Dr. Capadoso. The Dissertations are intended "as an incentive to inquiry suggestive of a form." The Memoirs are interesting; and fully prove, what hardly requires proof, that there is nothing in science which tends to lessen men's faith in the Divine doctrines of the Christian Revelation, or deter them from fulfilling all its obligations. Dr. Brown's book will doubtless be read with interest by many who are not members of the profession, as well as by physicians.

From the Christian Observer, Philadelphia.—It affords us pleasure to call attention to this interesting volume. It contains an impressive argument for the truth and excellence of the Gospel, drawn from the lives of scientific men. It shows that faith in the teaching of the Scriptures is not merely a persuasion, but a power, stronger than the innate passions of our nature—a Divine power manifested in the development of all that is pure and lovely and of good report in real life. The memorials of these excellent men show conclusively, that science and religion are not, as a few sciolists have imagined, incompatible with each other. The Preliminary Dissertation is rich in thought, suggestive, adapted to awaken inquiry on the most important subject.

From the Western Christian Advocate, Cincinnati.—No book of a similar character is before the American public, and we trust it will find a good sale, not among physicians merely, but among all lovers of healthy, religious biography.

From the Pittsburg Christian Advocate.—The narrative of the closing scenes in the life of Dr. Gordon, of Hull, is of itself worth double the price of the book. Medical men, whose time is necessarily engrossed with professional engagements, will appreciate the aim of the author in collecting and condensing more extended memoirs of their worthy brothers in similar toils; and when they would not take up a long and laboured production, they can find in this volume that which will refresh and strengthen in the midst of their unceasing labours. Ministers and others, who sometimes wish to testify their high appreciation of the faithful services of the physician, will recognise in this volume a testimonial which cannot but be regarded as beautiful, appropriate, and valuable.

From the Christian Chronicle, Philadelphia.—The object of these pages is to show that there is a harmony between religion and science. It is decidedly a religious book, abounding with the most useful lessons from the highest authority. The Dissertation that precedes is a valuable production, much enhancing the value of the work.

From the National Magazine. New York and Cincinnati.—We commend the volume to the general reader; while, in the language of the preface, "To medical men of every class, these Memoirs come with singular force, involving, as they do, the modes of thought, the associations, and the difficulties common to the medical profession. Their testimony is as the united voice of brethren of the same toils, proclaiming a heavenly rest to the weary pilgrim. It comes, too, unembarrassed with any considerations of interest, or mere purpose of sect or calling."

From Rev. J. F. Berg, D. D.—The selection of a number of Memoirs of Physicians eminent for their piety, who have adorned their profession in our own country and in other lands, as examples of the living power of piety, is itself a happy thought; and the primary Dissertation on the Cross as the Key to all Knowledge will suggest valuable reflections to the mind of the thoughtful reader. It is an able presentation of the great theme of the Cross of Christ as the foundation of all genuine science.

The Bible Defended againſt the Objections of Infidelity.

Being an Examination of the Scientific, Historical, Chronological, and other Scripture Difficulties. By Rev. Wm. H. Brisbane. Price, 50 cts.

NOTICES.

From the Western Christian Advocate.—The work is on a plan somewhat original, and meets a want long felt by Sabbath School Teachers and Scholars, private Christians and others. We can most heartily commend the little manual to all seeking the truth as it is in the Gospel of Christ.

From the Christian Advocate & Journal.—The author, in the body of his work, commencing with the account of the Creation, as given in the book of Genesis, goes through the principal facts recorded in the Old and New Testaments, stating and answering the objections of infidelity cogently and logically, bringing to his aid the result of extensive reading and patient investigation. It is a small book.—so small that none will be deterred from reading it by its size: yet it condenses the most general objections to the Bible, with a clear statement of the refutation of them, by the best authors who have written on the subject.

From the National Magazine.—A small but good review of the chief infidel objections to the Bible has been published by Higgins & Perkinpine. It is by Rev. W. H. Brisbane, and examines the scientific, historical, chronological, and other difficulties alleged against the Scriptures. It is especially adapted to meet the wants of Sunday School and Bible Class Teachers.

From the Easton Star.—The title page indicates the character of this little volume, which has evidently been prepared with great care, by one who appears to have thoroughly investigated the subject, and whose researches well qualify him to elucidate the difficult questions reviewed. The style is chaste, perspicuous, and comprehensive, and the volume replete with original thoughts and pertinent quotations from the first biblical and scientific authors, to support the Divine authority of the Scriptures and refute the objections of sceptics. The book contains in a nutshell most of the points of difference be tween infidels and Christians and should be read by all who experience any difficulty in reconciling those texts of Scripture that are in apparent conflict, but which accord in beautiful harmony when explained by their contexts, and other subjects to which they relate. We take pleasure in commending it to those readers who have not the time to investigate heavier works, as a book that will amply repay a careful perusal.

Lectures on the Doctrine of Election.

By the Rev. A. C. RUTHERFORD, of Greenock, Scotland.

Price, 50 cts.

NOTICES.

From the National Magazine.—These Lectures are remarkable for logical acuteness and sagacity, and a comprehensive knowledge of the subject. There is a strong spice of Scottish acerbity, too, in their style. Arminian polemics will receive this volume as among the ablest vindication of their views produced in modern times.

From Rev. Bishop Scott.—I have carefully read through your late publication, entitled "Lectures on the Doctrine of Election, by Alexander C. Rutherford, of Scotland," which you were kind enough to put into my hands. I am very much pleased with it. It is an admirable book. It refutes the Calvinistic theories on this subject with, I must think, unanswerable force of argument, and unfolds and exhibits the true Bible theory with clearness and power. And, unlike many controversial works, it is a very readable book. The author's style is so clear, so natural, so easy and flowing, and withal so animated and forcible, and his manner and illustrations so interesting and striking, that one is led on from page to page, and from chapter to chapter, not only without weariness, but with increasing interest. The spirit of the book, too, I think, is excellent, independent, frank, candid, affectionate, exhibiting a profound regard for the unadulterated teachings of the Bible and a yearning love for souls. The author, indeed, sometimes uses harsh words, but almost only of theories and systems and dogmas—seldom, indeed, of persons. He treats his opponents with Christian courtesy, occasionally only rebuking them sharply, while he deals with a fearless and unsparing hand with their false and soul-destroying errors. This book ought to be sown broadcast over the land. I could wish that a copy of it should go into every family; especially at this time, when there seems a disposition in certain quarters to force on us again this wretched Calvinistic controversy.

From Zion's Herald.—The author of this work is a Scotch clergyman, who was formerly a Calvinist, but who, by honestly seeking the truth as rêvealed in God's Word, was led to embrace the more Scriptural tenets of the Arminian school. Having first spread his views before the religious public at Greenock and Glasgow, in a series of lectures delivered in 1847, he afterwards gave them to the world in form of a book, which is now, for the first time, reprinted in America. Bating some few inferior points of doctrine, we think the work to be a sound, strong, and vigorous expose of the Calvinistic theory. It is finely adapted for popular circulation; could it be scattered broadcast, it would doubtless aid in extirpating the stubborn errors of that theory from such portions of the community as are still afflicted by its presence.

The Sunday School Speaker;

Or, Exercises for Anniversaries and Celebrations: Consisting of Addresses, Dialogues, Recitations, Bible Class Lessons, Hymns, &c. Adapted to the various subjects to which Sabbath School Efforts are directed. By Rev. JOHN KENNADAY, D. D. Price, 38 cts.

The Minſtrel of Zion.

A Book of Religious Songs, accompanied with Appropriate Music, Chiefly Original. By Rev. William Hunter and Rev. Samuel Wakefield. Price, 38 cts.

Select Melodies.

Comprising the Best Hymns and Spiritual Songs in common use, and not generally found in standard Church Hymn Books; as also a number of Original Pieces, and Translations from the German. By Rev. Wm. Hunter. Price, 40 cts.

A Short Poem,

Containing a Descant on the Universal Plan. By John Peck. *Multum in Parvo.* To which is added

Univerſaliſm a very Ancient Doctrine;

With some Account of its Author. By Lemuel Haynes, A. M. Price, 6 cts.

The Calvinistic Doctrine of Predestination Examined and Refuted;

Being the substance of a series of Discourses delivered in St. George's Methodist Episcopal Church, Philadelphia, by Francis Hodgson, D. D. Price, 35 cts.

Prophecy and the Times;

Or, England and Armageddon: an Application of the Predictions of Daniel and St. John to Current Events. By Rev. Joseph F. Berg, D. D

Abaddon and Mahanaim;

Or, Dæmons and Guardian Angels. By Rev. Joseph F. Berg, D. D.

A liberal discount made to wholesale purchasers.

www.ingramcontent.com/pod-product-compliance
Lightning Source LLC
LaVergne TN
LVHW020101110826
845151LV00001B/41

* 9 7 8 1 4 2 5 5 4 4 5 5 3 *